CHEAT CODE

EXPLOSION

FOR CONSOLES

FLIP THIS BOOK OVER FOR HANDHELD SYSTEMS

Nintendo DS™ & 3DS™

PlayStation® Portable

LOOK FOR CODEY

When you see Codey's face, you've found the newest and coolest codes!

ANGRY BIRDS

There are 26 Golden Eggs hidden around the levels of Angry Birds. The following tells you how to get them all. Earlier versions of the game numbered the eggs, but the following are listed in a more logical order, so they do not match up with the earlier game.

Since the PSP doesn't have a touch screen, anything that requires tapping the screen needs a button press, which is covered in the following pages.

GOLDEN EGGS

1 WORLD SELECT

At the world select, tap the sun until another Golden Egg pops out. Press Down + ⬤ on the PSP.

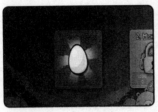

2 CREDITS

Select i from the Options and scroll up to find the Golden Egg. Let the credits roll through if you are unable to scroll up, such as on the PSP.

3 HELP SCREEN

This Golden Egg becomes available once you unlock the white bird. Then, during any level, pause the game and select the question mark. At the white bird help screen, touch the golden egg. For PSP, continue past this screen to automatically get the egg.

4 POACHED EGGS

Earn three stars on all of the Poached Eggs levels.

5 POACHED EGGS 1–8

Simply tap the treasure chest until you get the egg. On the PSP, press Down + ⬤.

6 POACHED EGGS 2–2

Destroy the beach ball that sits among the cubes of ice.

7 MIGHTY HOAX

Earn three stars on all of the Mighty Hoax levels.

8 MIGHTY HOAX 4-7

Zoom out to spot the egg on the right cliff. Launch the yellow bird into a high arc and tap when it lines up with the egg.

9 MIGHTY HOAX 5-19

The egg is located above the rocket ship. Zoom out and use a yellow or white bird to get it. Fire the yellow bird almost straight up and then tap when it reaches the clouds. If done correctly, the bird will get the egg as it comes back down.

10 DANGER ABOVE LEVEL SELECT

Select Danger Above and scroll the level select screens as far as you can to the right to find this egg.

11 DANGER ABOVE

Earn three stars on all of the Danger Above levels.

12 DANGER ABOVE 6-14

Pop the yellow balloon floating below the structure on the right to get this one. Send the boomerang bird over the house and tap to have it come back to the balloon. This requires very good timing with the boomerang.

13 DANGER ABOVE 8-15

The golden egg is located behind the two boxes below the slingshot. Zoom out to see it. Bounce a yellow bird off the pink cushion located to the right.

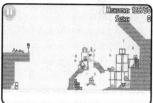

14 THE BIG SETUP

Earn three stars on all of The Big Setup levels.

15 THE BIG SETUP 9-14

This egg hides under a hard hat on the far side of the area. Send a bird over or through the structure to get it.

16 THE BIG SETUP 10-3
Destroy the rubber duck located below the bridge to get another Golden Egg.

UNAVAILABLE ON PSP

18 HAM 'EM HIGH
Earn three stars on all of the Ham 'Em High levels.

19 HAM 'EM HIGH 12-12
Destroy the cup that sits on the small platform below the big structure. Destroy the building and then send a bird through the opening to get it.

20 HAM 'EM HIGH 13-10
Zoom out to see the egg hanging on the far side of the map. Send the white bird toward the middle of the structure, just above the two concrete bars on top. At this time, tap the screen to send the bird into the egg.

21 HAM 'EM HIGH 13-12
You cannot see this egg until you get it. Zoom out so that you see the entire hill that you sit upon. Send a white bird to the left and quickly drop an explosive egg to reveal the Golden Egg.

22 HAM 'EM HIGH 14-4
Zoom out so that you can see the Golden Egg that sits high on the mountain in the upper-right corner. Launch the yellow bird at about a 60 degree angle and then tap the screen to send it toward the egg.

17 THE BIG SETUP 11-15

Zoom out to spot an egg below and to the left of your location. Fire the boomerang bird to the left and tap the screen to bring it back to the egg.

The Golden Eggs below this line are not available at the moment on the PSP version.

23 MINE AND DINE 15-12

Zoom out and an egg becomes visible in the top-right corner. Getting this one is very similar to 20. Send the yellow bird up and tap when it lines up with the egg.

24 MINE AND DINE 16-9

Zoom out to spot the egg on the rock formation to the right. Aim a yellow bird just to the left of the first platform above the slingshot. Immediately tap the screen and if done correctly, the bird will reach the egg on its descent.

25 MINE AND DINE

Earn three stars on all the Mine and Dine levels.

26 MINE AND DINE 17-12

Zoom out and a treasure chest can be seen on a rock high above. The first two birds cannot reach it, so use them up. Then fire the yellow bird at about a sixty degree angle up and to the right. As it lines up with the chest, tap the screen to get it.

GUITAR HERO & ROCK BAND

CHEAT CODE EXPLOSION FOR CONSOLES

GAMES LIST

BAND HERO

MOST CHARACTERS UNLOCKED
Select Input Cheats from the options and enter Blue, Yellow, Green, Yellow, Red, Green, Red, Yellow.

ELECTRIKA STEEL UNLOCKED
Select Input Cheats from the options and enter Blue, Blue, Red, Yellow, Red, Yellow, Blue, Blue.

ALL HOPO MODE
Select Input Cheats from the options and enter Red, Green, Blue, Green, Blue, Green, Red, Green.

ALWAYS SLIDE
Select Input Cheats from the options and enter Yellow, Green, Yellow, Yellow, Yellow, Red, Blue, Red.

AUTO KICK

Select Input Cheats from the options and enter Yellow, Green, Yellow, Blue, Blue, Red, Blue, Red.

FOCUS MODE

Select Input Cheats from the options and enter Yellow, Yellow, Green, Green, Red, Red, Blue, Blue.

HUD FREE MODE

Select Input Cheats from the options and enter Green, Red, Green, Red, Yellow, Blue, Green, Red.

PERFORMANCE MODE

Select Input Cheats from the options and enter Yellow, Yellow, Blue, Green, Blue, Red, Red, Red.

AIR INSTRUMENTS

Select Input Cheats from the options and enter Blue, Yellow, Blue, Red, Red, Yellow, Green, Yellow.

INVISIBLE ROCKER

Select Input Cheats from the options and enter Green, Red, Yellow, Green, Yellow, Blue, Yellow, Green.

GUITAR HERO

UNLOCK ALL

At the Main menu, press Yellow, Orange, Blue, Blue, Orange, Yellow, Yellow.

GUITAR HERO GUITAR CHEAT

At the Main menu, press Blue, Orange, Yellow, Blue, Blue.

CROWD METER CHEAT

At the Main menu, press Yellow, Blue, Orange, Orange, Blue, Blue, Yellow, Orange.

MONKEY HEAD CROWD CHEAT

At the Main menu, press Blue, Orange, Yellow, Yellow, Yellow, Blue, Orange.

SKULL HEAD CROWD CHEAT

At the Main menu, press Orange, Yellow, Blue, Blue, Orange, Yellow, Blue, Blue.

AIR GUITAR CHEAT

At the Main menu, press Orange, Orange, Blue, Yellow, Orange.

NO VENUE CHEAT

At the Main menu, press Blue, Yellow, Orange, Blue, Yellow, Orange.

GUITAR HERO II

AIR GUITAR

At the Main menu, press Yellow, Yellow, Blue, Orange, Yellow, Blue.

EYEBALL HEAD CROWD

At the Main menu, press Blue, Orange, Yellow, Orange, Yellow, Orange, Blue.

MONKEY HEAD CROWD

At the Main menu, press Orange, Blue, Yellow, Yellow, Orange, Blue, Yellow, Yellow.

FLAMING HEAD

At the Main menu, press Orange, Yellow, Orange, Orange, Yellow, Orange, Yellow, Yellow.

HORSE HEAD

At the Main menu, press Blue, Orange, Orange, Blue, Orange, Orange, Blue, Orange, Orange, Blue.

HYPER SPEED

At the Main menu, press Orange, Blue, Orange, Yellow, Orange, Blue, Orange, Yellow.

PERFORMANCE MODE

At the Main menu, press Yellow, Yellow, Blue, Yellow, Yellow, Orange, Yellow, Yellow.

GUITAR HERO III: LEGENDS OF ROCK

To enter the following cheats, strum the guitar while holding the listed buttons. For example, if the code lists Yellow + Orange, hold the Yellow and Orange buttons as you strum. Air Guitar, Precision Mode and Performance Mode can be toggled on and off from the Cheats menu. You can also change between five different levels of Hyperspeed at this menu.

UNLOCK EVERYTHING

Select Cheats from the Options. Choose Enter Cheat and enter the following (no sounds play while this code is entered):

Green + Red + Blue + Orange
Green + Red + Yellow + Blue
Green + Red + Yellow + Orange
Green + Yellow + Blue + Orange
Green + Red + Yellow + Blue
Red + Yellow + Blue + Orange
Green + Red + Yellow + Blue
Green + Yellow + Blue + Orange
Green + Red + Yellow + Blue
Green + Red + Yellow + Orange
Green + Red + Yellow + Orange
Green + Red + Yellow + Blue
Green + Red + Yellow + Orange

An easier way to illustrate this code is to represent Green as 1, progressing down the guitar neck to Orange as 5. For example, if you have 1345, you would hold Green + Yellow + Blue + Orange while strumming: 1245 + 1234 + 1235 + 1345 + 1234 + 2345 + 1234 + 1345 + 1234 + 1235 + 1235 + 1234 + 1235.

ALL SONGS

Select Cheats from the Options. Choose Enter Cheat and enter:

Yellow + Orange	Yellow + Blue
Red + Blue	Yellow + Orange
Red + Orange	Yellow + Orange
Green + Blue	Yellow + Blue
Red + Yellow	Yellow
Yellow + Orange	Red
Red + Yellow	Red + Yellow
Red + Blue	Red
Green + Yellow	Yellow
Green + Yellow	Orange
Yellow + Blue	

NO FAIL

Select Cheats from the Options. Choose Enter Cheat and enter:

Green + Red	Orange
Blue	Red + Yellow
Green + Red	Green + Yellow
Green + Yellow	Yellow
Blue	Green + Yellow
Green + Yellow	Green + Red
Red + Yellow	

AIR GUITAR

Select Cheats from the Options. Choose Enter Cheat and enter:

Blue + Yellow	Red + Yellow
Green + Yellow	Blue + Yellow
Green + Yellow	Green + Yellow
Red + Blue	Green + Yellow
Red + Blue	Red + Blue
Red + Yellow	Red + Blue

Red + Yellow	
Red + Yellow	
Green + Yellow	
Green + Yellow	
Red + Yellow	
Red + Yellow	

HYPERSPEED

Select Cheats from the Options. Choose Enter Cheat and enter:

Orange	Orange
Blue	Blue
Orange	Orange
Yellow	Yellow

PERFORMANCE MODE

Select Cheats from the Options. Choose Enter Cheat and enter:

Red + Yellow	Red + Yellow
Red + Blue	Green + Blue
Red + Orange	Red + Yellow
Red + Blue	Red + Blue

EASY EXPERT

Select Cheats from the Options. Choose Enter Cheat and enter:

Green + Red	Blue + Orange
Green + Yellow	Yellow + Orange
Yellow + Blue	Red + Yellow
Red + Blue	Red + Blue

PRECISION MODE

Select Cheats from the Options. Choose Enter Cheat and enter:

Green + Red	Green + Red
Green + Red	Green + Red
Green + Red	Green + Red
Red + Yellow	Red + Yellow
Red + Yellow	Red + Yellow
Red + Blue	Red + Blue
Red + Blue	Red + Blue
Yellow + Blue	Yellow + Blue
Yellow + Orange	Yellow + Orange
Yellow + Orange	Yellow + Orange

BRET MICHAELS SINGER

Select Cheats from the Options. Choose Enter Cheat and enter:

Green + Red	Red
Green + Red	Red + Blue
Green + Red	Red
Green + Blue	Red
Green + Blue	Red
Green + Blue	Red + Blue
Red + Blue	Red
Red	Red
Red	Red

9

GUITAR HERO & ROCK BAND

CHEAT CODE EXPLOSION FOR CONSOLES

GUITAR HERO 5

ALL HOPOS
Select Input Cheats from the Options menu and enter Green, Green, Blue, Green, Green, Green, Yellow, Green.

ALWAYS SLIDE
Select Input Cheats from the Options menu and enter Green, Green, Red, Red, Yellow, Blue, Yellow, Blue.

AUTO KICK
Select Input Cheats from the Options menu and enter Yellow, Green, Red, Blue, Blue, Blue, Blue, Red.

FOCUS MODE
Select Input Cheats from the Options menu and enter Yellow, Green, Red, Green, Yellow, Blue, Green, Green.

HUD FREE MODE
Select Input Cheats from the Options menu and enter Green, Red, Green, Green, Yellow, Green, Green, Green.

PERFORMANCE MODE
Select Input Cheats from the Options menu and enter Yellow, Yellow, Blue, Red, Blue, Green, Red, Red.

AIR INSTRUMENTS
Select Input Cheats from the Options menu and enter Red, Red, Blue, Yellow, Green, Green, Green, Yellow.

INVISIBLE ROCKER
Select Input Cheats from the Options menu and enter Green, Red, Yellow, Yellow, Yellow, Blue, Blue, Green.

ALL CHARACTERS
Select Input Cheats from the Options menu and enter Blue, Blue, Green, Green, Red, Green, Red, Yellow.

CONTEST WINNER 1
Select Input Cheats from the Options menu and enter Green, Green, Red, Red, Yellow, Red, Yellow, Blue.

GUITAR HERO ENCORE: ROCKS THE 80S

UNLOCK EVERYTHING
At the Main menu, press Blue, Orange, Yellow, Red, Orange, Yellow, Blue, Yellow, Red, Yellow, Blue, Yellow, Red, Yellow, Blue, Yellow.

HYPERSPEED
At the Main menu, press Yellow, Blue, Orange, Orange, Blue, Yellow, Yellow, Orange.

PERFORMANCE MODE
At the Main menu, press Blue, Blue, Orange, Yellow, Yellow, Blue, Orange, Blue.

AIR GUITAR
At the Main menu, press Yellow, Blue, Yellow, Orange, Blue, Blue.

EYEBALL HEAD CROWD
At the Main menu, press Yellow, Blue, Orange, Orange, Orange, Blue, Yellow.

MONKEY HEAD CROWD
At the Main menu, press Blue, Blue, Orange, Yellow, Blue, Blue, Orange, Yellow.

FLAME HEAD
At the Main menu, press Yellow, Orange, Yellow, Orange, Yellow, Orange, Blue, Orange.

HORSE HEAD
At the Main menu, press Blue, Orange, Orange, Blue, Yellow, Blue, Orange, Orange, Blue, Yellow.

The following cheats can be toggled on and off at the Cheats menu.

QUICKPLAY SONGS

Select Cheats from the Options menu, choose Enter New Cheat and press Blue, Blue, Red, Green, Green, Blue, Blue, Yellow.

ALWAYS SLIDE

Select Cheats from the Options menu, choose Enter New Cheat and press Green, Green, Red, Red, Yellow, Red, Yellow, Blue.

AT&T BALLPARK

Select Cheats from the Options menu, choose Enter New Cheat and press Yellow, Green, Red, Red, Green, Blue, Red, Yellow.

AUTO KICK

Select Cheats from the Options menu, choose Enter New Cheat and press Yellow, Green, Red, Blue (x4), Red.

EXTRA LINE 6 TONES

Select Cheats from the Options menu, choose Enter New Cheat and press Green, Red, Yellow, Blue, Red, Yellow, Blue, Green.

FLAME COLOR

Select Cheats from the Options menu, choose Enter New Cheat and press Green, Red, Green, Blue, Red, Red, Yellow, Blue.

GEM COLOR

Select Cheats from the Options menu, choose Enter New Cheat and press Blue, Red, Red, Green, Red, Green, Red, Yellow.

STAR COLOR

Select Cheats from the Options menu, choose Enter New Cheat and press Red, Red, Yellow, Red, Blue, Red, Red, Blue.

AIR INSTRUMENTS

Select Cheats from the Options menu, choose Enter New Cheat and press Red, Red, Blue, Yellow, Green (x3), Yellow.

HYPERSPEED

Select Cheats from the Options menu, choose Enter New Cheat and press Green, Blue, Red, Yellow, Yellow, Red, Green, Green. These show up in the menu as HyperGuitar, HyperBass, and HyperDrums.

PERFORMANCE MODE

Select Cheats from the Options menu, choose Enter New Cheat and press Yellow, Yellow, Blue, Red, Blue, Green, Red, Red.

INVISIBLE ROCKER

Select Cheats from the Options menu, choose Enter New Cheat and press Green, Red, Yellow (x3), Blue, Blue, Green.

VOCAL FIREBALL

Select Cheats from the Options menu, choose Enter New Cheat and press Red, Green, Green, Yellow, Blue, Green, Yellow, Green.

AARON STEELE!

Select Cheats from the Options menu, choose Enter New Cheat and press Blue, Red, Yellow (x5), Green.

JONNY VIPER

Select Cheats from the Options menu, choose Enter New Cheat and press Blue, Red, Blue, Blue, Yellow (x3), Green.

NICK

Select Cheats from the Options menu, choose Enter New Cheat and press Green, Red, Blue, Green, Red, Blue, Blue, Green.

RINA

Select Cheats from the Options menu, choose Enter New Cheat and press Blue, Red, Green, Green, Yellow (x3), Green.

GUITAR HERO: AEROSMITH

To enter the following cheats, strum the guitar while holding the listed buttons. For example, if the codes lists Yellow + Orange, hold Yellow and Orange as you strum. Air Guitar, Precision Mode, and Performance Mode can be toggled on and off from the Cheats menu. You can also change between five different levels of Hyperspeed at this menu.

ALL SONGS

Red + Yellow
Green + Red
Green + Red
Red + Yellow
Red + Yellow
Green + Red
Red + Yellow
Red + Yellow
Green + Red
Green + Red
Red + Yellow
Red + Yellow
Green + Red
Red + Yellow
Red + Blue

AIR GUITAR

Red + Yellow
Green + Red
Red + Yellow
Red + Yellow
Red + Blue
Red + Blue
Red + Blue
Red + Blue
Red + Blue
Yellow + Blue
Yellow + Blue
Yellow + Orange

HYPERSPEED

Yellow + Orange
Yellow + Orange
Yellow + Orange
Yellow + Orange
Yellow + Orange
Red + Yellow
Red + Yellow
Red + Yellow
Red + Yellow
Red + Blue
Red + Blue
Red + Blue
Red + Blue
Red + Blue
Yellow + Blue
Yellow + Orange
Yellow + Orange

NO FAIL

Green + Red
Blue
Green + Red
Green + Yellow
Blue
Green + Yellow
Red + Yellow
Orange
Red + Yellow
Green + Yellow
Yellow
Green + Yellow
Green + Red

PERFORMANCE MODE

Green + Red
Green + Red
Red + Orange
Red + Blue
Green + Red
Green + Red
Red + Orange
Red + Blue

PRECISION MODE

Red + Yellow
Red + Blue
Red + Blue
Red + Yellow
Red + Yellow
Yellow + Blue
Yellow + Blue
Yellow + Blue
Red + Yellow
Red + Yellow
Red + Blue
Red + Blue
Red + Yellow
Red + Yellow
Yellow + Blue
Yellow + Blue
Yellow + Blue
Red + Blue

GUITAR HERO: METALLICA

Once entered, the cheats must be activated in the Cheats menu.

METALLICA COSTUMES
Select Cheats from Settings and enter Green, Red, Yellow, Blue, Blue, Yellow, Red, Green.

HYPERSPEED
Select Cheats from Settings and enter Green, Blue, Red, Yellow, Yellow, Red, Green, Green.

PERFORMANCE MODE
Select Cheats from Settings and enter Yellow, Yellow, Blue, Red, Blue, Green, Red, Red.

INVISIBLE ROCKER
Select Cheats from Settings and enter Green, Red, Yellow (x3), Blue, Blue, Green.

AIR INSTRUMENTS
Select Cheats from Settings and enter Red, Red, Blue, Yellow, Green (x3), Yellow.

ALWAYS DRUM FILL
Select Cheats from Settings and enter Red (x3), Blue, Blue, Green, Green, Yellow.

AUTO KICK
Select Cheats from Settings and enter Yellow, Green, Red, Blue (x4), Red. With this cheat activated, the bass pedal is automatically hit.

ALWAYS SLIDE
Select Cheats from Settings and enter Green, Green, Red, Red, Yellow, Red, Yellow, Blue. All Guitar Notes Become Touch Pad Sliding Notes.

BLACK HIGHWAY
Select Cheats from Settings and enter Yellow, Red, Green, Red, Green, Red, Red, Blue.

FLAME COLOR
Select Cheats from Settings and enter Green, Red, Green, Blue, Red, Red, Yellow, Blue.

GEM COLOR
Select Cheats from Settings and enter Blue, Red, Red, Green, Red, Green, Red, Yellow.

STAR COLOR
Select Cheats from Settings and enter Press Red, Red, Yellow, Red, Blue, Red, Red, Blue.

ADDITIONAL LINE 6 TONES
Select Cheats from Settings and enter Green, Red, Yellow, Blue, Red, Yellow, Blue, Green.

VOCAL FIREBALL
Select Cheats from Settings and enter Red, Green, Green, Yellow, Blue, Green, Yellow, Green.

GUITAR HERO: SMASH HITS

Enter the following in the cheats menu which can be found in the options menu.

ALWAYS DRUM FILL
Green, Green, Red, Red, Blue, Blue, Yellow, Yellow

ALWAYS SLIDE
Blue, Yellow, Red, Green, Blue, Green, Green, Yellow

HYPERSPEED
Red, Green, Blue, Yellow, Green, Yellow, Red, Red

AIR INSTRUMENTS
Yellow, Red, Blue, Green, Yellow, Red, Red, Red

INVISIBLE ROCKER
Blue, Red, Red, Red, Red, Yellow, Blue, Green

GEM COLOR
Red, Red, Red, Blue, Blue, Blue, Yellow, Green

STAR COLOR
Green, Red, Green, Yellow, Green, Blue, Yellow, Red

LINE 6 UNLOCK
Green, Red, Yellow, Blue, Red, Yellow, Blue, Green

VOCAL FIREBALL
Green, Blue, Red, Red, Yellow, Yellow, Blue, Blue

GUITAR HERO: VAN HALEN

ALWAYS DRUM FILL
Select Input Cheats from the Options menu and enter Red, Red, Red, Blue, Blue, Green, Green, Yellow.

ALWAYS SLIDE
Select Input Cheats from the Options menu and enter Green, Green, Red, Red, Yellow, Red, Yellow, Blue.

AUTO KICK
Select Input Cheats from the Options menu and enter Yellow, Green, Red, Blue, Blue, Blue, Blue, Red.

HYPERSPEED
Select Input Cheats from the Options menu and enter Green, Blue, Red, Yellow, Yellow, Red, Green, Green. This allows you to enable Hyperguitar, Hyperbass, and Hyperdrums.

PERFORMANCE MODE
Select Input Cheats from the Options menu and enter Yellow, Yellow, Blue, Red, Blue, Green, Red, Red.

AIR INSTRUMENTS
Select Input Cheats from the Options menu and enter Red, Red, Blue, Yellow, Green, Green, Green, Yellow.

INVISIBLE ROCKER
Select Input Cheats from the Options menu and enter Green, Red, Yellow, Yellow, Yellow, Blue, Blue, Green.

BLACK HIGHWAY
Select Input Cheats from the Options menu and enter Yellow, Red, Green, Red, Green, Red, Red, Blue.

FLAME COLOR

Select Input Cheats from the Options menu and enter Green, Red, Green, Blue, Red, Red, Yellow, Blue.

GEM COLOR

Select Input Cheats from the Options menu and enter Blue, Red, Red, Green, Red, Green, Red, Yellow.

STAR COLOR

Select Input Cheats from the Options menu and enter Red, Red, Yellow, Red, Blue, Red, Red, Blue.

VOCAL FIREBALL

Select Input Cheats from the Options menu and enter Red, Green, Green, Yellow, Blue, Green, Yellow, Green.

EXTRA LINE 6 TONES

Select Input Cheats from the Options menu and enter Green, Red, Yellow, Blue, Red, Yellow, Blue, Green.

GUITAR HERO: WARRIORS OF ROCK

Select Extras from Options to toggle the following on and off. Some cheats will disable Achievements.

ALL CHARACTERS

Select Cheats from the Options menu and enter Blue, Green, Green, Red, Green, Red, Yellow, Blue.

ALL VENUES

Select Cheats from the Options menu and enter Red, Blue, Blue, Red, Red, Blue, Blue, Red.

ALWAYS SLIDE

Select Cheats from the Options menu and enter Blue, Green, Green, Red, Red, Yellow, Blue, Yellow.

ALL HOPOS

Select Cheats from the Options menu and enter Green (x3), Blue, Green (x3), Yellow. Most notes become hammer-ons or pull-offs.

INVISIBLE ROCKER

Select Cheats from the Options menu and enter Green, Green, Red, Yellow (x3), Blue, Blue.

AIR INSTRUMENTS

Select Cheats from the Options menu and enter Yellow, Red, Red, Blue, Yellow, Green (x3).

FOCUS MODE

Select Cheats from the Options menu and enter Green, Yellow, Green, Red, Green, Yellow, Blue, Green. This removes the busy background.

HUD FREE MODE

Select Cheats from the Options menu and enter Green, Green, Red, Green, Green, Yellow, Green, Green.

PERFORMANCE MODE

Select Cheats from the Options menu and enter Red, Yellow, Yellow, Blue, Red, Blue, Green, Red.

COLOR SHUFFLE

Select Cheats from the Options menu and enter Blue, Green, Blue, Red, Yellow, Green, Red, Yellow.

MIRROR GEMS

Select Cheats from the Options menu and enter Blue, Blue, Red, Blue, Green, Green, Red, Green.

RANDOM GEMS

Select Cheats from the Options menu and enter Green, Green, Red, Red, Yellow, Red, Yellow, Blue.

ROCK BAND

ALL SONGS

At the title screen, press Red, Yellow, Blue, Red, Red, Blue, Blue, Red, Yellow, Blue. Saving and all network features are disabled with this code.

TRANSPARENT INSTRUMENTS

Complete the hall of fame concert with that instrument.

GOLD INSTRUMENT

Complete the solo tour with that instrument.

SILVER INSTRUMENT

Complete the bonus tour with that instrument.

ROCK BAND 2

Most of these codes disable saving, achievements, and Xbox LIVE play.

UNLOCK ALL SONGS

Select Modify Game from the Extras menu, choose Enter Unlock Code and press Red, Yellow, Blue, Red, Red, Blue, Blue, Red, Yellow, Blue or 🅨, 🅑, 🅧, 🅨, 🅨, 🅧, 🅧, 🅨, 🅑, 🅧. Toggle this cheat on or off from the Modify Game menu.

SELECT VENUE SCREEN

Select Modify Game from the Extras menu, choose Enter Unlock Code and press Blue, Orange, Orange, Blue, Yellow, Blue, Orange, Orange, Blue, Yellow or (for Xbox 360) 🅧, Left Bumper, Left Bumper, 🅧, 🅑, 🅧, Left Bumper, Left Bumper, 🅧, 🅑. Toggle this cheat on or off from the Modify Game menu.

NEW VENUES ONLY

Select Modify Game from the Extras menu, choose Enter Unlock Code and press Red, Red, Red, Red, Yellow, Yellow, Yellow, Yellow or (for Xbox 360) 🅨 (x4), 🅑 (x4). Toggle this cheat on or off from the Modify Game menu.

PLAY THE GAME WITHOUT A TRACK

Select Modify Game from the Extras menu, choose Enter Unlock Code and press Blue, Blue, Red, Red, Yellow, Yellow, Blue, Blue or (for Xbox 360) ❌, ❌, ❓, ❓, Ⓑ, Ⓑ, ❌, ❌. Toggle this cheat on or off from the Modify Game menu.

AWESOMENESS DETECTION

Select Modify Game from the Extras menu, choose Enter Unlock Code and press Yellow, Blue, Orange, Yellow, Blue, Orange, Yellow, Blue, Orange or (for Xbox 360) Ⓑ, ❌, Left Bumper, Ⓑ, ❌, Left Bumper, Ⓑ, ❌, Left Bumper. Toggle this cheat on or off from the Modify Game menu.

STAGE MODE

Select Modify Game from the Extras menu, choose Enter Unlock Code and press Blue, Yellow, Red, Blue, Yellow, Red, Blue, Yellow, Red or (for Xbox 360) ❌, Ⓑ, ❓, ❌, Ⓑ, ❓, ❌, Ⓑ, ❓. Toggle this cheat on or off from the Modify Game menu.

ROCK BAND 3

GUILD X-79 GUITAR

At the main menu, press Blue, Orange, Orange, Blue, Orange, Orange, Blue, Blue.

OVATION D-2010 GUITAR

At the main menu, press Orange, Blue, Orange, Orange, Blue, Blue, Orange, Blue.

THE BEATLES: ROCK BAND

BONUS PHOTOS

At the title screen, press Blue, Yellow, Orange, Orange, Orange, Blue, Blue, Blue, Yellow, Orange.

CONTENTS

2010 FIFA WORLD CUP SOUTH AFRICA

ADIDAS U11 TEAM
Go to EA Extras in My 2010 FIFA World Cup. Select Unlockable Code Entry and enter WSBJPJYODFYQIIGK.

FINAL MATCH BALL
Go to EA Extras in My 2010 FIFA World Cup. Select Unlockable Code Entry and enter FGWIXGFXTNSICLSS.

ADIDAS ADIPURE III TRX (BLACK/SUN)
Go to EA Extras in My 2010 FIFA World Cup. Select Unlockable Code Entry and enter HHDOPWPMIXZQOJOZ.

ADIDAS F50 ADIZERO (BLACK/SUN/SUN)
Go to EA Extras in My 2010 FIFA World Cup. Select Unlockable Code Entry and enter SGFSTZPPXCHHMJMH.

ADIDAS F50 ADIZERO (CHAMELEON)
Go to EA Extras in My 2010 FIFA World Cup. Select Unlockable Code Entry and enter VOKMNEZTJOQPULUT.

ADIDAS F50 ADIZERO (SUN/BLACK/GOLD)
Go to EA Extras in My 2010 FIFA World Cup. Select Unlockable Code Entry and enter YOZCCVIFJGKQJWTW.

ADIDAS PREDATOR X (BLACK/SUN)
Go to EA Extras in My 2010 FIFA World Cup. Select Unlockable Code Entry and enter OCEGZCUHXOBSBNFU.

COCA-COLA CELEBRATIONS
Go to EA Extras in My 2010 FIFA World Cup. Select Unlockable Code Entry and enter the following:

CELEBRATION	CODE	HOW TO PERFORM
Baby Cradle	UGSIMLBHLFPUBFJY	L2 + ✖
Dance	KBRRWKUIRSTWUJQW	L2 + ⬤
Dying Fly	DVMNJPBTLHJZGECP	L2 + ⬤
Flying Dive	DBQDUXQTRWTVXYDC	L2 + 🔺

CELEBRATION	CODE	HOW TO PERFORM
Prancing Bird	TWVBIXYACAOLGOWO	R1 + ●
River Dance	MIKAKPUMEEWNTQVE	R1 + ●
Side Slide	VNDWDUDLMGRNHDNV	R1 + ▲
Speed Skating	LHEHJZTPYYQDJQXB	R1 + ✖

3D DOT GAME HEROES

HIDE SHIELD
Pause the game and press Up, Up, Down, Down, Left, Right, Left, Right, ●, ▲. Re-enter the code to show the shield again.

TOGGLE SWAY IN WALKING
Pause the game and press L1, R1, L1, R1, L1, L1, R1, R1, ●. Re-enter to turn this back on.

SPELUNKER MODE
Enter your name as SPELUNKER. In this mode, you will die with one hit—along with some dialogue changes.

BAJA: EDGE OF CONTROL

CAREER COMPLETE 100%
Select Cheat Codes from the Options menu and enter SHOWTIME.

INSTALL ALL PARTS
Select Cheat Codes from the Options menu and enter SUPERMAX.

BAKUGAN BATTLE BRAWLERS

1,000 BP
Enter 33204429 as your name.

10,000 BP
Enter 46836478 as your name.

100,000 BP
Enter 18499753 as your name.

5,000 BP
Enter 42348294 as your name.

500,000 BP
Enter 26037947 as your name.

BEJEWELED 2

TOGGLE CLASSIC STYLE GEMS
During a game, hold L1 + L2 + R1 + R2 and press ✖.

TOGGLE GAME BORDERS
During a game, hold L1 + L2 + R1 + R2 and press ●.

BEN 10 ULTIMATE ALIEN: COSMIC DESTRUCTION

These cheats disable Trophies. To remove the cheats, you will need to start a new game.

1,000,000 DNA
Pause the game, select Cheats, and enter Cash.

REGENERATE HEALTH
Pause the game, select Cheats, and enter Health.

REGENERATE ENERGY
Pause the game, select Cheats, and enter Energy.

UPGRADE EVERYTHING
Pause the game, select Cheats, and enter Upgrade.

ALL LEVELS
Pause the game, select Cheats, and enter Levels.

ENEMIES DO DOUBLE DAMAGE/PLAYER DOES ½ DAMAGE
Pause the game, select Cheats, and enter Hard.

UNLOCKS FOUR ARMS
Pause the game, select Cheats, and enter Classic.

THE BIGS

START A ROOKIE WITH HIGHER STATS
When you create a rookie, name him HOT DOG. His stats will be higher than when you normally start.

BLAZING ANGELS 2: SECRET MISSIONS OF WWII

ALL MISSIONS AND PLANES UNLOCKED
At the main menu, hold L2 + R2, and press ●, L1, R1, ▲, ▲, R1, L1, ●.

GOD MODE
Pause the game, hold L2, and press ●, ▲, ▲, ●. Release L2, hold R2 and press ▲, ●, ●, ▲. Re-enter the code to disable it.

INCREASED DAMAGE WITH ALL WEAPONS
Pause the game, hold L2, and press L1, L1, R1. Release L2, hold R2, and press R1, R1, L1. Re-enter the code to disable it.

BLUR

CONCEPT 1 SERIES TII CHROME
In the Multiplayer Showroom, highlight the BMW Concept 1 Series tii and press L2, R2, L2, R2.

FULLY UPGRADE FORD BRONCO
In the Multiplayer Showroom, highlight the Ford Bronco and press L2, R2, L2, R2.

BOLT
Many of the following cheats can be toggled on/off by pausing the game and selecting Cheats.

LEVEL SELECT
Select Cheats from the Extras menu and enter Right, Up, Left, Right, Up, Right.

ALL MINIGAMES
Select Cheats from the Extras menu and enter Right, Up, Right, Right.

UNLIMITED ENHANCED VISION
Select Cheats from the Extras menu and enter Left, Right, Up, Down.

UNLIMITED GROUND POUND
Select Cheats from the Extras menu and enter Right, Up, Right, Up, Left, Down.

UNLIMITED INVULNERABILITY
Select Cheats from the Extras menu and enter Down, Down, Up, Left.

UNLIMITED GAS MINES
Select Cheats from the Extras menu and enter Right, Left, Left, Up, Down, Right.

UNLIMITED LASER EYES
Select Cheats from the Extras menu and enter Left, Left, Up, Right.

UNLIMITED STEALTH CAMO
Select Cheats from the Extras menu and enter Left, Down (x3).

UNLIMITED SUPERBARK
Select Cheats from the Extras menu and enter Right, Left, Left, Up, Down, Up.

BURNOUT PARADISE

BEST BUY CAR

Pause the game and select Sponsor Product Code from the Under the Hood menu. Enter Bestbuy. Need A License to use this car offline.

CIRCUIT CITY CAR

Pause the game and select Sponsor Product Code from the Under the Hood menu. Enter Circuitcity. Need Burnout Paradise License to use this car offline.

GAMESTOP CAR

Pause the game and select Sponsor Product Code from the Under the Hood menu. Enter Gamestop. Need A License to use this car offline.

WALMART CAR

Pause the game and select Sponsor Product Code from the Under the Hood menu.. Enter Walmart. Need Burnout Paradise License to use this car offline.

"STEEL WHEELS" GT

Pause the game and select Sponsor Product Code from the Under the Hood menu. Enter G23X 5K8Q GX2V 04B1 or E60J 8Z7T MS8L 51U6.

LICENSES

LICENSE	NUMBER OF WINS NEEDED
D	2
C	7
B	16
A	26
Burnout Paradise	45
Elite License	All events

CARS 2: THE VIDEO GAME

ALL MODES AND TRACKS

Select Enter Codes from the Options and enter 959595.

LASER GUIDED

Select Enter Codes from the Options and enter 123456. Select Cheats to toggle the cheat on and off.

UNLIMITED ENERGY

Select Enter Codes from the Options and enter 721953. Select Cheats to toggle the cheat on and off.

CARS MATER-NATIONAL

ALL ARCADE RACES, MINI-GAMES, AND WORLDS

Select Codes/Cheats from the options and enter PLAYALL.

ALL CARS

Select Codes/Cheats from the options and enter MATTEL07.

ALTERNATE LIGHTNING MCQUEEN COLORS

Select Codes/Cheats from the options and enter NCEDUDZ.

ALL COLORS FOR OTHERS

Select Codes/Cheats from the options and enter PAINTIT.

UNLIMITED TURBO

Select Codes/Cheats from the options and enter ZZOOOOM.

EXTREME ACCELERATION

Select Codes/Cheats from the options and enter OTO200X.

EXPERT MODE

Select Codes/Cheats from the options and enter VRYFAST.

ALL BONUS ART

Select Codes/Cheats from the options and enter BUYTALL.

DIRT 2

Win the given events to earn the following cars:

GET THIS CAR	BY WINNING THIS EVENT
Ford RS200 Evolution	Rally Cross World Tour
Toyota Stadium Truck	Landrush World Tour
Mitsubishi Pajero Dakar 1993	Raid World Tour
Dallenbach Special	Trailblazer World Tour
1995 Subaru Impreza WRX STi	Colin McRae Challenge
Colin McRae R4 [X Games]	X Games Europe
Mitsubishi Lancer Evolution X [X Games]	X Games Asia
Subaru Impreza WRX STi [X Games]	X Games America
Ford Escort MKII and MG Metro 6R4	All X Games events

DISGAEA 4: A PROMISE UNFORGOTTEN

EXTRA CHARACTERS

After completing the story, extra battles become available from the Senate. Clear these to unlock the following characters.

CHARACTER	CLEAR EXTRA BATTLE
Axel	1
Flonne	2
Raspberyl	3
Etna	4
Laharl	5
Asagi	6
Kurtis	7
Zetta	9

DJ HERO

Select Cheats from Options and enter the following. Some codes will disable high scores and progress. Cheats cannot be used in tutorials and online.

UNLOCK ALL CONTENT
Enter tol0.

ALL CHARACTER ITEMS
Enter uNA2.

ALL VENUES
Enter Wv1u.

ALL DECKS
Enter LAuP.

ALL HEADPHONES
Enter 62Db.

ALL MIXES
Enter 82xl.

AUTO SCRATCH
Enter it6j.

AUTO EFFECTS DIAL
Enter ab1l.

AUTO FADER
Enter sl5d.

AUTO TAPPER
Enter zith.

AUTO WIN EUPHORIA
Enter r3a9.

BLANK PLINTHS
Enter ipr0.

HAMSTER SWITCH
Enter 7geo.

HYPER DECK MODE
Enter 76st.

SHORT DECK
Enter 51uc.

BLACK AND WHITE
Enter b!99.

EDGE EFFECT
Enter 2u4u.

INVISIBLE DJ
Enter oh5t.

MIDAS
Enter 4pe5.

PITCH BLACK OUT
Enter d4kr.

PLAY IN THE BEDROOM
Enter g7nh.

RAINBOW
Enter ?jy!.

ANY DJ, ANY SETLIST
Enter 0jj8.

DAFT PUNK'S CONTENT
Enter d1g?.

DJ AM'S CONTENT
Enter k07u.

DJ JAZZY JEFF'S CONTENT
Enter n1fz.

DJ SHADOW'S CONTENT
Enter omxv.

DJ Z-TRIP'S CONTENT
Enter 5rtg.

GRANDMASTER FLASH'S CONTENT
Enter ami8.

DJ HERO 2

ALL BONUS CONTENT
Select Cheats from the Options. Choose Retail Cheats and enter VIP Pass.

DAVID GUETTA
Select Cheats from the Options. Choose Retail Cheats and enter Guetta Blaster.

DEADMAU5
Select Cheats from the Options. Choose Retail Cheats and enter Open The Trap.

DRIVER: SAN FRANCISCO

MOVIE SCENE CHALLENGES
As you collect the 130 Movie Tokens in the game, Movie Scene Challenges are unlocked as shown below.

MOVIE SCENE CHALLENGE	VEHICLE GIVEN	# MOVIE TOKENS
Gone In 60 Seconds	1973 Ford Mustang Mach I	10
Starsky & Hutch	1974 Dodge Monaco Cop	20
Bullitt	1968 Ford Mustang GT Fastback	30
The French Connection	1971 Pontiac LeMans	40
Blues Brothers	1974 Dodge Monaco	50
Cannonball Run	1978 Lamborghini Countach LP400S	60
Dukes of Hazard	1969 Dodge Charger R/T	70
Vanishing Point	1970 Dodge Challenger R/T	80
The Driver	1965 Chevrolet S-10	90
Redline	2011 McLaren MP4-12C	100
Smokey & The Bandit	1977 Pontiac TransAm Firebird	110
Test Drive	1987 RUF CT-R Yellow Bird	120
The Italian Job	1972 Lamborghini Miura	130

EARTH DEFENSE FORCE: INSECT ARMAGEDDON

HIDDEN IMAGES IN GALLERY
Select Gallery from the Extras menu. At the gallery press ●, ●, ▲, ●, L1, R1.

G.I. JOE: THE RISE OF COBRA

CLASSIC DUKE
At the main menu, press Left, Up, ●, Up, Right, ▲.

SHANA "SCARLETT" O'HARA
At the main menu, press Right, Up, Down, Down, ▲.

GRID

ALL DRIFT CARS
Select Bonus Codes from the Options. Then choose Enter Code and enter TUN58396.

ALL MUSCLE CARS
Select Bonus Codes from the Options. Then choose Enter Code and enter MUS59279.

BUCHBINDER EMOTIONAL ENGINEERING BMW 320SI
Select Bonus Codes from the Options. Then choose Enter Code and enter F93857372. You can use this in Race Day or in GRID World once you've started your own team.

EBAY MOTORS MUSTANG
Select Bonus Codes from the Options. Then choose Enter Code and enter DAFJ55E01473M0. You can use this in Race Day or in GRID World once you've started your own team.

GAMESTATION BMW 320SI
Select Bonus Codes from the Options. Then choose Enter Code and enter G29782655. You can use this in Race Day or in GRID World once you've started your own team.

MICROMANIA PAGANI ZONDA R
Select Bonus Codes from the Options. Then choose Enter Code and enter M38572343. You can use this in Race Day or in GRID World once you've started your own team.

PLAY.COM ASTON MARTIN DBR9
Select Bonus Codes from the Options. Then choose Enter Code and enter P47203845. You can use this in Race Day or in GRID World once you've started your own team.

IRON MAN

CLASSIC ARMOR
Clear One Man Army vs. Mercs.

EXTREMIS ARMOR
Clear One Man Army vs. Maggia.

MARK II ARMOR
Clear One Man Army vs. Ten Rings.

HULKBUSTER ARMOR
Clear One Man Army vs. AIM-X. Can also be unlocked when clear game save data from Incredible Hulk is stored on the same console.

CLASSIC MARK I ARMOR
Clear One Man Army vs. AIM.

ULTIMATE ARMOR
Clear Mission 13: Showdown.

KUNG FU PANDA

UNLIMITED CHI
Select Cheats from the Extra menu and enter Down, Right, Left, Up, Down.

INVULNERABILITY
Select Cheats from the Extra menu and enter Down, Down, Right, Up, Left.

FULL UPGRADES
Select Cheats from the Extra menu and enter Left, Right, Down, Left, Up.

FULL AWESOME METER
Select Cheats from the Extra menu and enter Up, Down, Up, Right, Left. This gives Po 4X damage.

MULTIPLAYER CHARACTERS

Select Cheats from the Extra menu and enter Left, Down, Left, Right, Down.

OUTFITS

Select Cheats from the Extra menu and enter Right, Left, Down, Up, Right.

LARA CROFT AND THE GUARDIAN OF LIGHT

LARA CROFT HEAVY JUNGLE OUTFIT
Complete the game.

LARA CROFT JUNGLE OUTFIT
Score 1,410,000 points.

LARA CROFT BIKER OUTFIT
Score 1,900,000 points.

LARA CROFT LEGEND OUTFIT
Defeat Xolotl.

DOPPELGANGER OUTFIT
Score 2,400,000 points.

THE LEGEND OF SPYRO: DAWN OF THE DRAGON

UNLIMITED LIFE

Pause the game, hold **L1** and press Right, Right, Down, Down, Left with the Left Analog Stick.

UNLIMITED MANA

Pause the game, hold **R1** and press Up, Right, Up, Left, Down with the Left Analog Stick.

MAXIMUM XP

Pause the game, hold **R1** and press Left, Right, Right, Up, Up with the Left Analog Stick.

ALL ELEMENTAL UPGRADES

Pause the game, hold **L1** and press Left, Up, Down, Up, Right with the Left Analog Stick.

LEGO BATMAN

BATCAVE CODES

Using the computer in the Batcave, select Enter Code and enter the following codes.

CHARACTERS

CHARACTER	CODE	CHARACTER	CODE
Alfred	ZAQ637	Military Policeman	MKL382
Batgirl	JKR331	Nightwing	MVY759
Bruce Wayne	BDJ327	Penguin Goon	NKA238
Catwoman (Classic)	M1AAWW	Penguin Henchman	BJH782
Clown Goon	HJK327	Penguin Minion	KJP748
Commissioner Gordon	DDP967	Poison Ivy Goon	GTB899
Fishmonger	HGY748	Police Marksman	HKG984
Freeze Girl	XVK541	Police Officer	JRY983
Joker Goon	UTF782	Riddler Goon	CRY928
Joker Henchman	YUN924	Riddler Henchman	XEU824
Mad Hatter	JCA283	S.W.A.T.	HTF114
Man-Bat	NYU942	Sailor	NAV592

CHARACTER	CODE	CHARACTER	CODE
Scientist	JFL786	Yeti	NJL412
Security Guard	PLB946	Zoo Sweeper	DWR243
The Joker (Tropical)	CCB199		

VEHICLES

VEHICLE	CODE	VEHICLE	CODE
Bat-Tank	KNTT4B	Mr. Freeze's Kart	BCT229
Bruce Wayne's Private Jet	LEA664	Penguin Goon Submarine	BTN248
Catwoman's Motorcycle	HPLB26	Police Bike	LJP234
Garbage Truck	DUS483	Police Boat	PLC999
Goon Helicopter	GCH328	Police Car	KJL832
Harbor Helicopter	CHP735	Police Helicopter	CWR732
Harley Quinn's Hammer Truck	RDT637	Police Van	MAC788
Mad Hatter's Glider	HS000W	Police Watercraft	VJD328
Mad Hatter's Steamboat	M4DM4N	Riddler's Jet	HAHAHA
Mr. Freeze's Iceberg	ICYICE	Robin's Submarine	TTF453
The Joker's Van	JUK657	Two-Face's Armored Truck	EFE933

CHEATS

CHEAT	CODE	CHEAT	CODE
Always Score Multiply	9LRGNB	More Batarang Targets	XWP645
Fast Batarangs	JRBDCB	Piece Detector	KHJ554
Fast Walk	ZOLM6N	Power Brick Detector	MMN786
Flame Batarang	D8NYWH	Regenerate Hearts	HJH7HJ
Freeze Batarang	XPN4NG	Score x2	N4NR3E
Extra Hearts	ML3KHP	Score x4	CX9MAT
Fast Build	EVG26J	Score x6	MLVNF2
Immune to Freeze	JXUDY6	Score x8	WCCDB9
Invincibility	WYD5CP	Score x10	18HW07
Minikit Detector	ZXGH9J		

LEGO HARRY POTTER: YEARS 1-4

RED BRICK EXTRAS

Once you have access to The Leaky Cauldron, enter Wiseacre's Wizarding Supplies from Diagon Alley. Go upstairs to enter the following. Pause the game and select Extras to toggle the cheats on/off.

CHEAT	CODE	CHEAT	CODE
Carrot Wands	AUC8EH	Invincibility	QQWC6B
Character Studs	H27KGC	Red Brick Detector	7AD7HE
Character Token Detector	HA79V8	Regenerate Hearts	89ML2W
Christmas	T7PVVN	Score x2	74YKR7
Disguise	4DMK2R	Score x4	J3WHNK
Fall Rescue	ZEX7MV	Score x6	XK9ANE
Extra Hearts	J9U6Z9	Score x8	HUFV2H
Fast Dig	Z9BFAD	Score x10	H8X69Y
Fast Magic	FA3GQA	Silhouettes	HZBVX7
Gold Brick Detector	84QNQN	Singing Mandrake	BMEU6X
Hogwarts Crest Detector	TTMC6D	Stud Magnet	67FKWZ
Ice Rink	F88VUW		

WISEACRE SPELLS

Once you have access to The Leaky Cauldron, enter Wiseacre's Wizarding Supplies from Diagon Alley. Go upstairs to enter the following. You need to learn Wingardium Leviosa before you can use these cheats.

SPELL	CODE	SPELL	CODE
Accio	VE9VV7	Incarcerous	YEB9Q9
Anteoculatia	QFB6NR	Locomotor Mortis	2M2XJ6
Calvorio	6DNR6L	Multicorfors	JK6QRM
Colovaria	9GJ442	Redactum Skullus	UW8LRH
Engorgio Skullus	CD4JLX	Rictusempra	2UCA3M
Entomorphis	MYN3NB	Slugulus Eructo	U6EE8X
Flipendo	ND2L7W	Stupefy	UWDJ4Y
Glacius	ERA9DR	Tarantallegra	KWWQ44
Herbifors	H8FTHL	Trip Jinx	YZNRF6

EEYLOPS GOLD BRICKS

Once you have access to The Leaky Cauldron, enter Wiseacre's Wizarding Supplies from Diagon Alley. Go upstairs to enter the following. To access the LEGO Builder, visit Gringott's Bank at the end of Diagon Alley.

GOLD BRICK	CODE	GOLD BRICK	CODE
1	QE4VC7	7	XY6VYZ
2	FY8H97	8	TUNC4W
3	3MQT4P	9	EJ42Q6
4	PQPM7Z	10	GFJCV9
5	ZY2CPA	11	DZCY6G
6	3GMTP6		

LEGO INDIANA JONES: THE ORIGINAL ADVENTURES

CHARACTERS

Approach the blackboard in the Classsroom and enter the following codes.

CHARACTER	CODE	CHARACTER	CODE
Bandit	12N68W	Enemy Guard	VJ7R51
Bandit Swordsman	1MK4RT	Enemy Guard (Mountains)	YR47WM
Barranca	04EM94	Enemy Officer	572E61
Bazooka Trooper (Crusade)	MK83R7	Enemy Officer (Desert	2MK450
Bazooka Trooper (Raiders)	S93Y5R	Enemy Pilot	B84ELP
Belloq	CHN3YU	Enemy Radio Operator	1MF94R
Belloq (Jungle)	TDR197	Enemy Soldier (Desert)	4NSU7Q
Belloq (Robes)	VEO29L	Fedora	V75YSP
British Commander	B73EUA	First Mate	0GIN24
British Officer	VJ5TI9	Grail Knight	NE6THI
British Soldier	DJ5I2W	Hovitos Tribesman	H0V1SS
Captain Katanga	VJ3TT3	Indiana Jones (Desert Disguise)	4J8S4M
Chatter Lal	ENW936	Indiana Jones (Officer)	VJ850S
Chatter Lal (Thuggee)	CNH4RY	Jungle Guide	24PF34
Chen	3NK48T	Kao Kan	WM046L
Colonel Dietrich	2K9RKS	Kazim	NRH23J
Colonel Vogel	8EAL4H	Kazim (Desert)	3M29TJ
Dancing Girl	C7EJ21	Lao Che	2NK479
Donovan	3NFTU8	Maharajah	NFK5N2
Elsa (Desert)	JSNRT9	Major Toht	13NS01
Elsa (Officer)	VMJ5US	Masked Bandit	N48SF0
Enemy Boxer	8246RB	Mola Ram	FJUR31
Enemy Butler	VJ48W3	Monkey Man	3RF6YJ

CHARACTER	CODE
Pankot Assassin	2NKT72
Pankot Guard	VN28RH
Sherpa Brawler	VJ37WJ
Sherpa Gunner	ND762W
Slave Child	OE3ENW
Thuggee	VM683E
Thuggee Acolyte	T2R3F9

CHARACTER	CODE
Thuggee Slave Driver	VBS7GW
Village Dignitary	KD48TN
Village Elder	4682E1
Willie (Dinner Suit)	VK93R7
Willie (Pajamas)	MEN4IP
Wu Han	3NSLT8

EXTRAS

Approach the blackboard in the Classsroom and enter the following codes. Some cheats need to be enabled by selecting Extras from the pause menu.

CHEAT	CODE
Artifact Detector	VIKED7
Beep Beep	VNF59Q
Character Treasure	VIES2R
Disarm Enemies	VKRNS9
Disguises	4ID1N6
Fast Build	V83SLO
Fast Dig	378RS6
Fast Fix	FJ59WS
Fertilizer	B1GW1F
Ice Rink	33GM7J
Parcel Detector	VUT673
Poo Treasure	WWQ1SA

CHEAT	CODE
Regenerate Hearts	MDLP69
Secret Characters	3X44AA
Silhouettes	3HE85H
Super Scream	VN3R7S
Super Slap	OP1TA5
Treasure Magnet	H86LA2
Treasure x10	VI3PS8
Treasure x2	VM4TS9
Treasure x4	VLWEN3
Treasure x6	V84RYS
Treasure x8	A72E1M

LEGO INDIANA JONES 2: THE ADVENTURE CONTINUES

Pause the game, select Enter Secret Code from the Extras menu, and enter the following.

CHARACTERS

CHARACTER	CODE
Belloq (Priest)	FTL48S
Dovchenko	WL4T6N
Enemy Boxer	7EQF47
Henry Jones	4CSAKH
Indiana Jones	PGWSEA
Indiana Jones: 2	FGLKYS
Indiana Jones (Collect)	DZFY9S
Indiana Jones (Desert)	M4C34K
Indiana Jones (Desert Disguise)	2W8QR3
Indiana Jones (Dinner Suit)	QUNZUT
Indiana Jones (Kali)	J2XS97
Indiana Jones (Officer)	3FQFKS
Interdimensional Being	PXT4UP
Lao Che	7AWX3J
Mannequin (Boy)	2UJQWC
Mannequin (Girl)	3PGSEL
Mannequin (Man)	QPWDMM
Mannequin (Woman)	U7SMVK
Mola Ram	82RMC2
Mutt	2GKS62
Salah	E88YRP
Willie	94RUAJ

EXTRAS

EFFECT	CODE
Beep Beep	UU3VSC
Disguise	Y9TE98
Fast Build	SNXC2F
Fast Dig	XYAN83
Fast Fix	3Z7PJX
Fearless	TUXNZF
Ice Rink	TY9P4U
Invincibility	6JBB65
Poo Money	SZFAAE
Score x3	PEHHPZ
Score x4	UXGTB3
Score X6	XWLJEY
Score x8	S5UZCP
Score x10	V7JYBU
Silhouettes	FQGPYH
Snake Whip	2U7YCV
Stud Magnet	EGSM5B

LEGO PIRATES OF THE CARIBBEAN: THE VIDEO GAME

CODES

Pause the game and select Extras. Choose Enter Code and enter the following codes:

EFFECT	PASSWORD
Ammand the Corsair	EW8T6T
Angelica (Disguised)	DLRR45
Angry Cannibal	VGF32C
Blackbeard	D3DW0D
Clanker	ZM37GT
Clubba	644THF
Davy Jones	4DJLKR
Govorner Weatherby Swann	LD9454
Gunner	Y611WB

EFFECT	PASSWORD
Hungry Cannibal	64BNHG
Jack Sparrow (Musical)	VDJSPW
Jacoby	BW0656
Jimmy Legs	13GLW5
King George	RKED43
Koehler	RT093G
Mistress Ching	GDETDE
Phillip	WEV040
Quartermaster	RX58HU
The Spaniard	P861J0
Twigg	KDLFKD

LEGO STAR WARS: THE COMPLETE SAGA

The following still need to be purchase after entering the codes.

CHARACTERS

ADMIRAL ACKBAR

At the bar in Mos Eisley Cantina, select Enter Code and enter ACK646.

BATTLE DROID (COMMANDER)

At the bar in Mos Eisley Cantina, select Enter Code and enter KPF958.

BOBA FETT (BOY)

At the bar in Mos Eisley Cantina, select Enter Code and enter GGF539.

BOSS NASS

At the bar in Mos Eisley Cantina, select Enter Code and enter HHY697.

CAPTAIN TARPALS

At the bar in Mos Eisley Cantina, select Enter Code and enter QRN714.

COUNT DOOKU

At the bar in Mos Eisley Cantina, select Enter Code and enter DDD748.

DARTH MAUL

At the bar in Mos Eisley Cantina, select Enter Code and enter EUK421.

EWOK

At the bar in Mos Eisley Cantina, select Enter Code and enter EWK785.

GENERAL GRIEVOUS

At the bar in Mos Eisley Cantina, select Enter Code and enter PMN576.

GREEDO

At the bar in Mos Eisley Cantina, select Enter Code and enter ZZR636.

IG-88

At the bar in Mos Eisley Cantina, select Enter Code and enter GIJ989.

IMPERIAL GUARD

At the bar in Mos Eisley Cantina, select Enter Code and enter GUA850.

JANGO FETT

At the bar in Mos Eisley Cantina, select Enter Code and enter KLJ897.

KI-ADI MUNDI

At the bar in Mos Eisley Cantina, select Enter Code and enter MUN486.

LUMINARA

At the bar in Mos Eisley Cantina, select Enter Code and enter LUM521.

PADMÉ

At the bar in Mos Eisley Cantina, select Enter Code and enter VBJ322.

R2-Q5

At the bar in Mos Eisley Cantina, select Enter Code and enter EVILR2.

STORMTROOPER

At the bar in Mos Eisley Cantina, select Enter Code and enter NBN431.

TAUN WE

At the bar in Mos Eisley Cantina, select Enter Code and enter PRX482.

VULTURE DROID

At the bar in Mos Eisley Cantina, select Enter Code and enter BDC866.

WATTO

At the bar in Mos Eisley Cantina, select Enter Code and enter PLL967.

ZAM WESELL

At the bar in Mos Eisley Cantina, select Enter Code and enter 584HJF.

SKILLS

DISGUISE

At the bar in Mos Eisley Cantina, select Enter Code and enter BRJ437.

FORCE GRAPPLE LEAP

At the bar in Mos Eisley Cantina, select Enter Code and enter CLZ738.

VEHICLES

DROID TRIFIGHTER

At the bar in Mos Eisley Cantina, select Enter Code and enter AAB123.

IMPERIAL SHUTTLE

At the bar in Mos Eisley Cantina, select Enter Code and enter HUT845.

TIE INTERCEPTOR

At the bar in Mos Eisley Cantina, select Enter Code and enter INT729.

TIE FIGHTER

At the bar in Mos Eisley Cantina, select Enter Code and enter DBH897.

ZAM'S AIRSPEEDER

At the bar in Mos Eisley Cantina, select Enter Code and enter UUU875.

LITTLEBIGPLANET

CHEAT PAST ALL THE CREATE MODE TUTORIALS

As the credits roll press Down, Up, L1, L2, R2, R1, ●, ⊗.

LUCHA LIBRE AAA: HEROES DEL RING

LITTLE ONES

At the character select, press Up, Up, Down, Down, Left, Right, Left, Right. Play with them to unlock the Little Ones Can Too Trophy.

MADDEN NFL 12

MADDEN NFL 12 DEVELOPERS TEAM IN EXHIBITION

Select Exhibition from Play Now. At the team select, press the Random Team button, L2, until the Developers team shows up. Once you have entered a game as the team, they will always be on the list.

MARVEL ULTIMATE ALLIANCE

UNLOCK ALL SKINS
At the Team Menu, press Up, Down, Left, Right, Left, Right, Start.

UNLOCKS ALL HERO POWERS
At the Team Menu, press Left, Right, Up, Down, Up, Down, Start.

ALL HEROES TO LEVEL 99
At the Team Menu, press Up, Left, Up, Left, Down, Right, Down, Right, Start.

UNLOCK ALL HEROES
At the Team Menu, press Up, Up, Down, Down, Left, Left, Left, Start.

UNLOCK DAREDEVIL
At the Team Menu, press Left, Left, Right, Right, Up, Down, Up, Down, Start.

UNLOCK SILVER SURFER
At the Team Menu, press Down, Left, Left, Up, Right, Up, Down, Left, Start.

GOD MODE
During gameplay, press Up, Down, Up, Down, Up, Left, Down, Right, Start.

TOUCH OF DEATH
During gameplay, press Left, Right, Down, Down, Right, Left, Start.

SUPER SPEED
During gameplay, press Up, Left, Up, Right, Down, Right, Start.

FILL MOMENTUM
During gameplay, press Left, Right, Right, Left, Up, Down, Down, Up, Start.

UNLOCK ALL COMICS
At the Review menu, press Left, Right, Right, Left, Up, Up, Right, Start.

UNLOCK ALL CONCEPT ART
At the Review menu, press Down, Down, Down, Right, Right, Left, Down, Start.

UNLOCK ALL CINEMATICS
At the Review menu, press Up, Left, Left, Up, Right, Right, Up, Start.

UNLOCK ALL LOAD SCREENS
At the Review menu, press Up, Down, Right, Left, Up, Up Down, Start.

UNLOCK ALL COURSES
At the Comic Missions menu, press Up, Right, Left, Down, Up, Right, Left, Down, Start.

MARVEL ULTIMATE ALLIANCE 2

These codes will disable the ability to save.

GOD MODE
During a game, press Up, Down, Up, Down, Up, Left, Down, Right, Start.

UNLIMITED FUSION
During a game, press Right, Right, Up, Down, Up, Up, Left, Start.

UNLOCK ALL POWERS
During a game, press Left, Right, Up, Down, Up, Down, Start.

UNLOCK ALL HEROES
During a game, press Up, Up, Down, Down, Left, Left, Left, Start.

UNLOCK ALL SKINS
During a game, press Up, Down, Left, Right, Left, Right, Start.

UNLOCK JEAN GREY
During a game, press Left, Left, Right, Right, Up, Down, Up, Down, Start.

UNLOCK HULK
During a game, press Down, Left, Left, Up, Right, Up, Down, Left, Start.

UNLOCK THOR
During a game, press Up, Right, Right, Down, Right, Down, Left, Right, Start.

UNLOCK ALL AUDIO LOGS
At the main menu, press Left, Right, Right, Left, Up, Up, Right, Start.

UNLOCK ALL DOSSIERS
At the main menu, press Down, Down, Down, Right, Right, Left, Down, Start.

UNLOCK ALL MOVIES
At the main menu, press Up, Left, Left, Up, Right, Right, Up, Start.

MLB 08: THE SHOW

ALL CLASSIC STADIUMS
At the main menu, press Down, Right, Circle, Square, Left, Triangle, Up, **L1**. The controller will vibrate if entered correctly.

MLB 10: THE SHOW

SILENCE DAVE CAMPBELL
Pause the game and press Up, Up, Down, Down, Left, Right, Left, Up.

SILENCE MATT VASGERSIAN
Pause the game and press Up, Up, Down, Down, Left, Right, Left, Right.

SILENCE REX HUDLER
Pause the game and press Up, Up, Down, Down, Left, Right, Left, Left.

MODNATION RACERS

BOOST START
Press **L1** when GO appears.

MX VS. ATV REFLEX

MX VEHICLES FOR PURCHASE

Select Enter Cheat Code from the Options and enter brapbrap.

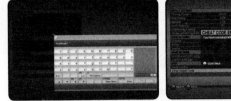

JUSTIN BRAYTON, KTM MX BIKES AND ATVS IN ARCADE MODE

Select Enter Cheat Code from the Options and enter readytorace.

ALL EVENT LOCATIONS IN ARCADE MODE

Select Enter Cheat Code from the Options and enter whereto.

ALL AI OPPONENTS

Select Enter Cheat Code from the Options and enter allai.

ATV VEHICLES FOR PURCHASE

Select Enter Cheat Code from the Options and enter couches.

ALL AVAILABLE RIDER GEAR

Select Enter Cheat Code from the Options and enter gearedup.

ALL AVAILABLE HELMETS

Select Enter Cheat Code from the Options and enter skullcap.

ALL AVAILABLE BOOTS

Select Enter Cheat Code from the Options and enter kicks.

ALL AVAILABLE GOGGLES

Select Enter Cheat Code from the Options and enter windows.

MX VS. ATV UNTAMED

ALL RIDING GEAR

Select Cheat Codes from the Options and enter crazylikea.

ALL HANDLEBARS

Select Cheat Codes from the Options and enter nohands.

NASCAR 08

ALL CHASE MODE CARS

Select cheat codes from the options menu and enter checkered flag.

EA SPORTS CAR

Select cheat codes from the options menu and enter ea sports car.

FANTASY DRIVERS

Select cheat codes from the options menu and enter race the pack.

WALMART CAR AND TRACK

Select cheat codes from the options menu and enter walmart everyday.

NASCAR 09

WAL-MART CAR & CHICAGO PIER RACETRACK

Select EA Extras from My Nascar, then choose Cheat Codes and enter WALMART EVERYDAY.

NASCAR THE GAME 2011

MARK MARTIN PAINT SCHEMES
At the garage main menu, press Down, Down, Up, Up, Right, Left, Right, Left. Enter godaddy.com.

KYLE BUSH NOS ENERGY DRINK CAR
At the garage main menu, press Down, Down, Up, Up, Right, Left, Right, Left. Enter drinknos.

NBA 09: THE INSIDE

EASTERN ALL-STARS 09 JERSEY
Select Extras from the Progression menu. Then choose nba.com from the Jerseys menu. Press ● and enter SHPNV2K699.

WESTERN ALL-STARS 09 JERSEY
Select Extras from the Progression menu. Then choose nba.com from the Jerseys menu. Press ● and enter K8AV6YMLNF.

L.A. LAKERS LATIN NIGHT JERSEY
Select Extras from the Progression menu. Then choose nba.com from the Jerseys menu. Press ● and enter NMTWCTC84S.

MIAMI HEAT LATIN NIGHT JERSEY
Select Extras from the Progression menu. Then choose nba.com from the Jerseys menu. Press ● and enter WCTGSA8SPD.

PHOENIX SUNS LATIN NIGHT JERSEY
Select Extras from the Progression menu. Then choose nba.com from the Jerseys menu. Press ● and enter LKUTSENFJH.

SAN ANTONIO SPURS LATIN NIGHT JERSEY
Select Extras from the Progression menu. Then choose nba.com from the Jerseys menu. Press ● and enter JFHSY73MYD.

NBA 2K8

ABA BALL
Select Codes from the Features menu and enter Payrespect.

2KSPORTS TEAM
Select Codes from the Features menu and enter 2ksports.

NBA DEVELOPMENT TEAM
Select Codes from the Features menu and enter nba2k.

SUPERSTARS TEAM
Select Codes from the Features menu and enter llmohffaae.

VISUAL CONCEPTS TEAM
Select Codes from the Features menu and enter Vcteam.

2008 ALL-STAR NBA JERSEYS
Select Codes from the Features menu and enter haeitgyebs.

BOBCATS RACING JERSEY
Select Codes from the Features menu and enter agtaccsinr.

PACERS SECOND ROAD JERSEY
Select Codes from the Features menu and enter cpares.

ST. PATRICK'S DAY JERSEYS
Select Codes from the Features menu and enter uclerehanp.

VALENTINE'S DAY JERSEYS
Select Codes from the Features menu and enter amcnreo.

NBA 2K9

2K SPORTS TEAM

Select Codes from the Features menu and enter 2ksports.

NBA 2K TEAM

Select Codes from the Features menu and enter nba2k.

SUPERSTARS

Select Codes from the Features menu and enter llmohffaae.

VC TEAM

Select Codes from the Features menu and enter vcteam.

ABA BALL

Select Codes from the Features menu and enter payrespect.

NBA 2K10

ABA BALL

Select Codes from the Options menu. Then select Enter Code and enter payrespect.

2K CHINA TEAM

Select Codes from the Options menu. Then select Enter Code and enter 2kchina.

NBA 2K TEAM

Select Codes from the Options menu. Then select Enter Code and enter nba2k.

2K SPORTS TEAM

Select Codes from the Options menu. Then select Enter Code and enter 2ksports.

VISUAL CONCEPTS TEAM

Select Codes from the Options menu. Then select Enter Code and enter vcteam.

2010 ALL-STAR UNIFORMS

Select Codes from the Options menu. Then select Enter Code and enter otnresla.

HARDWOOD CLASSIC UNIFORMS

Select Codes from the Options menu. Then select Enter Code and enter wasshcicsl. This code gives Hardwood Classic Uniforms for the Cavaliers, Jazz, Magic, Raptors, timberwolves, Trail Blazers, and Warriors.

LATIN NIGHTS UNIFORMS

Select Codes from the Options menu. Then select Enter Code and enter aihinntslgt. This code gives Latin Nights jerseys for Bulls, Heat, Knicks, Lakers, Mavericks, Rockets, Spurs, and Suns.

NBA GREEN UNIFORMS

Select Codes from the Options menu. Then select Enter Code and enter nreogge. This code gives green uniforms for the Bobcats, Bulls, and Nuggets.

SECONDARY ROAD UNIFORMS

Select Codes from the Options menu. Then select Enter Code and enter eydonscar. This code gives Second Road Uniforms for the Grizzlies, Hawks, Mavericks, and Rockets.

ST. PATRICK'S DAY UNIFORMS

Select Codes from the Options menu. Then select Enter Code and enter riiasgerh. This code gives St. Patrick's Day jerseys for the Bulls, Celtics, Knicks, and Raptors.

BOBCATS RACING UNIFORM

Select Codes from the Options menu. Then select Enter Code and enter agsntrccai.

36

CAVALIERS CAVFANATICS UNIFORM

Select Codes from the Options menu. Then select Enter Code and enter aifnaatccv.

HORNETS MARDI GRAS UNIFORM

Select Codes from the Options menu. Then select Enter Code and enter asrdirmga.

TRAIL BLAZERS RIP CITY UNIFORM

Select Codes from the Options menu. Then select Enter Code and enter ycprtii.

NBA 2K11

MJ: CREATING A LEGEND

In Features, select Codes from the Extras menu. Choose Enter Code and enter icanbe23.

2K CHINA TEAM

In Features, select Codes from the Extras menu. Choose Enter Code and enter 2kchina.

2K SPORTS TEAM

In Features, select Codes from the Extras menu. Choose Enter Code and enter 2Ksports.

NBA 2K TEAM

In Features, select Codes from the Extras menu. Choose Enter Code and enter nba2k.

VC TEAM

In Features, select Codes from the Extras menu. Choose Enter Code and enter vcteam.

ABA BALL

In Features, select Codes from the Extras menu. Choose Enter Code and enter payrespect.

2011 ALL-STAR UNIFORMS

In Features, select Codes from the Extras menu. Choose Enter Code and enter wydololoh.

SECONDARY ROAD UNIFORM

In Features, select Codes from the Extras menu. Choose Enter Code and enter ronoilnm. This unlocks the secondary road uniform for the Hornets, Magic, and Timberwolves.

ORANGE SPLIT DUNK

In Features, select Codes from the Extras menu. Choose Enter Code and enter SPRITEDUNK1. Go to Sprite Slam Dunk Showdown and use the help menu to find out more.

SPIN TOMMY DUNK

In Features, select Codes from the Extras menu. Choose Enter Code and enter SPRITEDUNK2. Go to Sprite Slam Dunk Showdown and use the help menu to find out more.

THE VILLAIN DUNK

In Features, select Codes from the Extras menu. Choose Enter Code and enter SPRITEDUNK3. Go to Sprite Slam Dunk Showdown and use the help menu to find out more.

CHEAT CODE EXPLOSION FOR CONSOLES

NBA 2K12

ABA BALL
Select Extras from the Features menu. Choose Codes and enter payrespect. This can be toggled on and off from this Codes menu.

2K CHINA TEAM
Select Extras from the Features menu. Choose Codes and enter 2kchina.

2K SPORTS TEAM
Select Extras from the Features menu. Choose Codes and enter 2ksports.

UNLOCK NBA 2K TEAM
Select Extras from the Features menu. Choose Codes and enter nba2k.

VC TEAM
Select Extras from the Features menu. Choose Codes and enter vcteam.

JORDAN RETRO COLLECTION
Select Extras from the Features menu. Choose Codes and enter 23.

NBA LIVE 08

ADIDAS GIL-ZERO - ALL-STAR EDITION
Select NBA Codes from My NBA and enter 23DN1PPOG4.

ADIDAS TIM DUNCAN STEALTH - ALL-STAR EDITION
Select NBA Codes from My NBA and enter FE454DFJCC.

NBA LIVE 09

SUPER DUNKS MODE
Use the Sprite vending machine in the practice area and enter spriteslam.

NBA LIVE 10

CHARLOTTE BOBCATS' 2009/2010 RACE DAY ALTERNATE JERSEYS
Select Options from My NBA Live and go to Select Codes. Enter ceobdabacarstcy.

NEW ORLEANS HORNETS' 2009/2010 MARDI GRAS ALTERNATE JERSEYS
Select Options from My NBA Live and go to Select Codes. Enter nishrag1rosmad0.

ALTERNATE JERSEYS
Select Options from My NBA Live and go to Select Codes. Enter ndnba1rooaesdc0. This unlocks alternate jerseys for Atlanta Hawks, Dallas Mavericks, Houston Rockets, and Memphis Grizzlies.

MORE HARDWOOD CLASSICS NIGHTS JERSEYS
Select Options from My NBA Live and go to Select Codes. Enter hdogdrawhoticns. This unlocks Hardwood Classics Nights jerseys for Cleveland Cavaliers, Golden State Warriors, Minnesota Timberwolves, Orlando Magic, Philadelphia 76ers.

ADIDAS EQUATIONS
Select Options from My NBA Live and go to Select Codes. Enter adaodqauieints1.

ADIDAS TS CREATORS WITH ANKLE BRACES
Select Options from My NBA Live and go to Select Codes. Enter atciadsstsdhecf.

ADIDAS TS SUPERNATURAL COMMANDERS
Select Options from My NBA Live and go to Select Codes. Enter andsicdsmatdnsr.

ADIDAS TS SUPERNATURAL CREATORS
Select Options from My NBA Live and go to Select Codes. Enter ard8siscdnatstr.

AIR MAX LEBRON VII
Select Options from My NBA Live and go to Select Codes. Enter ere1nbvlaoeknii, 2ovnaebnkrielei, 3rioabeneikenvl, ri4boenanekilve, ivl5brieekaeonn, or n6ieirvalkeeobn.

KOBE V

Select Options from My NBA Live and go to Select Codes. Enter ovze1bimenkoko0, m0kveokoiebozn2, eev0nbimokk3ozo, or bmo4inozeeo0kvk.

JORDAN CP3 IIIS

Select Options from My NBA Live and go to Select Codes. Enter iaporcdian3ejis.

JORDAN MELO M6S

Select Options from My NBA Live and go to Select Codes. Enter emlarmeoo6ajdsn.

JORDAN SIXTY PLUSES

Select Options from My NBA Live and go to Select Codes. Enter aondsuilyjrspxt.

NIKE HUARACHE LEGIONS

Select Options from My NBA Live and go to Select Codes. Enter aoieuchrahelgn.

NIKE KD 2S

Select Options from My NBA Live and go to Select Codes. Enter kk2tesaosepinrd.

NIKE ZOOM FLIP'NS

Select Options from My NBA Live and go to Select Codes. Enter epfnozaeminolki.

NEED FOR SPEED PROSTREET

$2,000

Select Career and then choose Code Entry. Enter 1MA9X99.

$4,000

Select Career and then choose Code Entry. Enter W2IOLL01.

$8,000

Select Career and then choose Code Entry. Enter L1IS97A1.

$10,000

Select Career and then choose Code Entry. Enter 1MI9K7E1.

$10,000

Select Career and then choose Code Entry. Enter CASHMONEY.

$10,000

Select Career and then choose Code Entry. Enter REGGAME.

AUDI TT

Select Career and then choose Code Entry. Enter ITSABOUTYOU.

CHEVELLE SS

Select Career and then choose Code Entry. Enter HORSEPOWER.

COKE ZERO GOLF GTI

Select Career and then choose Code Entry. Enter COKEZERO.

DODGE VIPER

Select Career and then choose Code Entry. Enter WORLDSLONGESTLASTING.

MITSUBISHI LANCER EVOLUTION

Select Career and then choose Code Entry. Enter MITSUBISHIGOFAR.

UNLOCK ALL BONUSES

Select Career and then choose Code Entry. Enter UNLOCKALLTHINGS.

5 REPAIR MARKERS

Select Career and then choose Code Entry. Enter SAFETYNET.

ENERGIZER VINYL

Select Career and then choose Code Entry. Enter ENERGIZERLITHIUM.

CASTROL SYNTEC VINYL

Select Career and then choose Code Entry. Enter CASTROLSYNTEC. This also gives you $10,000.

NEED FOR SPEED UNDERCOVER

$10,000

Select Secret Codes from the Options menu and enter %%S3/".

DIE-CAST BMW M3 E92

Select Secret Codes from the Options menu and enter)B7@B=.

DIE-CAST LEXUS IS F

Select Secret Codes from the Options menu and enter 0;5M2;.

NEEDFORSPEED.COM LOTUS ELISE

Select Secret Codes from the Options menu and enter -KJ3=E.

DIE-CAST NISSAN 240SX (S13)
Select Secret Codes from the Options menu and enter ?P:COL.

DIE-CAST PORSCHE 911 TURBO
Select Secret Codes from the Options menu and enter >8P:I;.

SHELBY TERLINGUA
Select Secret Codes from the Options menu and enter NeedForSpeedShelbyTerlingua.

DIE-CAST VOLKWAGEN R32
Select Secret Codes from the Options menu and enter!2ODBJ:.

NHL 2K9

3RD JERSEYS
From the Features menu, enter R6y34bsH52 as a code.

NHL 10

THIRD JERSEYS
At the EA Extras screen, enter rwyhafwh6ekyjcmr

PHINEAS AND FERB: ACROSS THE 2ND DIMENSION

SKIN FOR AGENT P: PERRY THE PLATTYBORG
Pause the game, select Enter Code from Extras, and enter ⊙, ✕, ⊙, ▲, ■, ▲.

PRINCE OF PERSIA

SANDS OF TIME PRINCE/FARAH SKINS
Select Skin Manager from the Extras menu. Press ▲ and enter 52585854. This gives you the Sands of Time skin for the Prince and Farah from Sands of Time for the Princess. Access them from the Skin Manager

PRINCE ALTAIR IBN LA-AHAD SKIN
Create an Ubisoft account. Then select "Altair Skin for Prince" to unlock.

RATCHET & CLANK FUTURE: A CRACK IN TIME

DISCOUNT AT WEAPON VENDORS
Have a save game for Ratchet and Clank Future: Tools of Destruction.

PIRATE HAT SKIN
Have a save game for Ratchet and Clank Future: Quest for Booty.

BANCHO RATCHET SKIN
Pause the game and enter Up, Right, Down, Left, ▲, ■, ✕, ⊙, R3.

CHALLENGE MODE

After defeating the game, you can replay the game in Challenge Mode with all of Ratchet's current upgraded weapons and armor.

SKILL POINTS

Complete the following objectives to earn skill points. Each one is worth 10 to 40 points and you can use these points to unlock Cheats in the Cheats Menu. The following table lists the skill points with a location and description.

SKILL POINT	LOCATION	DESCRIPTION
Smashing Good Time	Cobalia	Destroy all crates and consumer bots in the trade port and gel factory.
I Should Have Gone Down in a Barrel	Cobalia	Jump into each of the two gel waterfall areas in Cobalia gel factory.
Giant Hunter	Cobalia	Kill several Basilisk Leviathans in the Cobalia wilderness.
Wrench Ninja 3	Stratus City	Use only the Omniwrench to get through the level to the Robo-Wings segment.
We Don't Need No Stinkin' Bridges!	Stratus City	Cross the tri-pad sequence using gel-cube bounces.
Surface-to-Air Plasma Beasts	Stratus City	Take out several flying targets using a specific weapon.
Been Around	Stratus City	Take off from every Robo-wing launch pad in Stratus City.
Collector's Addition	Voron	Be very thorough in your collection of goodies.
Minesweeper	Voron	Clear out a bunch of mines.
What's That, R2?	Voron	Barrel roll multiple times.
I Think I'm Gonna Be Sick	IFF	Ride the Ferris wheel for 5 loops without getting off or taking damage.
Fast and the Fire-ious	IFF	Use the Charge Boots to cross the bridge to the arena without being burned.
One Heckuva Peephole	IFF	Return after receiving the Geo-laser and complete the Geo-laser setup.
Alphabet City	Apogee	Teleport to each of the six asteroids in alphabetical order.
Knock You Down to Size	Apogee	Wrench Slam 5 centipedes.
Dancin' with the Stars	Apogee	Make 5 enemies dance at once on an asteroid.
Taste o' Yer Own Medicine	Pirate Base	Destroy all of the Shooter Pirates with the Combuster.
Preemptive Strike	Pirate Base	Destroy all of the "sleeping bats" while they are still sleeping.
It's Mutant-E Cap'n!	Pirate Base	Change 5 pirates into penguins in one blast.
You Sunk My Battleship!	Rakar	Shoot down a large percentage of the big destroyers.
Pretty Lights	Rakar	Complete the level without destroying any of the snatchers that fire beams at Ratchet.
I've Got Places To Be	Rakar	Destroy the boss in under 2:30.
The Consumer Is Not (Always) Right	Rykan V	Destroy a bunch of consumer bots in the level.
Live Strong	Rykan V	Complete the Gryo Cycle in 1:45.
Untouchable	Rykan V	Don't take damage in the Gyro-Cycle.
It Sounded Like a Freight Train	Sargasso	Get 10 Swarmers in one tornado.
Head Examiner	Sargasso	Land on all of the dinosaur heads in Sargasso.
Extinction	Sargasso	Kill all of the Sargasso Predators.
Lombaxes Don't Like Cold	Iris	Break all the breakable icicles.
Mow Down Ho-Down	Iris	Use turrets to destroy 10 dancing pirates.
Dancin' on the Ceiling	Zordoom	Successfully use a Groovitron while on a Magboot surface.
Seared Ahi	Zordoom	Use the Pyroblaster on 3 Drophid creatures after freeing them from their robotic suits.
Shocking Ascent	Zordoom	Destroy all enemies on the elevator using just the Shock Ravager.

SKILL POINT	LOCATION	DESCRIPTION
Expert Marksman	Borag	Kill 75% of all of the enemies.
Can't Touch This	Borag	Don't take damage before fighting the boss.
Pyoo, Pyoo!	Borag	Complete the level without secondary fire.
Dead Aim	Kerchu	Destroy several destructible towers while on the pirate barge.
Fire With Fire	Kerchu	Kill a few Kerchu Flamethrowers with the Pyro Blaster.
Rocket Jump	Kerchu	Successfully jump over a row of three rockets while on the grindrail during the boss fight in Kerchu City.
Your Friendly Neighborhood…	Slag Fleet	Destroy 5 enemies while on the grav ramp before Slag's ship.
Turret Times Two	Slag Fleet	Destroy at least 2 pirates with each turret in the level.
Six Gun Salute	Slag Fleet	Get six pirates in a row to salute Ratchet while in the Pirate Disguise.
Gotta Catch 'Em All	Cragmite Ruins	Hit all Cragmite soldiers with the Mag-Net Launcher.
Ratchet and Goliath	Cragmite Ruins	Destroy multiple walkers using just the Nano-Swarmers.
Ratchet &…Not Clank?!	Cragmite Ruins	Use Mr. Zurkon in Cragmite's Ratchet-only segment.
Stay Still So I Can Shoot You!	Meridian	Use strafe-flip 10 times while fighting the Cragmite soldiers.
Now Boarding…	Meridian	Complete the Gyro-Cycle in 55 seconds.
Low Flying Howls	Meridian	Fly under an electrified barrier in the Robo-wings segment.
Extreme Alien Makeover	Fastoon2	Turn 10 Cragmites into penguins.
Empty Bag o' Tricks	Fastoon2	Complete the level without using any devices.
Nowhere to Hide	Fastoon2	Destroy every piece of breakable cover.
No, Up Your Arsenal	Global	Upgrade every weapon to the max.
Roflcopter	Global	Turn enemies into penguins, then use the Visicopter to destroy the penguins.
Stir Fry	Global	Kill 2 different enemy types using the Shock Ravager while they are trapped in a tornado.
Golden Children	Overall	Find all of the Gold Bolts.
Sacagawea	Global	Complete all of the maps 100%, leaving no area undiscovered.
Cheapskate	Global	Purchase a single Combustor round.
Everybody Dance Now	Global	Make every type of enemy in the game dance.
F5 on the Fujita Scale	Global	Pick up more than 10 enemies with one tornado.
Chorus line	Global	Get 10+ enemies to dance together.
Happy Feet	Global	Get several penguins to dance on-screen.
Disco Inferno	Global	Use the Groovitron followed by the Pyro Blaster.
Bolts in the Bank	Global	Sell a bunch of Leviathan Souls to the Smuggler.
It's Like the North Pole Here	Global	Have at least 12-15 enemies and/or citizens turned into penguins at one time.
Say Hello to My Little Friend	Global	Kill 15 enemies with one RYNO shot.
For the Hoard!	Global	Get every item.
Promoted to Inspector	Global	Get every gadget.
Global Thermonuclear War	Global	Get every weapon.
It's Even Better the Second Time!	Global	Complete Challenge Mode.
The Hardest of Core	Global	Get all skill points and everything else in the game.

RESONANCE OF FATE

Once you have reached Chapter 7, search Leanne's closet. As she speaks her first line enter the following codes to unlock more outfits.

8-BIT GIRL SHIRT
Up, Up, Down, Down, Left, Right, Left, Right, ●, ■

CLUB FAMITSU SHIRT
●, ●, Up, Up, ●, ●, Left, Left, L1, R1

GEMAGA SHIRT
R2, L2, L1, R1, ●, ●, ●, ●, ●, Up

HIRAKOU SHIRT
●, ●, L1, L1, R1, R1, L3, L3, Up, Down

PLATFORM LOGO SHIRT
R2, R1, R3, L3, L1, L2, Right, Left, ●, ▲

POLITAN SUIT
R3, R3, R3, Right, Left, ▲, ●, L2, R2, L1. This requires you to have the Reindeer Suit first.

ROCK REVOLUTION

ALL CHARACTERS
At the main menu, press ●, ●, ●, ●, ●, ●, ●, ▲, ■.

ALL VENUES
At the main menu, press ●, ●, ▲, ●, ■, ●, ▲, ●, ▲.

ROCKET KNIGHT

ALL CHARACTER SKINS
At the title screen, press Up, Up, Down, Down, Left, Right, Left, Right, ●, ✖, Start.

SCOTT PILGRIM VS. THE WORLD: THE GAME

PLAY AS SAME CHARACTER
At the title screen, press Down, R1, Up, L1, ▲, ●.

HEART SWORD
At the title screen, press ●, ●, ●, ✖, ●, ✖, ▲

BLOOD MODE
At the title screen, press ✖, ●, ✖, ●, ✖, ●, ●.

BOSS RUSH MODE
Pause the game on the overworld and press Right, Right, ●, R1, Right, Right, ●, R1.

ZOMBIE MODE
At the title screen, press Down, Up, Right, Down, Up, Right, Down, Up, Right, Right, Right.

SOUND CHECK BONUS LEVEL
Pause the game on the overworld and press L1, L1, R1, R1, L1, L1, L1, R1, R1, R1, L1, R1.

CHANGE MONEY TO ANIMALS
At the title screen, press Up, Up, Down, Down, Up, Up, Up, Up.

SEGA SUPERSTARS TENNIS

UNLOCK CHARACTERS
Complete the following missions to unlock the corresponding character.

CHARACTER	MISSION TO COMPLETE
Alex Kidd	Mission 1 of Alex Kidd's World
Amy Rose	Mission 2 of Sonic the Hedgehog's World
Gilius	Mission 1 of Golden Axe's World
Gum	Mission 12 of Jet Grind Radio's World
Meemee	Mission 8 of Super Monkey Ball's World
Pudding	Mission 1 of Space Channel 5's World
Reala	Mission 2 of NiGHTs' World
Shadow The Hedgehog	Mission 14 of Sonic the Hedgehog's World

THE SIMPSONS GAME

After unlocking the following, the outfits can be changed at the downstairs closet in the Simpson's house. The Trophies can be viewed at different locations in the house: Bart's room, Lisa's room, Marge's room, and the garage.

BART'S OUTFITS AND TROPHIES (POSTER COLLECTION)

At the main menu, press Right, Left, ●, ●, ▲, R3.

HOMER'S OUTFITS AND TROPHIES (BEER BOTTLE COLLECTION)

At the main menu, press Left, Right, ▲, ▲, ●, L3.

LISA'S OUTFITS AND TROPHIES (DOLLS)

At the main menu, press ●, ▲, ●, ●, ●, ▲, L3.

MARGE'S OUTFITS AND TROPHIES (HAIR PRODUCTS)

At the main menu, press ▲, ●, ▲, ▲, ●, R3.

THE SIMS 3

CHEATS

Load your family, press Start, and hold L1 + L2 + R1 + R2. The game prompts you to save another file before activating the cheats. Spoot the Llama is now available in Misc Décor. Place it in your lot and click it to access the cheats. This disables Trophies and challenges.

THE SIMS 3: PETS

CREATION MODE

Pause the game and press L2 + L1 + R2 + R1. This disables trophies.

SKATE 2

BIG BLACK

Select Enter Cheat from the Extras menu and enter letsdowork.

3D MODE

Select Enter Cheat from the Extras menu and enter strangeloops. Use glasses to view in 3D.

SKATE 3

HOVERBOARD MODE

In Free Play, select Extras from the Options. Choose Enter Cheat Code and enter mcfly.

MINI SKATER MODE

In Free Play, select Extras from the Options. Choose Enter Cheat Code and enter miniskaters.

ZOMBIE MODE

In Free Play, select Extras from the Options. Choose Enter Cheat Code and enter zombie.

ISAAC CLARK FROM DEADSPACE

In Free Play, select Extras from the Options. Choose Enter Cheat Code and enter deadspacetoo.

DEM BONES

Beat most of the Hall of Meat Challenges.

MEAT MAN

Beat all Hall of Meat Challenges.

RESETS OBJECTS TO ORIGINAL POSITIONS

In Free Play, select Extras from the Options. Choose Enter Cheat Code and enter streetsweeper.

SLY 2: BAND OF THIEVES

RESTART CURRENT EPISODE
Pause the game and press Left, R1, Up, Down, Up, Left.

TUTORIAL
Pause the game and press Right, Left, Up, Up, Up, R1.

SKIP TO EPISODE 1
Pause the game and press Down, R1, Left, Right, R1, Down.

SKIP TO EPISODE 2
Pause the game and press R1, Left, Right, R1, Left, Down.

SKIP TO EPISODE 3
Pause the game and press Up, Left, Right, Left, Down, Up.

SKIP TO EPISODE 4
Pause the game and press Up, Right, Right, Up, Left, Left.

SKIP TO EPISODE 5
Pause the game and press Left, R1, Down, Down, Up, Right.

SKIP TO EPISODE 6
Pause the game and press Down, Up, R1, R1, Left, Down.

SKIP TO EPISODE 7
Pause the game and press Left, Left, Left, Down, Down, R1.

SKIP TO EPSIODE 8
Pause the game and press Down Up, Left, Left, R1, Right.

UNLOCK TOM GADGET
Pause the game and press Left, Left, Down, Right, Left, Right.

TIME RUSH ABILITY
Pause the game and press Down, Down, Up, Down, Right, Left.

SLY 3: HONOR AMONG THIEVES

FLY THE TOONAMI PLANE
While in the regular plane, pause the game and press R1, R1, Right, Down, Down, Right.

RESTART MISSIONS
Pause the game and enter the following codes to restart the corresponding missions:

RESTART THIS MISSION	ENTER THIS CODE
Episode 1, Day 1	Left, R2, Right, L1, R2, L1
Episode 1, Day 2	Down, L2, Up, Left, R2, L2
Episode 2, Day 1	Right, L2, Left, Up, Right, Down
Episode 2, Day 2	Down, Up, R1, Up, R2, L2
Episode 3, Day 1	R2, R1, L1, Left, L1, Down
Episode 3, Day 2	L2, R1, R2, L2, L1, Up
Episode 4, Day 1	Left, Right, L1, R2, Right, R2
Episode 4, Day 2	L1, Left, L2, Left, Up, L1
Episode 5, Day 1	Left, R2, Right, Up, L1, R2

RESTART THIS MISSION	ENTER THIS CODE
Episode 5, Day 2	R2, R1, L1, R1, R2, R1
Operation Laptop Retrieval	L2, Left, R1, L2, L1, Down
Operation Moon Crash	L2, Up, Left, L1, L2, L1
Operation Reverse Double Cross	Right, Left, Up, Left, R2, Left
Operation Tar Be-Gone	Down, L2, R1, L2, R1, Right
Operation Turbo Dominant Eagle	Down, Right, Left, L2, R1, Right
Operation Wedding Crasher	L2, R2, Right, Down, L1, R2

SPACE CHANNEL 5 PART 2

LET CPU TAKE OVER

Pause the game, hold L1 + R1 and press ●, ▲, ■. The CPU takes over, but trophies are disabled.

SPIDER-MAN: EDGE OF TIME

SHATTERED DIMENSIONS BONUS SUITS

If you have a saved game data for Spider-Man: Shattered Dimensions on your system, eight new Alternate Suits become available in the Bonus Gallery.

AMAZING SPIDER-MAN #500 SUIT (AMAZING)

Select Enter Code from VIP Unlock Code and enter laststand. Go to the Bonus Gallery to access the alternate suits.

BIG TIME SUIT (2099)

At the main menu, press Right, Down, Down, Up, Left, Down, Down, Right.

FUTURE FOUNDATION SUIT (AMAZING)

At the main menu, press Up, Down, Left, Up, Down, Left, Right, Left.

POISON SUIT (2099)

Select Enter Code from VIP Unlock Code and enter innerspider. Go to the Bonus Gallery to access the alternate suits.

SPIDER-MAN: SHATTERED DIMENSIONS

The following can be entered after completing the tutorial. The suits can be found in the Bonus Gallery under Alternate Suits.

IRON SPIDER SUIT

At the main menu, press Up, Right, Right, Right, Left, Left, Left, Down, Up.

SCARLET SPIDER SUIT

At the main menu, press Right, Up, Left, Right, Up, Left, Right, Up, Left, Right.

NEGATIVE ZONE SUIT

At the main menu, press Left, Right, Right, Down, Right, Down, Up, Left.

SPLIT/SECOND

HANZO FX350 CX (COMPUTER SPIELE) IN QUICK PLAY

At the Options menu, press ✖, Up, ✖, Up, ✖, Up.

RYBACK COYOTE AMX IN QUICK PLAY

At the Options menu, press Left, ✖, Left, ✖, Left, ✖ Left, ✖, Left, ✖, Left, ✖, Right.

RYBACK MOHAWK XDX (DISNEY XD) IN QUICK PLAY

At the Options menu, press ✖, Down, ✖, Down, ✖, Down.

STAR WARS THE CLONE WARS: REPUBLIC HEROES

BIG HEAD MODE

Pause the game, select Shop, and enter Up, Down, Left, Right, Left, Right, Down, Up in Cheats.

MINI-GUN

Pause the game, select Shop, and enter Down, Left, Right, Up, Right, Up, Left, Down in Cheats.

ULTIMATE LIGHTSABER

Pause the game, select Shop, and enter Right, Down, Down, Up, Left, Up, Up, Down in Cheats.

LIGHTSABER THROW UPGRADE

Pause the game, select Shop, and enter Left, Left, Right, Right, Up, Down, Down, Up in Combat Upgrades.

SPIDER DROID UPGRADE

Pause the game, select Shop, and enter Up, Left, Down, Left, Right, Left, Left, Left in Droid-Jak Upgrades.

STAR WARS: THE FORCE UNLEASHED: ULTIMATE SITH EDITION

CHEAT CODES

Pause the game and select Input Code. Here you can enter the following codes. Activating any of the following cheat codes will disable some unlockables, and you will be unable to save your progress.

CHEAT	CODE
All Force Powers at Max Power	KATARN
All Force Push Ranks	EXARKUN
All Saber Throw Ranks	ADEGAN
All Repulse Ranks	DATHOMIR
All Saber Crystals	HURRIKANE
All Talents	JOCASTA
Deadly Saber	LIGHTSABER

COMBOS

Pause the game and select Input Code. Here you can enter the following codes. Activating any of the following cheat codes will disable some unlockables, and you will be unable to save your progress.

COMBO	CODE
All Combos	MOLDYCROW
Aerial Ambush	VENTRESS
Aerial Assault	EETHKOTH
Aerial Blast	YADDLE
Impale	BRUTALSTAB
Lightning Bomb	MASSASSI
Lightning Grenade	RAGNOS
Saber Slam	PLOKOON
Saber Sling	KITFISTO
Sith Saber Flurry	LUMIYA
Sith Slash	DARAGON
Sith Throw	SAZEN
New Combo	FREEDON
New Combo	MARAJADE

ALL DATABANK ENTRIES

Pause the game and select Input Code. Enter OSSUS.

MIRRORED LEVEL

Pause the game and select Input Code. Enter MINDTRICK. Re-enter the code to return level to normal.

SITH MASTER DIFFICULTY

Pause the game and select Input Code. Enter SITHSPAWN.

COSTUMES

Pause the game and select Input Code. Here you can enter the following codes.

COSTUME	CODE
All Costumes	SOHNDANN
Bail Organa	VICEROY
Ceremonial Jedi Robes	DANTOOINE
Drunken Kota	HARDBOILED
Emperor	MASTERMIND
Incinerator Trooper	PHOENIX
Jedi Adventure Robe	HOLOCRON
Kashyyyk Trooper	TK421GREEN
Kota	MANDALORE

COSTUME	CODE
Master Kento	WOOKIEE
Proxy	PROTOTYPE
Scout Trooper	FERRAL
Shadow Trooper	BLACKHOLE
Sith Stalker Armor	KORRIBAN
Snowtrooper	SNOWMAN
Stormtrooper	TK421WHITE
Stormtrooper Commander	TK421BLUE

STAR WARS: THE FORCE UNLEASHED II

BOBA FETT COSTUME

Pause the game, select Cheat Codes from the Options, and enter MANDALORE.

DARK APPRENTICE COSTUME

Pause the game, select Cheat Codes from the Options, and enter VENTRESS.

GENERAL KOTA COSTUME

Pause the game, select Cheat Codes from the Options, and enter RAHM.

NEIMOIDIAN COSTUME

Pause the game, select Cheat Codes from the Options, and enter GUNRAY.

REBEL COMMANDO COSTUME

Pause the game, select Cheat Codes from the Options, and enter SPECFORCE.

REBEL SOLDIER COSTUME

Pause the game, select Cheat Codes from the Options, and enter REBELSCUM.

SABER GUARD COSTUME

Pause the game, select Cheat Codes from the Options, and enter MORGUKAI.

SITH ACOLYTE COSTUME

Pause the game, select Cheat Codes from the Options, and enter HAAZEN.

STORMTROOPER COSTUME

Pause the game, select Cheat Codes from the Options, and enter TK421.

TERROR TROOPER COSTUME

Pause the game, select Cheat Codes from the Options, and enter SHADOW.

TRAINING DROID COSTUME

Pause the game, select Cheat Codes from the Options, and enter HOLODROID.

REPULSE FORCE POWER

Pause the game, select Cheat Codes from the Options, and enter MAREK.

SABRE THROW

Pause the game, select Cheat Codes from the Options, and enter TRAYA.

WISDOM LIGHTSABER CRYSTALS

Pause the game, select Cheat Codes from the Options, and enter SOLARI.

TRAINING GEAR

Have a save game from Star Wars: The Force Unleashed.

CEREMONIAL ROBES

Have a save game from Star Wars: The Force Unleashed with the Light Side ending.

SITH STALKER ARMOR

Have a save game from Star Wars: The Force Unleashed with the Dark Side ending.

SUPER STREET FIGHTER IV

BARREL BUSTER AND CAR CRUSHER BONUS STAGES

Beat Arcade Mode in any difficulty

COLORS AND TAUNTS

Colors 1 and 2 plus the first taunt for each fighter are available from the start. For colors 11 & 12, start a game with a Street Fighter IV save game on your system. To earn the rest of the colors and taunts, you need to fight a certain number of matches with that character.

COLOR	# OF MATCHES
3	2
4	4
5	6
6	8
7	10
8	12
9	14
10	16

TAUNT	# OF MATCHES
2	1
3	3
4	5
5	7
6	9
7	11
8	13
9	15
10	16

THOR: GOD OF THUNDER

NEW GAME PLUS

After defeating the game, select New Game Plus to use your stats and powers from the beaten game.

TOM CLANCY'S HAWX

A-12 AVENGER II
At the hangar, hold **L2** and press ●, **L1**, ●, **R1**, ▲, ■.

F-18 HARV
At the hangar, hold **L2** and press **L1**, ▲, **L1**, ▲, **L1**, ■.

FB-22 STRIKE RAPTOR
At the hangar, hold **L2** and press **R1**, ●, **R1**, ●, **R1**, ▲.

THE TOMB RAIDER TRILOGY

TOMB RAIDER: LEGEND
The following codes must be unlocked in the game before using them.

BULLETPROOF
During a game, hold **L1** and press ✖, **R1**, ▲, **R1**, ●, **L2**.

DRAIN ENEMY HEALTH
During a game, hold **L1** and press ●, ●, ✖, **L2**, **R1**, ▲.

INFINITE ASSAULT RIFLE AMMO
During a game, hold **L2** and press ✖, ●, ✖, **L1**, ●, ▲.

INFINITE GRENADE LAUNCHER AMMO
During a game, hold **L2** and press **L1**, ▲, **R1**, ●, **L1**, ●.

INFINITE SHOTGUN AMMO
During a game, hold **L2** and press **R1**, ●, ●, **L1**, ●, ✖.

INFINITE SMG AMMO
During a game, hold **L2** and press ●, ▲, **L1**, **R1**, ✖, ●.

EXCALIBUR
During a game, hold **L2** and press ▲, ✖, ●, **R1**, ▲, **L1**.

SOUL REAVER
During a game, hold **L2**. Then press: ✖, **R1**, ●, **R1**, **L1**, ●.

ONE SHOT KILL
During a game, hold **L1** and press ▲, ✖, ▲, ●, **L2**, ●.

TEXTURELESS MODE
During a game, hold **L1** and press **L2**, ✖, ●, ✖, ▲, **R1**.

TOMB RAIDER: UNDERWORLD

INVINCIBLE
During a game, hold **L2** and press ✖, **R2**, ▲, **R2**, ●, **L1**.

ONE SHOT KILLS
During a game, hold **L2** and press hold **R2** and press ▲, ✖, ▲, ●, **L1**, ●.

SHOW ENEMY HEALTH
During a game, hold **L2** and press ●, ●, ✖, **L1**, **R2**, ▲.

TONY HAWK RIDE

RYAN SHECKLER
Select Cheats from the Options menu and enter SHECKLERSIG.

QUICKSILVER 80'S LEVEL
Select Cheats from the Options menu and enter FEELINGEIGHTIES.

TOY STORY 2: BUZZ LIGHTYEAR TO THE RESCUE!

LEVEL SELECT
At the Options menu, press Right, Left, ⦿, ⬢, ⬢.

ALL LEVELS
At the title screen, press Up (x4), Down, Down, Up, Up, Down (x3).

DEBUG MODE
At the title screen, press ✪, ⦿, ▣.

TRANSFORMERS: DARK OF THE MOON

RATCHET IN MULTIPLAYER
At the Unlockables screen, press Up, Right, Down, Left, Up, Start.

TRANSFORMERS REVENGE OF THE FALLEN

LOW GRAVITY MODE
Select Cheat Code and enter ✪, ▣, ⬢, L3, ⬢, L3.

NO WEAPON OVERHEAT
Select Cheat Code and enter L3, ▣, ✪, L3, ⬢, L1.

ALWAYS IN OVERDRIVE MODE
Select Cheat Code and enter L1, ⦿, L1, ✪, ▣, R3.

UNLIMITED TURBO
Select Cheat Code and enter ⦿, L3, ▣, R3, ✪, ⬢

NO SPECIAL COOLDOWN TIME
Select Cheat Code and enter R3, ▣, R3, R3, ▣, ✪.

INVINCIBILITY
Select Cheat Code and enter R3, ✪, ▣, L3, ▣, ⦿.

4X ENERGON FROM DEFEATED ENEMIES
Select Cheat Code and enter ⬢, ▣, ⦿, R3, ✪, ⬢.

INCREASED WEAPON DAMAGE(ROBOT FORM)
Select the Cheat Code option and enter ⬢, ⬢, R3, ✪, L1, ⬢.

INCREASED WEAPON DAMAGE(VEHICLE FORM)
Select Cheat Code and enter ⬢, ⦿, R1, ✪, R3, L3.

MELEE INSTANT KILLS
Select the Cheat Code option and enter R3, ✪. L1, ⦿, R3, L1.

LOWER ENEMY ACCURACY
Select Cheat Code and enter ✪, L3, R3, L3, R3, R1.

INCREASED ENEMY HEALTH
Select Cheat Code and enter ⦿, ✪, L1, ⦿, R3, ⬢.

INCREASED ENEMY DAMAGE
Select Cheat Code and enter L1, ⬢, ✪, ⬢, R3, R3.

INCREASED ENEMY ACCURACY
Select Cheat Code and enter ⬢, ⬢, ⦿, ✪, A, L1.

SPECIAL KILLS ONLY MODE
Select Cheat Code and enter ⦿, ⦿, R1, ⦿, ✪, L3.

UNLOCK ALL SHANGHAI MISSIONS & ZONES
Select Cheat Code and enter ⬢, L3, R3, L1, ⦿, ✪.

UNLOCK ALL WEST COAST MISSIONS & ZONES
Select Cheat Code and enter L1, R1, R3, ⬢, R3, ⦿.

UNLOCK ALL DEEP SIX MISSIONS & ZONES
Select Cheat Code and enter ✕, R1, ▲, ●, ✕, L1.

UNLOCK ALL EAST COAST MISSIONS & ZONES
Select Cheat Code and enter R3, L3, R1, ✕, ●, ✕.

UNLOCK ALL CAIRO MISSIONS & ZONES
Select Cheat Code and enter R3, ▲, ✕, ▲, L3, L1.

UNLOCK & ACTIVATE ALL UPGRADES
Select Cheat Code and enter L1, ▲, L1, ●, ✕, ✕.

UNCHARTED 2: AMONG THIEVES

In Uncharted 2: Among Thieves, upon opening the store you'll have the option to hit the Square button to check for Uncharted: Drake's Fortune save data. You'll obtain cash for having save data! This cash can be used in the single and multiplayer stores. Could be useful if you want a head start online!

$20,000
Have a saved game of Uncharted: Drake's Fortune.

$80,000
Have a saved game of Uncharted: Drake's Fortune with the story completed at least once.

WORLD OF OUTLAWS: SPRINT CARS

$5,000,000
Enter your name as CHICMCHIM.

ALL DRIVERS
Enter your name as MITYMASTA.

ALL TRACKS
Enter your name as JOEYJOEJOE.

WORLD SERIES OF POKER 2008: BATTLE FOR THE BRACELETS

PHILLIP J. HELLMUTH
Enter BEATTHEBRAT as the player name.

WWE SMACKDOWN VS. RAW 2010

THE ROCK
Select Cheat Codes from the Options and enter The Great One.

VINCE'S OFFICE AND DIRT SHEET FOR BACKSTAGE BRAWL
Select Cheat Codes from the Options menu and enter BonusBrawl.

SHAWN MICHAEL'S ALTERNATE COSTUME
Select Cheat Codes from the Options menu and enter Bow Down.

JOHN CENA'S ALTERNATE COSTUME
Select Cheat Codes from the Options menu and enter CENATION.

RANDY ORTON'S ALTERNATE COSTUME
Select Cheat Codes from the Options menu and enter ViperRKO.

SANTINO MARELLA'S ALTERNATE COSTUME
Select Cheat Codes from the Options menu and enter Milan Miracle.

TRIPLE H'S ALTERNATE COSTUME
Select Cheat Codes from the Options menu and enter Suck IT!.

WWE SMACKDOWN VS. RAW 2011

JOHN CENA (ENTRANCE/CIVILIAN)
In My WWE, select Cheat Codes from the Options and enter SLURPEE.

ALL OF RANDY ORTON'S COSTUMES
In My WWE, select Cheat Codes from the Options and enter apexpredator.

TRIBUTE TO THE TROOPS ARENA
In My WWE, select Cheat Codes from the Options and enter 8thannualtribute.

X-MEN DESTINY

JUGGERNAUT SUIT
At the title screen, hold L1 + R1 and press Down, Right, Up, Left, ▲, ●.

EMMA FROST SUIT
At the title screen, hold L1 + R1 and press Up, Down, Right, Left, ●, ▲.

NINTENDO Wii™

CONTENTS

DO Wii™

NINTENDO Wii™ VIRTUAL CONSOLE GAMES

CONTENTS

2010 FIFA WORLD CUP SOUTH AFRICA

WORLD CLASSIC XI TEAM

Earn at least Bronze against each team in Kazumi's Dream Team to play the World Classic XI Team. Beat them in best of three matches to play as the team in Hit the Pitch.

ASTRO BOY: THE VIDEO GAME

INVULNERABLE
Pause the game and press Up, Down, Down, Up, 1, 2.

MAX STATS
Pause the game and press Left, Left, 2, Down, Down, 1.

INFINITE SUPERS
Pause the game and press Left, 1, Right, 1, Up, Down.

INFINITE DASHES
Pause the game and press 2, 2, 1, 2, Left, Up.

DISABLE SUPERS
Pause the game and press 1, 1, 2, 2, 1, Left.

COSTUME SWAP (ARENA AND CLASSIC COSTUMES)
Pause the game and press 2, Up, 1, Up, Down, 2.

UNLOCK LEVELS
Pause the game and press Up, 1, Right, 1, Down, 1. This allows you to travel to any level from the Story menu.

AVATAR: THE LAST AIRBENDER—THE BURNING EARTH

DOUBLE DAMAGE
Go to the code entry section and enter 90210.

INFINITE LIFE
Go to the code entry section and enter 65049.

INFINITE SPECIAL ATTACKS
Go to the code entry section and enter 66206.

MAX LEVEL
Go to the code entry section and enter 89121.

ONE-HIT DISHONOR
Go to the code entry section and enter 28260.

ALL BONUS GAMES
Go to the code entry section and enter 99801.

ALL GALLERY ITEMS
Go to the code entry section and enter 85061.

AVATAR - THE LAST AIRBENDER: INTO THE INFERNO

After you have defeated the first level, The Awakening, go to Ember Island. Walk to the left past the volleyball net to a red and yellow door. Select Game Secrets and then Code Entry. Now you can enter the following cheats.

MAX COINS
Enter 66639224.

ALL ITEMS AVAILABLE FROM SHOP
Enter 34737253.

ALL CHAPTERS
Enter 52993833.

UNLOCK CONCEPT ART IN GALLERY
Enter 27858343.

BAKUGAN BATTLE BRAWLERS

1,000 BP
Enter 33204429 as your name.

5,000 BP
Enter 42348294 as your name.

10,000 BP
Enter 46836478 as your name.

100,000 BP
Enter 18499753 as your name.

500,000 BP
Enter 26037947 as your name.

BRONZE WARIUS
Enter 44982493 as your name.

BAKUGAN: DEFENDERS OF THE CORE

HIDDEN ITEMS
Select Unlock Codes from Collection and enter HXV6Y7BF. Now you can enter up to 8 of your unique Bakugan Dimensions codes.

The codes unlock the following:

10,000 Core Energy	2FKRRMNCDQ
Ten Vexos Passes	82D77YK6P8
Earthen Armor	HUUH8ST7AR
Fire Spirit	JJUZDEACXX
Light Arrow	QY8CLD5NJE
Tornado Vortex	TD4UMFSRW3
Water Pillar	YJ7RGG7WGZ
Zorch Thunder	YQLHBBSMDC

Here are 8 codes:

BATMAN: THE BRAVE AND THE BOLD – THE VIDEOGAME

BATMAN COSTUMES

Access the terminal on the left side of the Batcave and enter the following:

COSTUME	CODE
Dark Batsuit	3756448
Medieval Batsuit	5644863
Rainbow Suit	7629863

WEAPONS

WEAPON	CODE
Barrier	2525655
Belt Sword	2587973
Flashbangs	3527463
Smoke Pellets	7665336

CHALLENGE MAPS

CHALLENGE MAP	CODE
Gotham 1 & 2	4846348
Proto Sparring	6677686
Science Island 1 & 2	7262348

BEN 10: ALIEN FORCE VILGAX ATTACKS

LEVEL SKIP
Pause the game and enter Portal in the Cheats menu.

UNLOCK ALL SPECIAL ATTACKS FOR ALL FORMS
Pause the game and enter Everythingproof in the Cheats menu.

UNLOCK ALL ALIEN FORMS
Pause the game and enter Primus in the Cheats menu.

TOGGLE INVULNERABILITY ON AND OFF
Pause the game and enter Xlmrsmoothy in the Cheats menu.

GIVES PLAYER FULL HEALTH
Pause the game and enter Herotime in the Cheats menu.

QUICK ENERGY REGENERATION
Pause the game and enter Generator in the Cheats menu.

BEN 10: PROTECTOR OF EARTH

INVINCIBILITY
Select a game from the Continue option. Go to the Map Selection screen, press Plus and choose Extras. Select Enter Secret Code and enter XLR8, Heatblast, Wildvine, Fourarms.

ALL COMBOS
Select a game from the Continue option. Go to the Map Selection screen, press Plus and choose Extras. Select Enter Secret Code and enter Cannonblot, Heatblast, Fourarms, Heatblast.

ALL LOCATIONS
Select a game from the Continue option. Go to the Map Selection screen, press Plus and choose Extras. Select Enter Secret Code and enter Heatblast, XLR8, XLR8, Cannonblot.

DNA FORCE SKINS
Select a game from the Continue option. Go to the Map Selection screen, press Plus and choose Extras. Select Enter Secret Code and enter Wildvine, Fourarms, Heatblast, Cannonbolt.

DARK HEROES SKINS
Select a game from the Continue option. Go to the Map Selection screen, press Plus and choose Extras. Select Enter Secret Code and enter Cannonbolt, Cannonbolt, Fourarms, Heatblast.

ALL ALIEN FORMS
Select a game from the Continue option. Go to the Map Selection screen, press Plus and choose Extras. Select Enter Secret Code and enter Wildvine, Fourarms, Heatblast, Wildvine.

MASTER CONTROL
Select a game from the Continue option. Go to the Map Selection screen, press Plus and choose Extras. Select Enter Secret Code and enter Cannonbolt, Heatblast, Wildvine, Fourarms.

BEN 10 ULTIMATE ALIEN: COSMIC DESTRUCTION

To remove the cheats, you will need to start a new game.

1,000,000 DNA
Pause the game, select Cheats, and enter Cash.

REGENERATE HEALTH
Pause the game, select Cheats, and enter Health.

REGENERATE ENERGY
Pause the game, select Cheats, and enter Energy.

UPGRADE EVERYTHING
Pause the game, select Cheats, and enter Upgrade.

ALL LEVELS
Pause the game, select Cheats, and enter Levels.

ENEMIES DO DOUBLE DAMAGE/ PLAYER DOES ½ DAMAGE
Pause the game, select Cheats, and enter Hard.

BLAZING ANGELS: SQUADRONS OF WWII

ALL AIRCRAFT AND CAMPAIGNS
After you have chosen a pilot, hold Minus + Plus and press Left, Right, 1, 2, 2, 1.

GOD MODE
Pause the game, hold Minus and press 1, 2, 1, 2.

WEAPON DAMAGE INCREASED
Pause the game, hold Minus and press 2, 1, 1, 2.

BOOM BLOX

ALL TOYS IN CREATE MODE
At the title screen, press Up, Right, Down, Left to bring up a cheats menu. Enter Tool Pool.

SLOW-MO IN SINGLE PLAYER
At the title screen, press Up, Right, Down, Left to bring up a cheats menu. Enter Blox Time.

CHEERLEADERS BECOME PROFILE CHARACTER
At the title screen, press Up, Right, Down, Left to bring up a cheats menu. Enter My Team.

FLOWER EXPLOSIONS
At the title screen, press Up, Right, Down, Left to bring up a cheats menu. Enter Flower Power.

JINGLE BLOCKS
At the title screen, press Up, Right, Down, Left to bring up a cheats menu. Enter Maestro.

BOOM BLOX BASH PARTY

At the title screen, press Up, Right, Down, Left. Now you can enter the following codes:

UNLOCK EVERYTHING
Enter Nothing But Hope.

1 MILLION BOOM BUX
Enter Bailout.

TURN ON BLOX TIME
Enter Freeze Frame.

TURNS ALL SOUND EFFECTS INTO VIRUS BLOX SOUND EFFECTS
Enter Musical Fruit.

ALL COLORED BLOX
Enter Rainbow Blox.

BRATZ: MOVIE STARZ

FEELIN' PRETTY CLOTHING LINE
At the Cheat Computer enter PRETTY.

HIGH SCHOOL CLOTHING LINE
At the Cheat Computer enter SCHOOL.

HOLLYWOOD CLOTHING LINE
At the Cheat Computer enter MOVIES

PASSION FOR FASHION CLOTHING LINE
At the Cheat Computer enter ANGELZ.

PRINCESS CLOTHING LINE
At the Cheat Computer enter SPARKL.

BUILD-A-BEAR WORKSHOP: A FRIEND FUR ALL SEASONS

ALL ISLANDS, MINIGAMES, OUTFITS, AND ACCESSORIES
At the main menu, press Up, Down, Left, Right, A, B.

CARS 2: THE VIDEO GAME

ALL MODES AND TRACKS
Select Enter Codes from the Options and enter 959595.

UNLIMITED ENERGY
Select Enter Codes from the Options and enter 721953. Select Cheats to toggle the cheat on and off.

LASER GUIDED
Select Enter Codes from the Options and enter 123456. Select Cheats to toggle the cheat on and off.

CARS MATER-NATIONAL

ALL ARCADE RACES, MINI-GAMES, AND WORLDS
Select Codes/Cheats from the options and enter PLAYALL.

ALL CARS
Select Codes/Cheats from the options and enter MATTEL07.

ALTERNATE LIGHTNING MCQUEEN COLORS
Select Codes/Cheats from the options and enter NCEDUDZ.

ALL COLORS FOR OTHERS
Select Codes/Cheats from the options and enter PAINTIT.

UNLIMITED TURBO
Select Codes/Cheats from the options and enter ZZOOOOM.

EXTREME ACCELERATION
Select Codes/Cheats from the options and enter OTO200X.

EXPERT MODE
Select Codes/Cheats from the options and enter VRYFAST.

ALL BONUS ART
Select Codes/Cheats from the options and enter BUYTALL.

CARS RACE-O-RAMA

ALL ARCADE MODE EVENTS
Select Cheats from the Options menu and enter SLVRKEY.

ALL STORY MODE EVENTS
Select Cheats from the Options menu and enter GOLDKEY.

ALL OF LIGHTNING MCQUEEN'S FRIENDS
Select Cheats from the Options menu and enter EVRYBDY.

ALL LIGHTNING MCQUEEN CUSTOM KIT PARTS
Select Cheats from the Options menu and enter GR8MODS.

ALL PAINT JOBS FOR ALL NON-LIGHTNING MCQUEEN CHARACTERS
Select Cheats from the Options menu and enter CARSHOW.

CASTLEVANIA THE ADVENTURE REBIRTH

LEVEL SELECT
Select Game Start and hold Right for a few seconds. You can play any level you have already played.

CODE LYOKO: QUEST FOR INFINITY

UNLOCK EVERYTHING
Pause the game and press 2, 1, C, Z, 2, 1.

UNLIMITED HEALTH AND POWER
Pause the game and press 2, 2, Z, Z, 1, 1.

INCREASE SPEED
Pause the game and press Z, 1, 2, 1 (x3).

INCREASE DAMAGE
Pause the game and press 1, Z, Z, C (x3).

CONFIGURATION A
Pause the game and press 2, Z, 1, Z, C, Z.

CONFIGURATION B
Pause the game and press C, C, 1, C, Z, C.

ALL ABILITIES
Pause the game and press Z, C, Z, C (x3).

ALL BONUSES
Pause the game and press 1, 2, C, 2 (x3).

ALL GOODIES
Pause the game and press C, 2, 2, Z, C, Z.

CONTRA REBIRTH

DEBUG MENU

At the title screen, press Plus + 1 + 2.

CORALINE

UNLIMITED LEVEL SKIP

Select Cheats from the Options menu and enter Beldam.

UNLIMITED HEALTH

Select Cheats from the Options menu and enter beets.

UNLIMITED FIREFLYS

Select Cheats from the Options menu and enter garden.

FREE HALL PASSES

Select Cheats from the Options menu and enter well.

BUTTON EYE CORALINE

Select Cheats from the Options menu and enter cheese.

CRASH: MIND OVER MUTANT

A cheat can be deactivated by re-entering the code.

FREEZE ENEMIES WITH TOUCH

Pause the game, hold guard and press Down, Down, Down, Up.

ENEMIES DROP X4 DAMAGE

Pause the game, hold guard and press Up, Up, Up, Left.

ENEMIES DROP PURPLE FRUIT

Pause the game, hold guard and press Up, Down, Down, Up.

ENEMIES DROP SUPER KICK

Pause the game, hold guard and press Up, Right, Down, Left.

ENIMIES DROP WUMPA FRUIT

Pause the game, hold guard and press Right, Right, Right, Up.

SHADOW CRASH

Pause the game, hold guard and press Left, Right, Left, Right.

DEFORMED CRASH

Pause the game, hold guard and press Left, Left, Left, Down.

COSTUMES

Complete all of the following character's mini-games to unlock each costume.

COSTUME	DEFEAT MINI-GAMES OF
Magmadon	Little Bear
Ratcicle	Ratcicle Kid
Skeleton	Sludge Brother
Snipe	Crunch
Spike	Uka Uka

DE BLOB

INVULNERABILITY

During a game, hold C and press 1, 1, 1, 1. Re-enter the code to disable.

LIFE UP

During a game, hold C and press 1, 1, 2, 2

TIME BONUS

During a game, hold C and press 1, 2, 1, 2. This adds 10 minutes to your time.

ALL MOODS
At the main menu, hold C and press B, B, 1, 2, 1, 2, B, B.

ALL MULTIPLAYER LEVELS
At the main menu, hold C and press 2, 2, B, B, 1, 1, B, B.

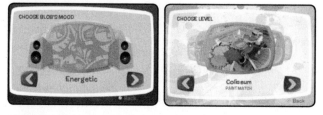

DISNEY PRINCESS: ENCHANTED JOURNEY

BELLE'S KINGDOM
Select Secrets and enter GASTON.

GOLDEN SET
Select Secrets and enter BLUEBIRD.

FLOWER WAND
Select Secrets and enter SLEEPY.

HEART WAND
Select Secrets and enter BASHFUL.

SHELL WAND
Select Secrets and enter RAJAH.

SHIELD WAND
Select Secrets and enter CHIP.

STAR WAND
Select Secrets and enter SNEEZY.

DJ HERO

Select Cheats from Options and enter the following. Some codes will disable high scores and progress. Cheats cannot be used in tutorials and online.

UNLOCK ALL CONTENT
Enter tol0.

ALL CHARACTER ITEMS
Enter uNA2.

ALL VENUES
Enter Wv1u.

ALL DECKS
Enter LAuP.

ALL HEADPHONES
Enter 62Db.

ALL MIXES
Enter 82xl.

AUTO SCRATCH
Enter IT6j.

AUTO EFFECTS DIAL
Enter ab1L.

AUTO FADER
Enter SL5d.

AUTO TAPPER
Enter ZitH.

AUTO WIN EUPHORIA
Enter r3a9.

BLANK PLINTHS
Enter ipr0.

HAMSTER SWITCH
Enter 7geo.

HYPER DECK MODE
Enter 76st.

SHORT DECK
Enter 51uC.

INVISIBLE DJ
Enter oh5T.

PITCH BLACK OUT
Enter d4kR.

PLAY IN THE BEDROOM
Enter g7nH.

ANY DJ, ANY SETLIST
Enter 0jj8.

DAFT PUNK'S CONTENT
Enter d1g?.

DJ AM'S CONTENT
Enter k07u.

DJ JAZZY JEFF'S CONTENT
Enter n1fz.

DJ SHADOW'S CONTENT
Enter oMxV.

DJ Z-TRIP'S CONTENT
Enter 5rtg.

GRANDMASTER FLASH'S CONTENT
Enter ami8.

DONKEY KONG COUNTRY 2: DIDDY'S KONG QUEST

SOUND TEST
Highlight Two Player and press Down (x5).

CHEAT MODE
Press Down (x5) again after getting Sound Test to access the cheat mode. Now you can enter the following:

50 LIVES
Press Y, A, Select, A, Down, Left, A, Down.

HARD MODE
Press B, A, Right, Right, A, Left, A, X. This gets rid of the barrels.

DRAGON BALL Z: BUDOKAI TENKAICHI 2

Hold Z + Minus to clear codes.

DOUBLE FIST POWER
At the Stage Select in vs mode, hold Z + Plus to start code input. Swing the Nunchuk Right, Wiimote Left, Wiimote Left + Nunchuk Right, Wiimote and Nunchuk Down.

TAIL POWER
At the Stage Select in vs mode, hold Z + Plus to start code input. Swing the Wiimote Down, Up, Left, Right.

DRAGON BALL Z: BUDOKAI TENKAICHI 3

SURVIVAL MODE
Clear 30 missions in Mission 100 mode.

EA SPORTS NBA JAM

Hold the Wii Remote vertically when entering the following. The teams can be found by pressing + at the team select.

BEASTIE BOYS
At the title screen, press Up, Up, Down, Down, Left, Right, Left, Right, B, +. This team includes Ad Rock, MCA, and Mike D.

J.COLE AND 9TH WONDER
At the title screen, press Up, Left, Down, Right, Up, Left, Down, Right, 1, 2.

DEMOCRATS TEAM
At the title screen, press Left (x13), +. This team includes Barack Obama, Joe Biden, Bill Clinton, and Hillary Clinton.

REPUBLICANS TEAM
At the title screen, press Right (x13), +. The team includes George W. Bush, Sarah Palin, and John McCain.

ESPN'S SPORTSNATION
Select Play Now. When entering the initials, enter ESP for P1 and NSN for P2. Advance to the Choose Teams screen and use + to find the team. This team includes the hosts of the show; Colin Cowherd and Michelle Beadle.

NBA MASCOTS
Select Play Now. When entering the initials, enter MAS for P1 and COT for P2. Advance to the Choose Teams screen and use + to find the team.

ORIGINAL GENERATION JAM
Select Play Now. When entering the initials, enter MJT for P1. Advance to the Choose Teams screen and use + to find the team. This team includes Mark Turmell and Tim Kitzrow.

EARTHWORM JIM

CHEAT MENU
Pause the game and press Y + Left, B, B, Y, Y + Right, B, B, Y. These are the button presses for the classic controller.

FAMILY FEUD 2010 EDITION

NEW WARDROBE
Select the lock tab from the Wardrobe screen and enter FAMILY.

FATAL FURY SPECIAL

SOUND TEST
Pause the game and press A, B, C, D, A.

FIGHTING STREET

+4 CREDITS, SIMPLIFIED SPECIAL MOVES, AND STAGE SELECT
After getting a high score, enter .SD as your initials. Then, at the title screen, hold Left + 1 + 2, and press Minus.

+4 CREDITS
After getting a high score, enter .HU as your initials. Then, at the title screen, hold Left + 1 + 2, and press Minus.

SIMPLIFIED SPECIAL MOVES
After getting a high score, enter .LK as your initials. Then, at the title screen, hold Left + 1 + 2, and press Minus.

STAGE SELECT
After getting a high score, enter .AS as your initials. Then, at the title screen, hold Left + 1 + 2, and press Minus.

GHOST SQUAD

COSTUMES
Reach the following levels in single-player to unlock the corresponding costume.

LEVEL	COSTUME
07	Desert Camouflage
10	Policeman
15	Tough Guy
18	Sky Camouflage
20	World War II
23	Cowboy

LEVEL	COSTUME
30	Urban Camouflage
34	Virtua Cop
38	Future Warrior
50	Ninja
60	Panda Suit
99	Gold Uniform

NINJA MODE
Play through Arcade Mode.

PARADISE MODE
Play through Ninja Mode.

GHOUL PATROL

PASSWORDS

LEVEL	PASSWORD
5	CP4V
9	7LBR
13	KVCY

G.I. JOE: THE RISE OF COBRA

CLASSIC DUKE
At the title screen press Left, Up, -, Up, Right, +.

CLASSIC SCARLETT
At the title screen press Right, Up, Down, Down, +.

GODZILLA UNLEASHED

UNLOCK ALL
At the main menu, press A + Up to bring up the cheat entry screen. Enter 204935.

90000 STORE POINTS
At the main menu, press A + Up to bring up the cheat entry screen. Enter 031406.

SET DAY
At the main menu, press A + Up to bring up the cheat entry screen. Enter 0829XX, where XX represents the day. Use 00 for day one.

SHOW MONSTER MOVES
At the main menu, press A + Up to bring up the cheat entry screen. Enter 411411.

VERSION NUMBER
At the main menu, press A + Up to bring up the cheat entry screen. Enter 787321.

MOTHERSHIP LEVEL
Playing as the Aliens, destroy the mothership in the Invasion level.

GRADIUS REBIRTH

4 OPTIONS
Pause the game and press Up, Up, Down, Down, Left, Right, Left, Right, Fire, Powerup. This code can be used once for each stage you have attempted.

GRAVITRONIX

VERSUS OPTIONS AND LEVEL SELECT
At the Options menu, press 1, 2, 2, 2, 1.

GREG HASTINGS PAINTBALL 2

PRO AND NEW GUN
Select Career, hold C, and press Up, Up, Down, Right, Left, Left, Right, Up.

HARRY POTTER AND THE HALF-BLOOD PRINCE

BONUS TWO-PLAYER DUELING ARENA CASTLE GATES
At the Rewards menu, press Right, Right, Down, Down, Left, Right, Left, Right, Left, Right, +.

HASBRO FAMILY GAME NIGHT 2

SECRET PRIZE
Have a saved file from the first Hasbro Family Game Night.

INDIANA JONES AND THE STAFF OF KINGS

FATE OF ATLANTIS GAME
At the main menu, hold Z and press A, Up, Up, B, Down, Down, Left, Right, Left, B.

IRON MAN

ARMOR SELECTION

Iron Man's different armor suits are unlocked by completing certain missions. Refer to the following tables for when each is unlocked. After selecting a mission to play, you get the opportunity to pick the armor you wish to use.

COMPLETE MISSION	SUIT UNLOCKED
1: Escape	Mark I
2: First Flight	Mark II
3: Fight Back	Mark III
6: Flying Fortress	Comic Tin Can
9: Home Front	Classic
13: Showdown	Silver Centurion

CONCEPT ART

Concept Art is unlocked after finding certain numbers of Weapon Crates.

CONCEPT ART UNLOCKED	NUMBER OF WEAPON CRATES FOUND
Environments Set 1	6
Environments Set 2	12
Iron Man	18
Environments Set 3	24
Enemies	30
Environments Set 4	36
Villains	42
Vehicles	48
Covers	50

IVY THE KIWI?

BONUS MODE AND PICTURE BOOK

Finish the main game.

DOG COSTUME

Collect 100 red feathers—50 from the main game and 50 from Bonus Mode.

KARAOKE REVOLUTION GLEE: VOLUME 2

ICE ICE BABY

Select Unlockables from the Options and enter A64112.

PINK HOUSES

Select Unlockables from the Options and enter DD6C62.

KUNG FU PANDA

INFINITE CHI

Select Cheats from the Extra menu and press Down, Right, Left, Up, Down.

INVINCIBILITY

Select Cheats from the Extra menu and press Down, Down, Right, Up, Left.

4X DAMAGE MULTIPLYER

Select Cheats from the Extra menu and press Up, Down, Up, Right, Left.

ALL MULTIPLAYER CHARACTERS

Select Cheats from the Extra menu and press Left, Down, Left, Right, Down.

DRAGON WARRIOR OUTFIT IN MULTIPLAYER

Select Cheats from the Extra menu and press Left, Down, Right, Left, Up.

THE LEGEND OF SPYRO: DAWN OF THE DRAGON

INFINITE HEALTH
Pause the game, hold Z and move the Nunchuk Right, Right, Down, Down, Left.

INFINITE MANA
Pause the game, hold Z and move the Nunchuk Up, Right, Up, Left, Down.

MAX XP
Pause the game, hold Z and move the Nunchuk Up, Left, Left, Down, Up.

ALL ELEMENTAL UPGRADES
Pause the game, hold Z and move the Nunchuk Left, Up, Down, Up, Right.

LEGO BATMAN

BATCAVE CODES
Using the computer in the Batcave, select Enter Code and enter the following codes.

CHARACTERS

CHARACTER	CODE	CHARACTER	CODE
Alfred	ZAQ637	Penguin Henchman	BJH782
Batgirl	JKR331	Penguin Minion	KJP748
Bruce Wayne	BDJ327	Poison Ivy Goon	GTB899
Catwoman (Classic)	M1AAWW	Police Marksman	HKG984
Clown Goon	HJK327	Police Officer	JRY983
Commissioner Gordon	DDP967	Riddler Goon	CRY928
Fishmonger	HGY748	Riddler Henchman	XEU824
Freeze Girl	XVK541	S.W.A.T.	HTF114
Joker Goon	UTF782	Sailor	NAV592
Joker Henchman	YUN924	Scientist	JFL786
Mad Hatter	JCA283	Security Guard	PLB946
Man-Bat	NYU942	The Joker (Tropical)	CCB199
Military Policeman	MKL382	Yeti	NJL412
Nightwing	MVY759	Zoo Sweeper	DWR243
Penguin Goon	NKA238		

VEHICLES

VEHICLE	CODE	VEHICLE	CODE
Bat-Tank	KNTT4B	Mr. Freeze's Kart	BCT229
Bruce Wayne's Private Jet	LEA664	Penguin Goon Submarine	BTN248
Catwoman's Motorcycle	HPL826	Police Bike	LJP234
Garbage Truck	DUS483	Police Boat	PLC999
Goon Helicopter	GCH328	Police Car	KJL832
Harbor Helicopter	CHP735	Police Helicopter	CWR732
Harley Quinn's Hammer Truck	RDT637	Police Van	MAC788
Mad Hatter's Glider	HS000W	Police Watercraft	VJD328
Mad Hatter's Steamboat	M4DM4N	Riddler's Jet	HAHAHA
Mr. Freeze's Iceberg	ICYICE	Robin's Submarine	TTF453
The Joker's Van	JUK657	Two-Face's Armored Truck	EFE933

CHEATS

CHEAT	CODE	CHEAT	CODE
Always Score Multiply	9LRGNB	More Batarang Targets	XWP645
Fast Batarangs	JRBDCB	Piece Detector	KHJ554
Fast Walk	ZOLM6N	Power Brick Detector	MMN786
Flame Batarang	D8NYWH	Regenerate Hearts	HJH7HJ
Freeze Batarang	XPN4NG	Score x2	N4NR3E
Extra Hearts	ML3KHP	Score x4	CX9MAT
Fast Build	EVG26J	Score x6	MLVNF2
Immune to Freeze	JXUDY6	Score x8	WCCDB9
Invincibility	WYD5CP	Score x10	18HW07
Minikit Detector	ZXGH9J		

LEGO HARRY POTTER: YEARS 1-4

RED BRICK EXTRAS

Once you have access to The Leaky Cauldron, enter Wiseacre's Wizarding Supplies from Diagon Alley. Go upstairs to enter the following. Pause the game and select Extras to toggle the cheats on/off.

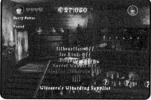

CHEAT	CODE
Carrot Wands	AUC8EH
Character Studs	H27KGC
Character Token Detector	HA79V8
Christmas	T7PVVN
Disguise	4DMK2R
Fall Rescue	ZEX7MV
Extra Hearts	J9U6Z9
Fast Dig	Z9BFAD
Fast Magic	FA3GQA
Gold Brick Detector	84QNQN
Hogwarts Crest Detector	TTMC6D
Ice Rink	F88VUW

CHEAT	CODE
Invincibility	QQWC6B
Red Brick Detector	7AD7HE
Regenerate Hearts	89ML2W
Score x2	74YKR7
Score x4	J3WHNK
Score x6	XK9ANE
Score x8	HUFV2H
Score x10	H8X69Y
Silhouettes	HZBVX7
Singing Mandrake	BMEU6X
Stud Magnet	67FKWZ

WISEACRE SPELLS

Once you have access to The Leaky Cauldron, enter Wiseacre's Wizarding Supplies from Diagon Alley. Go upstairs to enter the following. You need to learn Wingardium Leviosa before you can use these cheats.

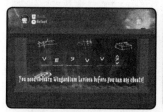

SPELL	CODE
Accio	VE9VV7
Anteoculatia	QFB6NR
Calvorio	6DNR6L
Colovaria	9GJ442
Engorgio Skullus	CD4JLX
Entomorphis	MYN3NB
Flipendo	ND2L7W
Glacius	ERA9DR

HERBIFORS	H8FTHL
Incarcerous	YEB9Q9
Locomotor Mortis	2M2XJ6
Multicorfors	JK6QRM
Redactum Skullus	UW8LRH
Rictusempra	2UCA3M
Slugulus Eructo	U6EE8X
Stupefy	UWDJ4Y
Tarantallegra	KWWQ44
Trip Jinx	YZNRF6

EEYLOPS GOLD BRICKS

Once you have access to The Leaky Cauldron, enter Wiseacre's Wizarding Supplies from Diagon Alley. Go upstairs to enter the following. To access the LEGO Builder, visit Gringott's Bank at the end of Diagon Alley.

GOLD BRICK	CODE	GOLD BRICK	CODE
1	QE4VC7	7	XY6VYZ
2	FY8H97	8	TUNC4W
3	3MQT4P	9	EJ42Q6
4	PQPM7Z	10	GFJCV9
5	ZY2CPA	11	DZCY6G
6	3GMTP6		

LEGO INDIANA JONES: THE ORIGINAL ADVENTURES

CHARACTERS

Approach the blackboard in the Classsroom and enter the following codes.

CHARACTER	CODE	CHARACTER	CODE
Bandit	12N68W	Fedora	V75YSP
Bandit Swordsman	1MK4RT	First Mate	0GIN24
Barranca	04EM94	Grail Knight	NE6THI
Bazooka Trooper (Crusade)	MK83R7	Hovitos Tribesman	HOV1SS
Bazooka Trooper (Raiders)	S93Y5R	Indiana Jones (Desert Disguise)	4J8S4M
Belloq	CHN3YU	Indiana Jones (Officer)	VJ850S
Belloq (Jungle)	TDR197	Jungle Guide	24PF34
Belloq (Robes)	VEO29L	Kao Kan	WMO46L
British Commander	B73EUA	Kazim	NRH23J
British Officer	VJ5TI9	Kazim (Desert)	3M29TJ
British Soldier	DJ5I2W	Lao Che	2NK479
Captain Katanga	VJ3TT3	Maharajah	NFK5N2
Chatter Lal	ENW936	Major Toht	13NSO1
Chatter Lal (Thuggee)	CNH4RY	Masked Bandit	N48SF0
Chen	3NK48T	Mola Ram	FJUR31
Colonel Dietrich	2K9RKS	Monkey Man	3RF6YJ
Colonel Vogel	8EAL4H	Pankot Assassin	2NKT72
Dancing Girl	C7EJ21	Pankot Guard	VN28RH
Donovan	3NFTU8	Sherpa Brawler	VJ37WJ
Elsa (Desert)	JSNRT9	Sherpa Gunner	ND762W
Elsa (Officer)	VMJ5US	Slave Child	OE3ENW
Enemy Boxer	8246RB	Thuggee	VM683E
Enemy Butler	VJ48W3	Thuggee Acolyte	T2R3F9
Enemy Guard	VJ7R51	Thuggee Slave Driver	VBS7GW
Enemy Guard (Mountains)	YR47WM	Village Dignitary	KD48TN
Enemy Officer	572E61	Village Elder	4682E1
Enemy Officer (Desert	2MK450	Willie (Dinner Suit)	VK93R7
Enemy Pilot	B84ELP	Willie (Pajamas)	MEN4IP
Enemy Radio Operator	1MF94R	Wu Han	3NSLT8
Enemy Soldier (Desert)	4NSU7Q		

EXTRAS

Approach the blackboard in the Classsroom and enter the following codes. Some cheats need to be enabled by selecting Extras from the pause menu.

CHEAT	CODE	CHEAT	CODE
Artifact Detector	VIKED7	Disguises	4ID1N6
Beep Beep	VNF59Q	Fast Build	V83SL0
Character Treasure	VIES2R	Fast Dig	378RS6
Disarm Enemies	VKRNS9	Fast Fix	FJ59WS

CHEAT	CODE
Fertilizer	B1GW1F
Ice Rink	33GM7J
Parcel Detector	VUT673
Poo Treasure	WWQ1SA
Regenerate Hearts	MDLP69
Secret Characters	3X44AA
Silhouettes	3HE85H
Super Scream	VN3R7S

CHEAT	CODE
Super Slap	OP1TA5
Treasure Magnet	H86LA2
Treasure x10	VI3PS8
Treasure x2	VM4TS9
Treasure x4	VLWEN3
Treasure x6	V84RYS
Treasure x8	A72E1M

LEGO INDIANA JONES 2: THE ADVENTURE CONTINUES

Pause the game, select Enter Secret Code from the Extras menu, and enter the following.

CHARACTERS

CHARACTER	CODE
Bellog (Priest)	FTL48S
Dovchenko	WL4T6N
Enemy Boxer	7EQF47
Henry Jones	4CSAKH
Indiana Jones	PGWSEA
Indiana Jones: 2	FGLKYS
Indiana Jones (Collect)	DZFY9S
Indiana Jones (Desert)	M4C34K
Indiana Jones (Desert Disguise)	2W8QR3
Indiana Jones (Dinner Suit)	QUNZUT
Indiana Jones (Kali)	J2XS97
Indiana Jones (Officer)	3FQFKS
Interdimensional Being	PXT4UP
Lao Che	7AWX3J
Mannequin (Boy)	2UJQWC
Mannequin (Girl)	3PGSEL
Mannequin (Man)	QPWDMM
Mannequin (Woman)	U7SMVK
Mola Ram	82RMC2
Mutt	2GKS62
Salah	E88YRP
Willie	94RUAJ

EXTRAS

EFFECT	CODE
Beep Beep	UU3VSC
Disguise	Y9TE98
Fast Build	SNXC2F
Fast Dig	XYAN83
Fast Fix	3Z7PJX
Fearless	TUXNZF
Ice Rink	TY9P4U
Invincibility	6JBB65
Poo Money	SZFAAE
Score x3	PEHHPZ
Score x4	UXGTB3
Score X6	XWLJEY
Score x8	S5UZCP
Score x10	V7JYBU
Silhouettes	FQGPYH
Snake Whip	2U7YCV
Stud Magnet	EGSM5B

LEGO PIRATES OF THE CARIBBEAN: THE VIDEO GAME

CODES

Pause the game and select Extras. Choose Enter Code and enter the following codes:

EFFECT	PASSWORD	EFFECT	PASSWORD
Ammand the Corsair	EW8T6T	Jacoby	BW0656
Blackbeard	D3DW0D	Jimmy Legs	13GLW5
Clubba	644THF	Koehler	RT093G
Davy Jones	4DJLKR	Mistress Ching	GDETDE
Governor Weatherby Swann	LD9454	Philip	WEV040
Gunner	Y611WB	Quartermaster	RX58HU
Hungry Cannibal	64BNHG	The Spaniard	P861JO
Jack Sparrow	VDJSPW	Twigg	KDLFKD

LEGO STAR WARS: THE COMPLETE SAGA

The following still need to be purchase after entering the codes.

CHARACTERS

ADMIRAL ACKBAR
At the bar in Mos Eisley Cantina, select Enter Code and enter ACK646.

BATTLE DROID (COMMANDER)
At the bar in Mos Eisley Cantina, select Enter Code and enter KPF958.

BOBA FETT (BOY)
At the bar in Mos Eisley Cantina, select Enter Code and enter GGF539.

BOSS NASS
At the bar in Mos Eisley Cantina, select Enter Code and enter HHY697.

CAPTAIN TARPALS
At the bar in Mos Eisley Cantina, select Enter Code and enter QRN714.

COUNT DOOKU
At the bar in Mos Eisley Cantina, select Enter Code and enter DDD748.

DARTH MAUL
At the bar in Mos Eisley Cantina, select Enter Code and enter EUK421.

EWOK
At the bar in Mos Eisley Cantina, select Enter Code and enter EWK785.

GENERAL GRIEVOUS
At the bar in Mos Eisley Cantina, select Enter Code and enter PMN576.

GREEDO
At the bar in Mos Eisley Cantina, select Enter Code and enter ZZR636.

IG-88
At the bar in Mos Eisley Cantina, select Enter Code and enter GIJ989.

IMPERIAL GUARD
At the bar in Mos Eisley Cantina, select Enter Code and enter GUA850.

JANGO FETT
At the bar in Mos Eisley Cantina, select Enter Code and enter KLJ897.

KI-ADI MUNDI
At the bar in Mos Eisley Cantina, select Enter Code and enter MUN486.

LUMINARA
At the bar in Mos Eisley Cantina, select Enter Code and enter LUM521.

PADMÉ
At the bar in Mos Eisley Cantina, select Enter Code and enter VBJ322.

R2-Q5
At the bar in Mos Eisley Cantina, select Enter Code and enter EVILR2.

STORMTROOPER
At the bar in Mos Eisley Cantina, select Enter Code and enter NBN431.

TAUN WE
At the bar in Mos Eisley Cantina, select Enter Code and enter PRX482.

VULTURE DROID
At the bar in Mos Eisley Cantina, select Enter Code and enter BDC866.

WATTO
At the bar in Mos Eisley Cantina, select Enter Code and enter PLL967.

ZAM WESELL
At the bar in Mos Eisley Cantina, select Enter Code and enter 584HJF.

SKILLS

DISGUISE
At the bar in Mos Eisley Cantina, select Enter Code and enter BRJ437.

FORCE GRAPPLE LEAP
At the bar in Mos Eisley Cantina, select Enter Code and enter CLZ738.

VEHICLES

DROID TRIFIGHTER
At the bar in Mos Eisley Cantina, select Enter Code and enter AAB123.

IMPERIAL SHUTTLE
At the bar in Mos Eisley Cantina, select Enter Code and enter HUT845.

TIE INTERCEPTOR
At the bar in Mos Eisley Cantina, select Enter Code and enter INT729.

TIE FIGHTER
At the bar in Mos Eisley Cantina, select Enter Code and enter DBH897.

ZAM'S AIRSPEEDER
At the bar in Mos Eisley Cantina, select Enter Code and enter UUU875.

LEGO STAR WARS III: THE CLONE WARS

Pause the game, select Enter Code from Extras and enter the following:

CHARACTERS

CHARACTER	CODE
Aayla Secura	2VG95B
Adi Gallia	G2BFEN
Admiral Ackbar (Classic)	272Y9Q
Admiral Yularen	NG6PYX
Ahsoka	2VJ9TH
Anakin Skywalker	F9VUYJ
Anakin Skywalker (Geonosian Arena)	9AA4DW
Asajj Ventress	YG9DD7
Aurra Sing	M2V1JV
Bail Organa	GEHX6C
Barriss Offee	BTVTZ5
Battle Droid	5Y7MA4
Battle Droid Commander	LSU4LJ
Bib Fortuna	9U4TF3
Boba Fett (Classic)	TY2BYJ
Boil	Q5Q39P
Bossk	2KLW5R
C-3PO	574226
Cad Bane	NHME85
Captain Antilles (Classic)	D8SNGJ
Captain Rex	MW3QYH
Captain Typho	GD6FX3
Chancellor Palpatine	5C62YQ
Chewbacca (Classic)	66UU3T
Clone Pilot	HQ7BVD
Clone Shadow Trooper (Classic)	7GFNCQ
Clone Trooper	NP5GTT

CHARACTER	CODE
Commander Bly	7CB6NS
Commander Cody	SMN259
Commander Fil	U25HFC
Commander Ponds	JRPR2A
Commander Stone	5XZQSV
Commando Droid	QEGU64
Count Dooku	EWR7WM
Darth Maul (Classic)	QH68AK
Darth Sidious (Classic)	QXY5XN
Darth Vader (Classic)	FM4JB7
Darth Vader Battle Damaged (Classic)	NMJFBL
Destroyer Droid	9MUTS2
Dr. Nuvo Vindi	MB9EMW
Echo	JB9E5S
Eeth Koth	WUFDYA
Gammorean Guard	WSFZZQ
General Grievous	7FNU4T
Geonosian Guard	GAFZUD
Gold Super Battle Droid	2C8NHP
Gonk Droid	C686PK
Grand Moff Tarkin	NH2405
Greedo (Classic)	FUW4C2
Hailfire Droid	T7XF9Z
Han Solo (Classic)	KFDBXF
Heavy Super Battle Droid	G65KJJ
Heavy Weapons Clone Trooper	WXUTWY
Helios 3D	4AXTY4

CHARACTER	CODE
Hevy	EUB8UG
Hondo Ohnaka	5A7XYX
IG-86	EABPCP
Imperial Guard (Classic)	5W6FGD
Jango Fett	5KZQ4D
Jar Jar Binks	MESPTS
Jek	AYREC9
Ki-Adi-Mundi	HGBCTQ
Kit Fitso	PYWJ6N
Lando Calrissian (Classic)	ERAEWE
LEP Servent Droid	SM3Y9B
Lieutenant Thire	3NEUXC
Lok Durd	TKCYUZ
Luke Skywalker (Classic)	PG73HF
Luminara Unduli	MKUYQ8
Lurmen Villager	R35Y7N
Luxury Droid	V4WMJN
Mace Windu	8NVRWJ
MagnaGuard	2KEF2D
MSE-6	S6GRNZ
Nahdar Vebb	ZKXG43
Neimoidian	BJB94J
Nute Gunray	QFYXMC
Obi-Wan Kenobi	J9HNF9
Obi-Wan Kenobi (Classic)	FFBU5M
Obi-Wan Kenobi (Geonosian Arena)	5U9FJK
OG-9 Homing Spider Droid	7NEC36
Onaconda Farr	DB7ZQN
Padmé Amidala (Geonosian Arena)	SZ824Q
Padmé Amidala	8X87U6
Pirate Ruffian	BH2EHU
Plo Koon	BUD4VU

CHARACTER	CODE
Poggle The Lesser	4592WM
Princess Leia (Classic)	2D3D3L
Probe Droid	U2T4SP
Queen Neeyutnee	ZQRN85
Qui-Gon Jinn (Classic)	LKHD3B
R2-D2	RZ5HUV
R3-S6	Z87PAU
R4-P17	5MXSYA
R6-H5	7PMC3C
Rebel Commando (Classic)	PZMQNK
Robonino	2KLW5R
Rys	4PTP53
Savage Oppress	MELLO7
Senate Commando	EPBPLK
Senate Commando (Captain)	S4Y7VW
Senator Kharrus	EA4E9S
Senator Philo	9Q7YCT
Shahan Alama	G4N7C2
Sionver Boll	5C62YQ
Stormtrooper (Classic)	HPE7PZ
Super Battle Droid	MJKDV5
Tee Watt Kaa	FYVSHD
Turk Falso	HEBHW5
Tusken Raider (Classic)	GC2XSA
TX-20	PE7FGD
Undead Geonosian	QGENFD
Vader's Apprentice (Classic)	EGQQ4V
Waq Too	VRUVSZ
Wat Tambor	ZP8XVH
Waxer	BNJE79
Wedge Antilles (Classic)	DRGLWS
Whorm Loathsom	4VVYQV
Workout Clone Trooper	MP9DRE
Yoda	CSQTMB

VEHICLES

VEHICLE	CODE
Dwarf Spider Droid	NACMGG
Geonosian Solar Sailor	PJ2U3R
Geonosian Starfighter	EDENEC

VEHICLE	CODE
Slave I	KDDQVD
The Twilight	T4K5L4
Vulture Droid	7W7K7S

RED BRICKS

CHEAT	CODE
Character Studs	QD2C31
Dark Side	X1V4N2
Dual Wield	C4ES4R
Fast Build	GCHP7S
Glow in the Dark	4GT3VQ
Invincibility	J46P7A
Minikit Detector	CSD5NA
Perfect Deflect	3F5L56
Regenerate Hearts	2D7JNS

CHEAT	CODE
Score x2	YZPHUV
Score x4	43T5E5
Score x6	SEBHGR
Score x8	BYFSAQ
Score x10	N1CKR1
Stud Magnet	6MZ5CH
Super Saber Cut	BS828K
Super Speeders	B1D3W3

LOST IN SHADOW

GOBLIN HAND
As your game loads, hold Z.

KNIFE
As your game loads, hold C.

MADDEN NFL 10

UNLOCK EVERYTHING
Select Enter Game Code from Extras and enter THEWORKS.

FRANCHISE MODE
Select Enter Game Code from Extras and enter TEAMPLAYER.

SITUATION MODE
Select Enter Game Code from Extras and enter YOUCALLIT.

SUPERSTAR MODE
Select Enter Game Code from Extras and enter EGOBOOST.

PRO BOWL STADIUM
Select Enter Game Code from Extras and enter ALLSTARS.

SUPER BOWL STADIUM
Select Enter Game Code from Extras and enter THEBIGSHOW.

MARIO & SONIC AT THE OLYMPIC GAMES

UNLOCK 4X100M RELAY EVENT
Medal in Mercury, Venus, Jupiter, and Saturn.

UNLOCK SINGLE SCULLS EVENT
Medal in Mercury, Venus, Jupiter, and Saturn.

UNLOCK DREAM RACE EVENT
Medal in Mercury, Venus, Jupiter, and Saturn.

UNLOCK ARCHERY EVENT
Medal in Moonlight Circuit.

UNLOCK HIGH JUMP EVENT
Medal in Stardust Circuit.

UNLOCK 400M EVENT
Medal in Planet Circuit.

UNLOCK DREAM FENCING EVENT
Medal in Comet Circuit.

UNLOCK DREAM TABLE TENNIS EVENT
Medal in Satellite Circuit.

UNLOCK 400M HURDLES EVENT
Medal in Sunlight Circuit.

UNLOCK POLE VAULT EVENT
Medal in Meteorite Circuit.

UNLOCK VAULT EVENT
Medal in Meteorite Circuit.

UNLOCK DREAM PLATFORM EVENT
Medal in Cosmos Circuit.

CROWNS
Get all gold medals in all events with a character to unlock their crown.

MARIO KART WII

CHARACTERS

CHARACTER	HOW TO UNLOCK
Baby Daisy	Earn 1 Star in 50cc for Mushroom, Flower, Star, and Special Cups
Baby Luigi	Unlock 8 Expert Staff Ghost Data in Time Trials
Birdo	Race 16 different courses in Time Trials or win 250 versus races
Bowser Jr.	Earn 1 Star in 100cc for Shell, Banana, Leaf, and Lightning Cups
Daisy	Win 150cc Special Cup
Diddy Kong	Win 50cc Lightning Cup
Dry Bones	Win 100cc Leaf Cup
Dry Bowser	Earn 1 Star in 150cc for Mushroom, Flower, Star, and Special Cups
Funky Kong	Unlock 4 Expert Staff Ghost Data in Time Trials
King Boo	Win 50cc Star Cup
Mii Outfit A	Win 100cc Special Cup
Mii Outfit B	Unlock all 32 Expert Staff Ghost Data in Time Trials
Mii Outfit C	Get 15,000 points in Versus Mode
Rosalina	Have a Super Mario Galaxy save file and she is unlocked after 50 races or earn 1 Star in all Mirror Cups
Toadette	Race 32 different courses in Time Trials

KARTS

KART	HOW TO UNLOCK
Blue Falcon	Win Mirror Lightning Cup
Cheep Charger	Earn 1 Star in 50cc for Mushroom, Flower, Star, and Special Cups
Rally Romper	Unlock an Expert Staff Ghost Data in Time Trials
B Dasher Mk. 2	Unlock 24 Expert Staff Ghost Data in Time Trials
Royal Racer	Win 150cc Leaf Cup
Turbo Blooper	Win 50cc Leaf Cup
Aero Glider	Earn 1 Star in 150cc for Mushroom, Flower, Star, and Special Cups
Dragonetti	Win 150cc Lightning Cup
Piranha Prowler	Win 50cc Special Cup

BIKES

KART	HOW TO UNLOCK
Bubble Bike	Win Mirror Leaf Cup
Magikruiser	Race 8 different courses in Time Trials
Quacker	Win 150cc Star Cup
Dolphin Dasher	Win Mirror Star Cup
Nitrocycle	Earn 1 Star in 100cc for all cups
Rapide	Win 100cc Lightning Cup
Phantom	Win Mirror Special Cup
Torpedo	Unlock 12 Expert Staff Ghost Data in Time Trials
Twinkle Star	Win 100cc Star Cup

MARVEL SUPER HERO SQUAD

IRON MAN, BONUS COSTUME "WAR MACHINE"

Select Enter Code from the Options and enter 111111.

HULK, BONUS COSTUMES "GREY HULK" & "RED HULK"

Select Enter Code from the Options and enter 222222.

WOLVERINE, BONUS COSTUMES "WOLVERINE (BROWN COSTUME)" & "FERAL WOLVERINE"

Select Enter Code from the Options and enter 333333.

THOR, BONUS COSTUMES "THOR (CHAIN ARMOR)" & "LOKI-THOR"

Select Enter Code from the Options and enter 444444.

SILVER SURFER, BONUS COSTUMES "ANTI-SURFER" & "GOLD SURFER"

Select Enter Code from the Options and enter 555555.

FALCON, BONUS COSTUME "ULTIMATES FALCON"

Select Enter Code from the Options and enter 666666.

CHEAT "SUPER KNOCKBACK"

Select Enter Code from the Options and enter 777777.

CHEAT "NO BLOCK MODE"

Select Enter Code from the Options and enter 888888.

DOCTOR DOOM, BONUS COSTUMES "ULTIMATES DOCTOR DOOM" & "PROFESSOR DOOM"

Select Enter Code from the Options and enter 999999.

CAPTAIN AMERICA, BONUS COSTUME "ULTIMATE CAPTAIN AMERICA COSTUME"

Select Enter Code from the Options and enter 177674

A.I.M. AGENT, BONUS COSTUME "BLUE SUIT A.I.M."

Select Enter Code from the Options and enter 246246

CHEAT "GROUNDED"

Select Enter Code from the Options and enter 476863

CHEAT "ONE-HIT TAKEDOWN"
Select Enter Code from the Options and enter 663448

CHEAT "INFINITE SHARD DURATION"
Select Enter Code from the Options and enter 742737

CHEAT "THROWN OBJECT TAKEDOWN"
Select Enter Code from the Options and enter 847936

MARVEL ULTIMATE ALLIANCE

UNLOCK ALL SKINS
At the Team menu, press Up, Down, Left, Right, Left, Right, Plus.

UNLOCKS ALL HERO POWERS
At the Team menu, press Left, Right, Up, Down, Up, Down, Plus.

ALL HEROES TO LEVEL 99
At the Team menu, press Up, Left, Up, Left, Down, Right, Down, Right, Plus.

UNLOCK ALL HEROES
At the Team menu, press Up, Up, Down, Down, Left, Left, Left, Plus.

UNLOCK DAREDEVIL
At the Team menu, press Left, Left, Right, Right, Up, Down, Up, Down, Plus.

UNLOCK SILVER SURFER
At the Team menu, press Down, Left, Left, Up, Right, Up, Down, Left, Plus.

GOD MODE
During gameplay, press Up, Down, Up, Down, Up, Left, Down, Right, Plus.

TOUCH OF DEATH
During gameplay, press Left, Right, Down, Down, Right, Left, Plus.

SUPER SPEED
During gameplay, press Up, Left, Up, Right, Down, Right, Plus.

FILL MOMENTUM
During gameplay, press Left, Right, Right, Left, Up, Down, Down, Up, Plus.

UNLOCK ALL COMICS
At the Review menu, press Left, Right, Right, Left, Up, Up, Right, Plus.

UNLOCK ALL CONCEPT ART
At the Review menu, press Down, Down, Down, Right, Right, Left, Down, Plus.

UNLOCK ALL CINEMATICS
At the Review menu, press Up, Left, Left, Up, Right, Right, Up, Plus.

UNLOCK ALL LOAD SCREENS
At the Review menu, press Up, Down, Right, Left, Up, Up Down, Plus.

UNLOCK ALL COURSES
At the Comic Missions menu, press Up, Right, Left, Down, Up, Right, Left, Down, Plus.

MARVEL ULTIMATE ALLIANCE 2

GOD MODE
At any point during a game, press Up, Up, Down, Down, Left, Right, Down.

GIVE MONEY
At the Team Select or Hero Details screen press Up, Up, Down, Down, Up, Up, Up, Down.

UNLOCK ALL POWERS
At the Team Select or Hero Details screen press Up, Up, Down, Down, Left, Right, Right, Left.

ADVANCE ALL CHARACTERS TO L99
At the Hero Details screen press Down, Up, Left, Up, Right, Up, Left, Down.

UNLOCK ALL BONUS MISSIONS
While using the Bonus Mission Simulator, press Up, Right, Down, Left, Left, Right, Up, Up.

ADD 1 CHARACTER LEVEL
During a game, press Down, Up, Right, Up, Right, Up, Right, Down.

ADD 10 CHARACTER LEVELS
During a game, press Down, Up, Left, Up, Left, Up, Left, Down.

MEGA MAN 5

ALL WEAPONS AND ITEMS PASSWORD
Enter Blue B4 D6 F1 and Red C1 D4 F6 as a password.

METROID: OTHER M

HARD MODE
Finish the game with all items.

THEATER MODE
Defeat final boss.

CHAPTERS	HOW TO UNLOCK
1-26	Defeat final boss
27-30	After the credits, finish bonus area and boss

GALLERY MODE
Defeat final boss.

GALLERY PAGES	HOW TO UNLOCK
1-4	Defeat final boss
5-7	After the credits, finish bonus area and boss
8	Finish the game with all items

MLB POWER PROS

EXTRA FORMS
At the main menu, press Right, Left, Up, Down, Down, Right, Right, Up, Up, Left, Down, Left.

VIEW MLB PLAYERS AT CUSTOM PLAYER MENU
Select View or Delete Custom Players/Password Display from My Data and press Up, Up, Down, Down, Left, Right, Left, Right, 1, 2.

MONSTER LAIR

CONTINUE
At the game over screen, press Left, Right, Down, Up, Select + Left.

UNLIMITED CONTINUES
Enter 68K as your initials.

SOUND TEST
At the title screen, hold 1 + 2 and press Run.

MYSIMS AGENTS

ASTRONAUT SUIT
At the Create-a-Sim screen, press Up, Down, Up, Down, Left, Right, Left, Right.

BLACK NINJA OUTFIT
At the Create-a-Sim screen, press Right, Up, Right, Up, Down, Left, Down, Left.

STEALTH SUIT
At the Create-a-Sim screen, press Left, Right, Left, Right, Up, Down, Up, Down.

MYSIMS KINGDOM

DETECTIVE OUTFIT
Pause the game and press Left, Right, Left, Right, Left, Right.

SWORDSMAN OUTFIT
Pause the game and press Down, Up, Down, Up, Down, Up, Down, Up.

TATTOO VEST OUTFIT
Pause the game and press C, Z, C, Z, B, A, B, A.

NARUTO SHIPPUDEN: CLASH OF NINJA REVOLUTION III

RYO BONUS
A 50,00 starting Ryo bonus is given if you have a saved data from Naruto Shippuden: Clash of Ninja Revolution 1 or 2 on your Nintendo Wii.

78

NASCAR THE GAME 2011

MARK MARTIN PAINT SCHEMES

At the garage main menu, press Down, Down, Up, Up, Right, Left, Right, Left. Enter godaddy.com.

NASCAR KART RACING

JOEY LOGANO

Select Enter Cheat from the Profile Info menu and enter 426378.

NBA 2K10

ABA BALL

Select Codes from the Options menu. Then select Enter Code and enter payrespect.

2K CHINA TEAM

Select Codes from the Options menu. Then select Enter Code and enter 2kchina.

NBA 2K TEAM

Select Codes from the Options menu. Then select Enter Code and enter nba2k.

2K SPORTS TEAM

Select Codes from the Options menu. Then select Enter Code and enter 2ksports.

VISUAL CONCEPTS TEAM

Select Codes from the Options menu. Then select Enter Code and enter vcteam.

2010 ALL-STAR UNIFORMS

Select Codes from the Options menu. Then select Enter Code and enter otnresla.

HARDWOOD CLASSIC UNIFORMS

Select Codes from the Options menu. Then select Enter Code and enter wasshcicsl. This code gives Hardwood Classic Uniforms for the Cavaliers, Jazz, Magic, Raptors, timberwolves, Trail Blazers, and Warriors.

LATIN NIGHTS UNIFORMS

Select Codes from the Options menu. Then select Enter Code and enter aihinntslgt. This code gives Latin Nights jerseys for Bulls, Heat, Knicks, Lakers, Mavericks, Rockets, Spurs, and Suns.

NBA GREEN UNIFORMS

Select Codes from the Options menu. Then select Enter Code and enter nreogge. This code gives green uniforms for the Bobcats, Bulls, and Nuggets.

SECONDARY ROAD UNIFORMS
Select Codes from the Options menu. Then select Enter Code and enter eydonscar. This code gives Second Road Uniforms for the Grizzlies, Hawks, Mavericks, and Rockets.

ST. PATRICK'S DAY UNIFORMS
Select Codes from the Options menu. Then select Enter Code and enter riiasgerh. This code gives St. Patrick's Day jerseys for the Bulls, Celtics, Knicks, and Raptors.

BOBCATS RACING UNIFORM
Select Codes from the Options menu. Then select Enter Code and enter agsntrccai.

CAVALIERS CAVFANATICS UNIFORM
Select Codes from the Options menu. Then select Enter Code and enter aifnaatccv.

HORNETS MARDI GRAS UNIFORM
Select Codes from the Options menu. Then select Enter Code and enter asrdirmga.

TRAIL BLAZERS RIP CITY UNIFORM
Select Codes from the Options menu. Then select Enter Code and enter ycprtii.

NBA 2K11

MJ: CREATING A LEGEND
In Features, select Codes from the Extras menu. Choose Enter Code and enter icanbe23.

2K CHINA TEAM
In Features, select Codes from the Extras menu. Choose Enter Code and enter 2kchina.

2K SPORTS TEAM
In Features, select Codes from the Extras menu. Choose Enter Code and enter 2Ksports.

NBA 2K TEAM
In Features, select Codes from the Extras menu. Choose Enter Code and enter nba2k.

VC TEAM
In Features, select Codes from the Extras menu. Choose Enter Code and enter vcteam.

ABA BALL
In Features, select Codes from the Extras menu. Choose Enter Code and enter payrespect.

NBA 2K12

ABA BALL
Select Extras from the Features menu. Choose Codes and enter payrespect. This can be toggled on and off from this Codes menu.

2K CHINA TEAM
Select Extras from the Features menu. Choose Codes and enter 2kchina.

2K SPORTS TEAM
Select Extras from the Features menu. Choose Codes and enter 2ksports.

UNLOCK NBA 2K TEAM
Select Extras from the Features menu. Choose Codes and enter nba2k.

VC TEAM
Select Extras from the Features menu. Choose Codes and enter vcteam.

NEED FOR SPEED PROSTREET

$2,000
Select Career and then choose Code Entry. Enter 1MA9X99.

$4,000
Select Career and then choose Code Entry. Enter W2IOLL01.

$8,000
Select Career and then choose Code Entry. Enter L1IS97A1.

$10,000
Select Career and then choose Code Entry. Enter 1MI9K7E1.

$10,000
Select Career and then choose Code Entry. Enter CASHMONEY.

$10,000
Select Career and then choose Code Entry. Enter REGGAME.

AUDI TT
Select Career and then choose Code Entry. Enter ITSABOUTYOU.

CHEVELLE SS
Select Career and then choose Code Entry. Enter HORSEPOWER.

COKE ZERO GOLF GTI
Select Career and then choose Code Entry. Enter COKEZERO.

DODGE VIPER
Select Career and then choose Code Entry. Enter WORLDSLONGESTLASTING.

MITSUBISHI LANCER EVOLUTION
Select Career and then choose Code Entry. Enter MITSUBISHIGOFAR.

UNLOCK ALL BONUSES
Select Career and then choose Code Entry. Enter UNLOCKALLTHINGS.

5 REPAIR MARKERS
Select Career and then choose Code Entry. Enter SAFETYNET.

ENERGIZER VINYL
Select Career and then choose Code Entry. Enter ENERGIZERLITHIUM.

CASTROL SYNTEC VINYL
Select Career and then choose Code Entry. Enter CASTROLSYNTEC. This also gives you $10,000.

NERF N-STRIKE

BLACK HEART VENGEANCE
Select Codes from the main menu and enter BHDETA8.

CRUSHER SAD-G
Select Codes from the main menu and enter CRUSH14.

FIREFLY ELITE
Select Codes from the main menu and enter HELIOX6.

GOLIATHAN NITRO
Select Codes from the main menu and enter FIERO2.

HABANERO
Select Codes from the main menu and enter 24KGCON4.

HYDRA
Select Codes from the main menu and enter HRANGEL3.

LONGSHOT STREET
Select Codes from the main menu and enter LONGST5.

MAVERICK CRYSTAL
Select Codes from the main menu and enter CRISTOL10.

MAVERICK MIDNIGHT
Select Codes from the main menu and enter MAVMID7.

MERCURIO
Select Codes from the main menu and enter RSMERC9.

SEMPER FIRE ULTRA
Select Codes from the main menu and enter CROMO1.

SPARTAN NCS-12
Select Codes from the main menu and enter THISIS12.

STAMPEDE
Select Codes from the main menu and enter DOGIE15.

VULCAN MAGMA
Select Codes from the main menu and enter MAGMA3.

NERF: N-STRIKE ELITE

Select Codebook and enter the following codes.

10 CANISTERS
Enter NERF.

UNLIMITED AMMO
Enter DART. This can be toggled on and off.

CERBERUS CS-12
Enter DUDE.

CRUSHER SAD-G
Enter RUSH.

GOLITHAN UB-1
Enter ROCK.

HAMMERHEAD GL-1
Enter PONG.

HYDRA SG-7
Enter WIDE.

ICARUS HM-7
Enter DOOM.

LONGSHOT CS-6
Enter IDOL.

LONGSTRIKE CS-6
Enter PING.

RECON CS-6
Enter DIRT.

SEMPERFIRE RF-100
Enter FLEX.

SPARTAN NCS-12
Enter ICON.

VULCAN EBF-25
Enter LOTS.

NHL 2K9

3RD JERSEYS
At the codes menu enter R6y34bsH52.

NHL 2K10

THIRD JERSEYS
Select Cheats from the Extras menu and enter G8r23Bty56.

VISUAL CONCEPTS TEAM
Select Cheats from the Extras menu and enter vcteam.

NICKTOONS: ATTACK OF THE TOYBOTS

DAMAGE BOOST
Select Cheats from the Extras menu. Choose Enter Cheat Code and enter 456645.

INVULNERABILITY
Select Cheats from the Extras menu. Choose Enter Cheat Code and enter 313456.

UNLOCK EXO-HUGGLES 9000
Select Cheats from the Extras menu. Choose Enter Cheat Code and enter 691427.

UNLOCK MR. HUGGLES
Select Cheats from the Extras menu. Choose Enter Cheat Code and enter 654168.

UNLIMITED LOBBER GOO
Select Cheats from the Extras menu. Choose Enter Cheat Code and enter 118147.

UNLIMITED SCATTER GOO
Select Cheats from the Extras menu. Choose Enter Cheat Code and enter 971238.

UNLIMITED SPLITTER GOO
Select Cheats from the Extras menu. Choose Enter Cheat Code and enter 854511.

PHINEAS AND FERB: ACROSS THE 2ND DIMENSION

SKIN FOR AGENT P: PERRY THE PLATYBORG
During a game, press the Minus button to bring up the pause menu. Select Enter Code from Extras and enter BAB121.

PINBALL HALL OF FAME – THE GOTTLIEB COLLECTION

UNLOCK TABLES IN FREEPLAY, EXTRA OPTIONS, AND PAYOUT MODE

Select Enter Code from the Main Menu and enter the following:

EFFECTS	CODE
Aces High Freeplay	UNO
Big Shot Freeplay	UJP
Black Hole Freeplay	LIS
Central Park Freeplay	NYC
Goin' Nuts Freeplay	PHF
Love Machine Freeplay	HOT
Playboy Freeplay	HEF

EFFECTS	CODE
Strikes 'N Spares Freeplay	PBA
Tee'd Off Freeplay	PGA
Xolten Freeplay	BIG
Custom Balls in Options	CKF
Optional Tilt in Options	BZZ
Payout Mode	WGR

PIRATES PLUNDARRR

CHEAT MENU

Press + to pause the game. Enter Up, Up, Down, Down, Left, Right, Left, Right, 2, 1. A new Cheat option appears at the bottom of the menu.

AMAZON

Defeat Tecciztecatl, Witch Doctor.

SPECTRAL

Defeat Nanauatl, Hero of the Sun.

POKEMON RUMBLE

POKEMON PASSWORDS

Go to the recruitment building in the terminal and enter the following passwords to get the corresponding Pokemon.

POKEMON	PASSWORD
Blastoise	9580-1423
Charizard	7968-4528
Charmander	7927-6161
Cherrim Positive Forme	7540-5667
Chimchar	8109-8384
Eevee	0511-0403
Giratina (Origin Form)	8322-3706
Mew	9561-8808

POKEMON	PASSWORD
Piplup	9900-2455
Shaymin (Sky Form)	5468-6284
Shiny Bidoof	5575-2435
Shiny Rattata	9849-3731
Squirtle	6824-2045
Turtwig	8672-1076
Venusaur	1589-3955

POKEPARK WII: PIKACHU'S ADVENTURE

CELEBI APPEARS

Enter 58068773 as a password.

DARKRAI APPEARS

Enter 65967413 as a password.

GROUDON APPEARS

Enter 49446209 as a password.

JIRACHI APPEARS

Enter 73938790 as a password.

PIKACHU'S BALLOONS

Enter 99930457 as a password.

PIKACHU'S SNOWBOARD

Enter 67446162 as a password.

PIKACHU'S SURFBOARD

Enter 02970626 as a password.

PRESS YOUR LUCK 2010 EDITION

WARDROBE PIECES FOR AVATAR

Select the lock tab from the Wardrobe screen and enter SECRET.

THE PRICE IS RIGHT 2010 EDITION

AVATAR UPGRADES

Select the lock tab from the Wardrobe screen and enter PRIZES.

PRINCESS TOMATO IN THE SALAD KINGDOM

DEBUG BATTLE PASSWORD

Enter GG62 as a password.

PUNCH-OUT!!

REGAIN HEALTH BETWEEN ROUNDS

Press minus between rounds to regain health at the start of the next round.

DONKEY KONG IN EXHIBITION

Fight Donkey Kong in Last Stand mode.

CHAMPIONS MODE

Win 10 bouts in Mac's Last Stand.

RABBIDS GO HOME

ASSASSIN RABBID

Finish Nick of Time to unlock the Rabbid customization option. Enter this option and select a Rabbid. Go to the menu and select Manage Figurines from the Figurines screen. Hold C + Z and press 2, 2, 1, 1, A, A, 1, 1.

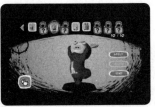

BEST BUY RABBID

Finish Nick of Time to unlock the Rabbid customization option. Enter this option and select a Rabbid. Go to the menu and select Manage Figurines from the Figurines screen. Hold C + Z and press B, 1, 1, B, A, 2, 2, A.

GEEK SQUAD RABBID

Finish Nick of Time to unlock the Rabbid customization option. Enter this option and select a Rabbid. Go to the menu and select Manage Figurines from the Figurines screen. Hold C + Z and press A, A, 1, 1, 1, 1, 2, 2.

KANGAROO RABBID

Finish Nick of Time to unlock the Rabbid customization option. Enter this option and select a Rabbid. Go to the menu and select Manage Figurines from the Figurines screen. Hold C + Z and press 1, 1, 1, 1, 1, 2, 1, 2.

LEONARDO RABBID

Finish Nick of Time to unlock the Rabbid customization option. Enter this option and select a Rabbid. Go to the menu and select Manage Figurines from the Figurines screen. Hold C + Z and press 1, 1, 2, 2, A, A, 1, 1.

PRINCE RABBID

Finish Nick of Time to unlock the Rabbid customization option. Enter this option and select a Rabbid. Go to the menu and select Manage Figurines from the Figurines screen. Hold C + Z and press 1, 2, 1, 2, 1, 2, A, A.

SPLINTER CELL RABBID

Finish Nick of Time to unlock the Rabbid customization option. Enter this option and select a Rabbid. Go to the menu and select Manage Figurines from the Figurines screen. Hold C + Z and press B, B, B, B, A, A, A, A.

RAYMAN RAVING RABBIDS 2

FUNKYTOWN
Play each game at least once.

RABBID COSTUMES
Costumes are unlocked as you score 12,000 points in certain games and when you shoot the correct rabbid in the shooting games.

COSTUME	MINIGAME	HOW TO UNLOCK
Cossack	Chess	Earn 12,000 points
Crash Test Dummy	Shopping Cart Downhill	Earn 12,000 points
Cupid	Burgerinnii	Earn 12,000 points
Doctor	Anesthetics	Earn 12,000 points
Fireman	Paris, Pour Troujours	Shoot fireman rabbid
French Maid	Little Chemist	Earn 12,000 points
Fruit-Hat Dancer	Year of the Rabbids	Shoot rabbid wearing fruit hat
Gingerbread	Hot Cake	Earn 12,000 points
HAZE Armor	Big City Fights	Shoot rabbid with armor
Indiana Jones	Rolling Stone	Earn 12,000 points
Jet Trooper	Greatest Hits	Earn 12,000 points
Ken	RRR Xtreme Beach Volleyball	Earn 12,000 points
Martian	Bumper Cars	Earn 12,000 points
Party Girl	Paris, Mon Amour	Once inside boat, shoot girl rabbid
Raider's	American Football	Earn 12,000 points
Sam Fisher	Rabbid School	Earn 12,000 points
Samurai	The Office	Earn 12,000 points
Space	Year of the Rabbids	Earn 12,000 points
Spider-	Spider Rabbid	Play the "Spider Rabbid" Game
TMNT, Leonardo	Usual Rabbids	Earn 12,000 points
Transformer	Plumber Rabbids	Earn 12,000 points
Vegas Showgirl	Burp	Earn 12,000 points
Voodoo	Voodoo Rabbids	Earn 12,000 points
Wrestler	Greatest Hits	Shoot rabbid in green outfit

RUBIK'S PUZZLE WORLD

ALL LEVELS AND CUBIES
At the main menu, press A, B, B, A, A.

RUGBY LEAGUE 3

$100,000,000 SALARY CAP
Go to Create a Player and enter SOMBRERO as the name.

PRESS Z FOR MAX SPEED
Go to Create a Player and enter RSI as the name.

UNLIMITED FUNDING
Go to Create a Player and enter Sugar Daddy as the name.

STRONG WIND
Go to Create a Player and enter Beans & Eggs as the name.

HUGE MUSCLES
Go to Create a Player and enter i'll be back as the name.

ONE TACKLE THEN HANDOVER
Go to Create a Player and enter Force Back as the name.

SCOOBY-DOO! AND THE SPOOKY SWAMP

BIG HEAD

Enter the clubhouse and select Codes from the Extras menu. Enter 2654.

CHIPMUNK TALK

Enter the clubhouse and select Codes from the Extras menu. Enter 3293.

DOUBLE DAMAGE

Enter the clubhouse and select Codes from the Extras menu. Enter 9991.

SLOW MOTION

Enter the clubhouse and select Codes from the Extras menu. Enter 1954.

SCOOBY-DOO! FIRST FRIGHTS

DAPHNE'S SECRET COSTUME

Select Codes from the Extras menu and enter 2839.

FRED'S SECRET COSTUME

Select Codes from the Extras menu and enter 4826.

SCOOBY DOO'S SECRET COSTUME

Select Codes from the Extras menu and enter 1585.

SHAGGY'S SECRET COSTUME

Select Codes from the Extras menu and enter 3726.

VELMA'S SECRET COSTUME

Select Codes from the Extras menu and enter 6588.

THE SECRET SATURDAYS: BEASTS OF THE 5TH SUN

ALL LEVELS

Select Enter Secret Code from the Secrets menu and enter Zon, Zon, Zon, Zon.

UNLOCK AMAROK TO BE SCANNED IN LEVEL 2

Select Enter Secret Code from the Secrets menu and enter Fiskerton, Zak, Zon, Komodo.

UNLOCK BISHOPVILLE LIZARDMAN TO BE SCANNED IN LEVEL 3

Select Enter Secret Code from the Secrets menu and enter Komodo, Zon, Zak, Komodo.

UNLOCK NAGA TO BE SCANNED IN LEVEL 7

Select Enter Secret Code from the Secrets menu and enter Zak, Zak, Zon, Fiskerton.

UNLOCK RAKSHASA TO BE SCANNED IN LEVEL 8

Select Enter Secret Code from the Secrets menu and enter Zak, Komodo, Fiskerton, Fiskerton.

UNLOCK BILOKO TO BE SCANNED IN LEVEL 9

Select Enter Secret Code from the Secrets menu and enter Zon, Zak, Zon, Fiskerton.

SHOCKMAN

REFILL ENERGY

Pause the game and press Left + Select + 2

SOUND TEST

After completing the game at the To Be Continued screen, hold Select and press Up or Down.

SIMANIMALS

FERRET

Begin a game in an unlocked forest area, press 2 to pause, and select Enter Codes. Enter Ferret.

PANDA

Begin a game in an unlocked forest area, press 2 to pause, and select Enter Codes. Enter PANDA.

RED PANDA

Begin a game in an unlocked forest area, press 2 to pause, and select Enter Codes. Enter Red Panda.

SIMCITY CREATOR

EGYPTIAN BUILDING SET

Name your city Mummy's desert.

GREEK BUILDING SET

Name your city Ancient culture.

JUNGLE BUILDING SET

Name your city Become wild.

SCI-FI BUILDING SET

Name your city Future picture.

THE SIMPSONS GAME

UNLIMITED POWER FOR ALL CHARACTERS

At the Extras menu, press Plus, Left, Right, Plus, Minus, Z.

ALL MOVIES

At the Extras menu, press Minus, Left, Minus, Right, Plus, C.

ALL CLICHÉS

At the Extras menu, press Left, Minus, Right, Plus, Right, Z.

SIN AND PUNISHMENT: STAR SUCCESSOR

ISA & KACHI MODE

Defeat the game as Isa and as Kachi. Use the − button to switch between the two.

SONIC COLORS

EXTRA LIVES

After completing a level, the results screen shows how well you did. Jump through the numbers until they break apart revealing gold rings and extra lives.

SPACE HARRIER

CONTINUE AFTER GAME OVER

At the Game Over screen, press Up, Up, Down, Down, Left, Right, Left, Right, Down, Up, Down, Up.

SPECTROBES: ORIGINS

METALIC LEO AND RYZA

At the title screen, before creating a game save, press Up, Down, Left, Right, A.

SPEED RACER

INVULNERABILITY

Select Enter Code from the Options menu and enter A, B, A, Up, Left, Down, Right.

UNLIMITED BOOST

Select Enter Code from the Options menu and enter B, A, Down, Up, B, A, Down.

LAST 3 CARS

Select Enter Code from the Options menu and enter 1, 2, 1, 2, B, A, Plus.

GRANITE CAR

Select Enter Code from the Options menu and enter B, Up, Minus, Plus, 1, Up, Plus.

MONSTER TRUCK

Select Enter Code from the Options menu and enter B, Up, Minus, 2, B, Up, Minus.

AGGRESSIVE OPPONENTS

Select Enter Code from the Options menu and enter Up, Left, Down, Right, Up, Left, Down.

PACIFIST OPPONENTS

Select Enter Code from the Options menu and enter Up, Right, Down, Left, Up, Right, Down.

TINY OPPONENTS

Select Enter Code from the Options menu and enter B, A, Left, Down, Minus, Up, Minus.

HELIUM

Select Enter Code from the Options menu and enter Minus, Up, Minus, 2, Minus, Up, Minus.

MOON GRAVITY

Select Enter Code from the Options menu and enter Up, Plus, Up, Right, Minus, Up, Minus.

OVERKILL

Select Enter Code from the Options menu and enter A, Minus, Plus, Down, Up, Plus, 1.

PSYCHEDELIC

Select Enter Code from the Options menu and enter Left, A, Right, Down, B, Up, Minus.

SPIDER-MAN: EDGE OF TIME

SHATTERED DIMENSIONS BONUS SUITS

If you have a saved game data for Spider-Man: Shattered Dimensions on your system, new Alternate Suits become available in the Bonus Gallery.

BIG TIME SUIT (2099)

At the main menu, press Right, Down, Down, Up, Left, Down, Down, Right.

FUTURE FOUNDATION SUIT (AMAZING)

At the main menu, press Up, Down, Left, Up, Down, Left, Right, Left.

SPIDER-MAN: SHATTERED DIMENSIONS

The following can be entered after completing the tutorial.

IRON SPIDER SUIT
At the main menu, press Up, Right, Right, Right, Left, Left, Left, Down, Up.

NEGATIVE ZONE SUIT
At the main menu, press Left, Right, Right, Down, Right, Down, Up, Left.

SCARLET SPIDER SUIT
At the main menu, press Right, Up, Left, Right, Up, Left, Right, Up, Left, Right.

SPONGEBOB SQUAREPANTS FEATURING NICKTOONS: GLOBS OF DOOM

When entering the following codes, the order of the characters going down is: SpongeBob SquarePants, Nicolai Technus, Danny Phantom, Dib, Zim, Tlaloc, Tak, Beautiful Gorgeous, Jimmy Neutron, Plankton. These names are shortened to the first name in the following.

ATTRACT COINS
Using the Upgrade Machine on the bottom level of the lair, select "Input cheat codes here". Enter Tlaloc, Plankton, Danny, Plankton, Tak. Coins are attracted to you making them much easier to collect.

DON'T LOSE COINS
Using the Upgrade Machine on the bottom level of the lair, select "Input cheat codes here". Enter Plankton, Jimmy, Beautiful, Jimmy, Plankton. You don't lose coins when you get knocked out.

GOO HAS NO EFFECT
Using the Upgrade Machine on the bottom level of the lair, select "Input cheat codes here". Enter Danny, Danny, Danny, Nicolai, Nicolai. Goo does not slow you down.

MORE GADGET COMBO TIME
Using the Upgrade Machine on the bottom level of the lair, select "Input cheat codes here". Enter SpongeBob, Beautiful, Danny, Plankton, Nicolai. You have more time to perform gadget combos.

PATRICK TUX IN STARFISHMAN TO THE RESCUE
Select Cheat Codes from the Extras menu and enter PATRICK. Select Activate Bonus Items to enable this bonus item.

SPONGEBOB PLANKTON IN SUPER-SIZED PATTY
Select Cheat Codes from the Extras menu and enter PANTS. Select Activate Bonus Items to enable this bonus item.

PATRICK LASER COLOR IN ROCKET RODEO
Select Cheat Codes from the Extras menu and enter ROCKET. Select Activate Bonus Items to enable this bonus item.

PATRICK ROCKET SKIN COLOR IN ROCKET RODEO
Select Cheat Codes from the Extras menu and enter SPACE. Select Activate Bonus Items to enable this bonus item.

PLANKTON ASTRONAUT SUIT IN REVENGE OF THE GIANT PLANKTON MONSTER
Select Cheat Codes from the Extras menu and enter ROBOT. Select Activate Bonus Items to enable this bonus item.

PLANKTON EYE LASER COLOR IN REVENGE OF THE GIANT PLANKTON MONSTER

Select Cheat Codes from the Extras menu and enter LASER. Select Activate Bonus Items to enable this bonus item.

PIRATE PATRICK IN ROOFTOP RUMBLE

Select Cheat Codes from the Extras menu and enter PIRATE. Select Activate Bonus Items to enable this bonus item.

HOVERCRAFT VEHICLE SKIN IN HYPNOTIC HIGHWAY—PLANKTON

Select Cheat Codes from the Extras menu and enter HOVER. Select Activate Bonus Items to enable this bonus item.

STAR WARS: THE FORCE UNLEASHED

CHEATS

Once you have accessed the Rogue Shadow, select Enter Code from the Extras menu. Now you can enter the following codes:

CHEAT	CODE
Invincibility	CORTOSIS
Unlimited Force	VERGENCE
1,000,000 Force Points	SPEEDER
All Force Powers	TYRANUS

CHEAT	CODE
Max Force Power Level	KATARN
Max Combo Level	COUNTDOOKU
Stronger Lightsaber	LIGHTSABER

COSTUMES

Once you have accessed the Rogue Shadow, select Enter Code from the Extras menu. Now you can enter the following codes:

COSTUME	CODE
All Costumes	GRANDMOFF
501st Legion	LEGION
Aayla Secura	AAYLA
Admiral Ackbar	ITSATWAP
Anakin Skywalker	CHOSENONE
Asajj Ventress	ACOLYTE
Ceremonial Jedi Robes	DANTOOINE
Chop'aa Notimo	NOTIMO
Classic stormtrooper	TK421
Count Dooku	SERENNO
Darth Desolous	PAUAN
Darth Maul	ZABRAK
Darth Phobos	HIDDENFEAR
Darth Vader	SITHLORD
Drexl Roosh	DREXLROOSH
Emperor Palpatine	PALPATINE
General Rahm Kota	MANDALORE
Han Solo	NERFHERDER
Heavy trooper	SHOCKTROOP

COSTUME	CODE
Juno Eclipse	ECLIPSE
Kento's Robe	WOOKIEE
Kleef	KLEEF
Lando Calrissian	SCOUNDREL
Luke Skywalker	T16WOMPRAT
Luke Skywalker (Yavin)	YELLOWJCKT
Mace Windu	JEDIMASTER
Mara Jade	MARAJADE
Maris Brook	MARISBROOD
Navy commando	STORMTROOP
Obi Wan Kenobi	BENKENOBI
Proxy	HOLOGRAM
Qui Gon Jinn	MAVERICK
Shaak Ti	TOGRUTA
Shadow trooper	INTHEDARK
Sith Robes	HOLOCRON
Sith Stalker Armor	KORRIBAN
Twi'lek	SECURA

STREET FIGHTER ALPHA 2

AUSTRALIA STAGE

In versus mode, highlight Sagat, hold Start, and press any button.

CHUN-LI'S HIDDEN COSTUME

At the character select, highlight Chun-li, hold Start and press any button.

SUPER MARIO GALAXY

PLAY AS LUIGI
Collect all 120 stars and fight Bowser. After the credits you will get a message that Luigi is playable.

GRAND FINALE GALAXY
Collect all 120 stars with Luigi and beat Bowser.

STAR 121
Collect 100 purple coins.

SUPER MARIO GALAXY 2

ALL LUIGI GHOSTS
Collect 9999 coins.

BANKER TOAD
Depositing star bits with Banker Toad changes his outfit as follows.

ITEM	# OF STAR BITS DEPOSITED
Glasses	1000
Spear/shield	2000
Pickaxe	4000
Scuba suit	6000
Explorer outfit	8000

GREEN STARS
Collect 120 stars to unlock 120 green stars.

WORLD S
After the game ending, you unlock World S.

GRANDMASTER GALAXY
Collect 120 stars and 120 green stars.

GRANDMASTER GALAXY COMET – THE PERFECT RUN
Deposit 9999 star bits with Banker Toad.

TEENAGE MUTANT NINJA TURTLES: SMASH-UP

NINJA RABBID AND UNDERGROUND STAGE
At the Bonus Content menu, press Up, Up, Down, Down, Down, Right, Up, Left, Right, Left.

SHREDDER AND CYBER SHREDDER OUTFIT
At the Bonus Content menu, press Up, Down, Right, Up, Down, Right, Left, Up, Right, Down.

THRILLVILLE: OFF THE RAILS

$50,000
During a game, press C, Z, B, C, Z, B, A.

500 THRILL POINTS
During a game, press Z, C, B, Z, C, B, C.

ALL MISSIONS
During a game, press C, Z, B, C, Z, B, Z.

ALL PARKS
During a game, press C, Z, B, C, Z, B, C.

ALL RIDES
During a game, press C, Z, B, C, Z, B, B.

ALL MINIGAMES
During a game, press C, Z, B, C, Z, B, Right.

TIGER WOODS PGA TOUR 09 ALL-PLAY

SPECTATORS BIG HEAD MODE
Select EA SPORTS Extras from My Tiger '09, choose Password and enter cephalus.

TIGER WOODS PGA TOUR 10

TW ITEMS IN PRO SHOP
Select Password from the Options and enter eltigre.

TONY HAWK RIDE

RYAN SHECKLER
Select Cheats from the Options menu and enter SHECKLERSIG.

QUICKSILVER 80'S LEVEL
Select Cheats from the Options menu and enter FEELINGEIGHTIES.

WALL-E

The following cheats will disable saving. The five possible characters starting with Wall-E and going down are: Wall-E, Auto, EVE, M-O, GEL-A Steward.

ALL BONUS FEATURES UNLOCKED
Select Cheats from the Bonus Features menu and enter Wall-E, Auto, EVE, GEL-A Steward.

ALL GAME CONTENT UNLOCKED
Select Cheats from the Bonus Features menu and enter M-O, Auto, GEL-A Steward, EVE.

ALL SINGLE-PLAYER LEVELS UNLOCKED
Select Cheats from the Bonus Features menu and enter Auto, GEL-A Steward, M-O, Wall-E.

ALL MULTIPLAYER MAPS UNLOCKED
Select Cheats from the Bonus Features menu and enter EVE, M-O, Wall-E, Auto.

ALL HOLIDAY COSTUMES UNLOCKED
Select Cheats from the Bonus Features menu and enter Auto, Auto, GEL-A Steward, GEL-A Steward.

ALL MULTIPLAYER COSTUMES UNLOCKED
Select Cheats from the Bonus Features menu and enter GEL-A Steward, Wall-E, M-O, Auto.

UNLIMITED HEALTH UNLOCKED
Select Cheats from the Bonus Features menu and enter Wall-E, M-O, Auto, M-O.

WALL-E: MAKE ANY CUBE AT ANY TIME
Select Cheats from the Bonus Features menu and enter Auto, M-O, Auto, M-O.

WALL-EVE: MAKE ANY CUBE AT ANY TIME
Select Cheats from the Bonus Features menu and enter M-O, GEL-A Steward, EVE, EVE.

WALL-E WITH A LASER GUN AT ANY TIME
Select Cheats from the Bonus Features menu and enter Wall-E, EVE, EVE, Wall-E.

WALL-EVE WITH A LASER GUN AT ANY TIME
Select Cheats from the Bonus Features menu and enter GEL-A Steward, EVE, M-O, Wall-E.

WALL-E: PERMANENT SUPER LASER UPGRADE
Select Cheats from the Bonus Features menu and enter Wall-E, Auto, EVE, M-O.

EVE: PERMANENT SUPER LASER UPGRADE
Select Cheats from the Bonus Features menu and enter EVE, Wall-E, Wall-E, Auto.

CREDITS
Select Cheats from the Bonus Features menu and enter Auto, Wall-E, GEL-A Steward, M-O.

WII PARTY

SPOT THE SNEAK IN MINIGAMES
Play all of the 4-player minigames.

WII SPORTS

BOWLING BALL COLOR
After selecting your Mii, hold the following direction on the D-pad and press A at the warning screen:

DIRECTION	COLOR
Up	Blue
Right	Gold
Down	Green
Left	Red

NO HUD IN GOLF
Hold 2 as you select a course to disable the power meter, map, and wind speed meter.

BLUE TENNIS COURT
After selecting your Mii, hold 2 and press A at the warning screen.

WII SPORTS RESORT

MODIFY EVENTS
At the Select a Mii screen, hold 2 while pressing A while on "OK." This will make the following modifications to each event.

EVENT	MODIFICATION
Air Sports Island Flyover	No balloons or I points
Air Sports Skydiving	Play intro event
Archery	More difficult; no aiming reticule
Basketball Pickup Game	Nighttime
Frisbee Golf	No wind display or distance
Golf	No wind display or distance
Swordplay Duel	Evening
Table Tennis Match	11-point match

WIPEOUT: THE GAME

JOHN ANDERSON AND MOST LIKELY TO SUCCEED (SECOND OUTFIT)
Play a single player game.

MAD COWGIRL, VALLEY GIRL (SECOND OUTFIT) AND GRASSHOPPER
Play a multiplayer game.

CHEF MUTTEN
Defeat Wipeout Zone within 1:00.

WWE SMACKDOWN VS. RAW 2010

THE ROCK
Select Cheat Codes from the Options and enter The Great One.

VINCE'S OFFICE AND DIRT SHEET FOR BACKSTAGE BRAWL
Select Cheat Codes from the Options menu and enter BonusBrawl.

HBK/SHAWN MICHAEL'S ALTERNATE COSTUME
Select Cheat Codes from the Options menu and enter Bow Down.

JOHN CENA'S ALTERNATE COSTUME
Select Cheat Codes from the Options menu and enter CENATION.

RANDY ORTON'S ALTERNATE COSTUME
Select Cheat Codes from the Options menu and enter ViperRKO.

SANTINO MARELLA'S ALTERNATE COSTUME
Select Cheat Codes from the Options menu and enter Milan Miracle.

TRIPLE H'S ALTERNATE COSTUME
Select Cheat Codes from the Options menu and enter Suck IT!.

WWE SMACKDOWN VS. RAW 2011

JOHN CENA (ENTRANCE/CIVILIAN)
In My WWE, select Cheat Codes from the Options and enter SLURPEE.

ALL OF RANDY ORTON'S COSTUMES
In My WWE, select Cheat Codes from the Options and enter apexpredator.

TRIBUTE TO THE TROOPS ARENA
In My WWE, select Cheat Codes from the Options and enter 8thannualtribute.

CRUISERWEIGHT TITLE, HARDCORE TITLE, AND MILLION DOLLAR TITLE
In My WWE, select Cheat Codes from the Options and enter Historicalbelts.

Nintendo Wii™: Virtual Console

For the Virtual Console games, a Classic Controller may be needed to enter some codes.

ALTERED BEAST

LEVEL SELECT
At the Title screen, press B + Start.

BEAST SELECT
At the Title screen, hold A + B + C + Down/Left and press Start.

SOUND TEST
At the Title screen, hold A + C + Up/Right and press Start.

CHEW MAN FU

GAME COMPLETE PASSWORDS
Select Password and enter 573300 or 441300.

COMIX ZONE

STAGE SELECT
At the Jukebox menu, press C on the following numbers:
14, 15, 18, 5, 13, 1, 3, 18, 15, 6
A voice says "Oh Yeah" when entered correctly. Then, press C on 1 through 6 to warp to that stage.

INVINCIBLE
At the Jukebox menu, press C on the following numbers:
3, 12, 17, 2, 2, 10, 2, 7, 7, 11
A voice says "Oh Yeah" when entered correctly.

CREDITS
At the Options menu press A + B + C.

DR. ROBOTNIK'S MEAN BEAN MACHINE

EASY PASSWORDS

STAGE	PASSWORD
02: Frankly	Red Bean, Red Bean, Red Bean, Has Bean
03: Humpty	Clear Bean, Purple Bean, Clear Bean, Green Bean
04: Coconuts	Red Bean, Clear Bean, Has Bean, Yellow Bean
05: Davy Sprocket	Clear Bean, Blue Bean, Blue Bean, Purple Bean
06: Skweel	Clear Bean, Red Bean, Clear Bean, Purple Bean
07: Dynamight	Purple Bean, Yellow Bean, Red Bean, Blue Bean
08: Grounder	Yellow Bean, Purple Bean, Has Bean, Blue Bean
09: Spike	Yellow Bean, Purple Bean, Has Bean, Blue Bean
10: Sir Ffuzy-Logik	Red Bean, Yellow Bean, Clear Bean, Has Bean
11: Dragon Breath	Green Bean, Purple Bean, Blue Bean, Clear Bean
12: Scratch	Red Bean, Has Bean, Has Bean, Yellow Bean
13: Dr. Robotnik	Yellow Bean, Has Bean, Blue Bean, Blue Bean

NORMAL PASSWORDS

STAGE	PASSWORD
02: Frankly	Has Bean, Clear Bean, Yellow Bean, Yellow Bean
03: Humpty	Blue Bean, Clear Bean, Red Bean, Yellow Bean
04: Coconuts	Yellow Bean, Blue Bean, Clear Bean, Purple Bean
05: Davy Sprocket	Has Bean, Green Bean, Blue Bean, Yellow Bean
06: Skweel	Green Bean, Purple Bean, Purple Bean, Yellow Bean
07: Dynamight	Purple Bean, Blue Bean, Green Bean, Has Bean
08: Grounder	Green Bean, Has Bean, Clear Bean, Yellow Bean
09: Spike	Blue Bean, Purple Bean, Has Bean, Has Bean
10: Sir Ffuzy-Logik	Has Bean, Red Bean, Yellow Bean, Clear Bean
11: Dragon Breath	Clear Bean, Red Bean, Red Bean, Blue Bean
12: Scratch	Green Bean, Green Bean, Clear Bean, Yellow Bean
13: Dr. Robotnik	Purple Bean, Yellow Bean, Has Bean, Clear Bean

HARD PASSWORDS

STAGE	PASSWORD
02: Frankly	Clear Bean, Green Bean, Yellow Bean, Yellow Bean
03: Humpty	Yellow Bean, Purple Bean, Clear Bean, Purple Bean
04: Coconuts	Blue Bean, Green Bean, Clear Bean, Blue Bean
05: Davy Sprocket	Red Bean, Purple Bean, Green Bean, Green Bean
06: Skweel	Yellow Bean, Yellow Bean, Clear Bean, Green Bean
07: Dynamight	Purple Bean, Clear Bean, Blue Bean, Blue Bean
08: Grounder	Clear Bean, Yellow Bean, Has Bean, Yellow Bean
09: Spike	Purple Bean, Blue Bean, Blue Bean, Green Bean
10: Sir Ffuzy-Logik	Clear Bean, Green Bean, Red Bean, Yellow Bean
11: Dragon Breath	Blue Bean, Yellow Bean, Yellow Bean, Has Bean
12: Scratch	Green Bean, Clear Bean, Clear Bean, Blue Bean
13: Dr. Robotnik	Has Bean, Clear Bean, Purple Bean, Has Bean

HARDEST PASSWORDS

STAGE	PASSWORD
02: Frankly	Blue Bean, Blue Bean, Green Bean, Yellow Bean
03: Humpty	Green Bean, Yellow Bean, Green Bean, Clear Bean
04: Coconuts	Purple Bean, Purple Bean, RedBean, Has Bean
05: Davy Sprocket	Green Bean, Red Bean, Purple Bean, Blue Bean
06: Skweel	Purple Bean, Clear Bean, Green Bean, Yellow Bean
07: Dynamight	Blue Bean, Purple Bean, Green Bean, Has Bean
08: Grounder	Clear Bean, Purple Bean, Yellow Bean, Has Bean
09: Spike	Purple Bean, Green Bean, Has Bean, Clear Bean
10: Sir Ffuzy-Logik	Green Bean, Blue Bean, Yellow Bean, Has Bean
11: Dragon Breath	Green Bean, Purple Bean, Has Bean, Red Bean
12: Scratch	Red Bean, Green Bean, Has Bean, Blue Bean
13: Dr. Robotnik	Red Bean, Red Bean, Clear Bean, Yellow Bean

ECCO THE DOLPHIN

DEBUG MENU

Pause the game with Ecco facing the screen and press Right, B, C, B, C, Down, C, Up.

INFINITE AIR

Enter LIFEFISH as a password.

PASSWORDS

LEVEL	PASSWORD	LEVEL	PASSWORD
The Undercaves	WEFIDNMP	Deep City	DDXPQQLJ
The Vents	BQDPXJDS	City of Forever	MSDBRQLA
The Lagoon	JNSBRIKY	Jurassic Beach	IYCBUNLB
Ridge Water	NTSBZTKB	Pteranodon Pond	DMXEUNLI
Open Ocean	YWGTTJNI	Origin Beach	EGRIUNLB
Ice Zone	HZIFZBMF	Trilobite Circle	IELMUNLB
Hard Water	LRFJRQLI	Dark Water	RKEQUNLN
Cold Water	UYNFRQLC	City of Forever 2	HPQIGPLA
Island Zone	LYTIOQLZ	The Tube	JUMFKMLB
Deep Water	MNOPOQLR	The Machine	GXUBKMLF
The Marble	RJNTQQLZ	The Last Fight	TSONLMLU
The Library	RTGXQQLE		

F-ZERO X

ALL TRACKS, VEHICLES, AND DIFFICULTIES

At the Mode Select screen, press Up on the D-pad, L, R, Up on the Right control stick, X, Y, ZR, Plus.

GOLDEN AXE

LEVEL SELECT

At the Character Select screen, in Arcade mode, hold Down/Left and press B + Start.

START WITH 9 CONTINUES

At the Character Select screen, in Arcade mode, hold Down/Left and then hold A + C. Release the buttons and select a character.

GRADIUS

MAX OUT WEAPONS

Pause the game and press Up, Up, Down, Down, Left, Right, Left, Right, B, A.

GRADIUS III

FULL POWER-UP

Pause the game and press Up, Up, Down, Down, L, R, L, R, B, A.

Pause the game and press Up, Up, Down, Down, Left, Right, Left, Right, B, A.

SUICIDE

MILITARY MADNESS

PASSWORDS

LEVEL	PASSWORD	LEVEL	PASSWORD
01	REVOLT	06	SENECA
02	ICARUS	07	SABINE
03	CYRANO	08	ARATUS
04	RAMSEY	09	GALIOS
05	NEWTON	10	DARWIN

LEVEL	PASSWORD	LEVEL	PASSWORD
11	PASCAL	22	ARBINE
12	HALLEY	23	RECTOS
13	BORMAN	24	YEANTA
14	APOLLO	25	MONOGA
15	KAISER	26	ATTAYA
16	NECTOR	27	DESHTA
17	MILTON	28	NEKOSE
18	IRAGAN	29	ERATIN
19	LIPTUS	30	SOLCIS
20	INAKKA	31	SAGINE
21	TETROS	32	WINNER

SOUND TEST
Enter ONGAKU as a password.

RISTAR

Select Passwords from the Options menu and enter the following:

LEVEL SELECT
ILOVEU

BOSS RUSH MODE
MUSEUM

TIME ATTACK MODE
DOFEEL

TOUGHER DIFFICULTY
SUPER

ONCHI MUSIC
MAGURO. Activate this from the Sound Test.

CLEARS PASSWORD
XXXXXX

GAME COPYRIGHT INFO
AGES

SONIC THE HEDGEHOG

LEVEL SELECT
At the Title screen, press Up, Down, Left, Right. A sound of a ring being collected plays if the code is entered correctly. Hold A and press Start to access the Level Select.

CONTROL MODE
At the Title screen, press Up, C, Down, C, Left, C, Right, C. Then, hold A and press Start.

DEBUG MODE
After entering the Control Mode, hold A and press Start. Press A to change Sonic into another sprite. Press B to change back to Sonic. Press C to place that sprite. Pause the game and press A to restart. Hold B for slow motion and press C to advance a frame.

CHANGE DEMO
During the demo, hold C and Sonic will start making mistakes.

WARIO'S WOODS

HARD BATTLES
Highlight VS. Computer Mode, hold Left and press Start.

XBOX 360™

TABLE OF CONTENTS

2010 FIFA WORLD CUP SOUTH AFRICA

ADIDAS U11 TEAM

Go to EA Extras in My 2010 FIFA World Cup. Select Unlockable Code Entry and enter WSBJPJYODFYQIIGK.

FINAL MATCH BALL

Go to EA Extras in My 2010 FIFA World Cup. Select Unlockable Code Entry and enter FGWIXGFXTNSICLSS

ADIDAS ADIPURE III TRX (BLACK/SUN)

Go to EA Extras in My 2010 FIFA World Cup. Select Unlockable Code Entry and enter HHDOPWPMIXZQOJOZ

ADIDAS F50 ADIZERO (BLACK/SUN/SUN)

Go to EA Extras in My 2010 FIFA World Cup. Select Unlockable Code Entry and enter SGFSTZPPXCHHMJMH

ADIDAS F50 ADIZERO (CHAMELEON)

Go to EA Extras in My 2010 FIFA World Cup. Select Unlockable Code Entry and enter VOKMNEZTJOQPULUT

ADIDAS F50 ADIZERO (SUN/BLACK/GOLD)

Go to EA Extras in My 2010 FIFA World Cup. Select Unlockable Code Entry and enter YOZCCVIFJGKQJWTW

ADIDAS PREDATOR X (BLACK/SUN)

Go to EA Extras in My 2010 FIFA World Cup. Select Unlockable Code Entry and enter OCEGZCUHXOBSBNFU

COCA-COLA CELEBRATIONS

Go to EA Extras in My 2010 FIFA World Cup. Select Unlockable Code Entry and enter the following:

CELEBRATION	CODE	HOW TO PERFORM
Baby Cradle	UGSIMLBHLFPUBFJY	Left Trigger + A
Dance	KBRRWKUIRSTWUJQW	Left Trigger + B
Dying Fly	DVMNJPBTLHJZGECP	Left Trigger + X
Flying Dive	DBQDUXQTRWTVXYDC	Left Trigger + Y
Prancing Bird	TWVBIXYACAOLGOWO	RB + B
River Dance	MIKAKPUMEEWNTQVE	RB + X
Side Slide	VNDWDUDLMGRNHDNV	RB + Y
Speed Skating	LHEHJZTPYYQDJQXB	RB + A

AVATAR: THE LAST AIRBENDER - THE BURNING EARTH

UNLIMITED HEALTH

Select Code Entry from the Extras menu and enter 65049.

DOUBLE DAMAGE

Select Code Entry from the Extras menu and enter 90210.

MAXIMUM LEVEL

Select Code Entry from the Extras menu and enter 89121.

UNLIMITED SPECIALS

Select Code Entry from the Extras menu and enter 66206.

ONE-HIT DISHONOR

Select Code Entry from the Extras menu and enter 28260.

ALL BONUS GAMES

Select Code Entry from the Extras menu and enter 99801.

UNLOCKS GALLERY

Select Code Entry from the Extras menu and enter 85061.

BAJA: EDGE OF CONTROL

ALL VEHICLES AND TRACKS

Select Cheat Codes from the Options menu and enter SHOWTIME.

ALL PARTS

Select Cheat Codes from the Options menu and enter SUPERMAX.

BAKUGAN BATTLE BRAWLERS

1,000 BP

Enter 33204429 as your name.

5,000 BP

Enter 42348294 as your name.

10,000 BP

Enter 46836478 as your name.

100,000 BP

Enter 18499753 as your name.

500,000 BP

Enter 26037947 as your name.

BAKUGAN: DEFENDERS OF THE CORE

HIDDEN ITEMS

Select Unlock Codes from Collection and enter HXV6Y7BF. Now you can enter up to 8 of your unique Bakugan Dimensions codes.

The codes unlock the following:	Here are 8 codes:
10,000 Core Energy	2FKRRMNCDQ
Ten Vexos Passes	82D77YK6P8
Earthen Armor	HUUH8ST7AR
Fire Spirit	JJUZDEACXX
Light Arrow	QY8CLD5NJE
Tornado Vortex	TD4UMFSRW3
Water Pillar	YJ7RGG7WGZ
Zorch Thunder	YQLHBBSMDC

BANJO-KAZOOIE

In Treasure Trove Cove, enter the Sandcastle and spell CHEAT by using your Beak Buster on the desired letter. A sound will confirm the entry of the letter. The following cheats will now be available for you. Two things to keep in mind. The first is that no sound will confirm the correct letter. Secondly, ignore the spaces in the phrases…just spell the entire phrase out.

AREA OPENING CHEATS

ACCESS CLANKER'S CAVERN
THERES NOWHERE DANKER THAN IN WITH CLANKER

ACCESS MAD MONSTER MANSION
THE JIGGYS NOW MADE WHOLE INTO THE MANSION YOU CAN STROLL

ACCESS GOBI'S VALLEY
GOBIS JIGGY IS NOW DONE TREK ON IN AND GET SOME SUN

ACCESS RUSTY BUCKET BAY
WHY NOT TAKE A TRIP INSIDE GRUNTYS RUSTY SHIP

ACCESS CLICK CLOCK WOOD
THIS ONES GOOD AS YOU CAN ENTER THE WOOD

ACCESS FREEZEEZY PEAK
THE JIGGYS DONE SO OFF YOU GO INTO FREEZEEZY PEAK AND ITS SNOW

ACCESS BUBBLEGLOOP SWAMP
NOW INTO THE SWAMP YOU CAN STOMP

HIDDEN EGG CHEATS

The Hidden Egg cheats will only work if you have been to the level previously.

REVEAL THE BLUE EGG IN GOBI'S VALLEY BEHIND THE LOCKED GATE IN THE ROCK WALL
A DESERT DOOR OPENS WIDE ANCIENT SECRETS WAIT INSIDE

REVEAL THE PURPLE EGG IN TREASURE TROVE COVE IN SHARKFOOD ISLAND
OUT OF THE SEA IT RISES TO REVEAL MORE SECRET PRIZES

REVEAL THE ICE KEY IN FREEZEEZY PEAK IN THE ICE CAVE
NOW YOU CAN SEE A NICE ICE KEY WHICH YOU CAN HAVE FOR FREE

REVEAL THE LIGHT BLUE EGG IN GRUNTILDA'S LAIR-YOU'LL FIND IT IN THE CASK MARKED WITH AN X
DONT YOU GO AND TELL HER ABOUT THE SECRET IN HER CELLAR

REVEAL THE GREEN EGG IN MAD MONSTER MANSION IN THE SAME ROOM AS LOGGO THE TOILET
AMIDST THE HAUNTED GLOOM A SECRET IN THE BATHROOM

REVEAL THE YELLOW EGG IN CLICK CLOCK WOOD IN NABNUTS' TREE HOUSE
NOW BANJO WILL BE ABLE TO SEE IT ON NABNUTS TABLE

REVEAL THE RED EGG IN RUSTY BUCKET BAY IN THE CAPTAIN'S CABIN
THIS SECRET YOULL BE GRABBIN IN THE CAPTAINS CABIN

NOTE DOOR CHEATS

These will pop those note doors open without having to find the required notes.

DOOR 2
THESE GO RIGHT ON THROUGH NOTE DOOR TWO

DOOR 3
NOTE DOOR THREE GET IN FOR FREE

DOOR 4
TAKE A TOUR THROUGH NOTE DOOR FOUR

DOOR 5
USE THIS CHEAT NOTE DOOR FIVE IS BEAT

DOOR 6
THIS TRICKS USED TO OPEN NOTE DOOR SIX

DOOR 7
THE SEVENTH NOTE DOOR IS NOW NO MORE

SWITCH AND OBSTACLE CHEATS FOR GRUNTILDA'S LAIR

These will allow you to alter certain obstacles throughout Gruntilda's Lair. Sometimes, the cheat will even remove them completely.

RAISE THE PIPES NEAR CLANKER'S CAVERN
BOTH PIPES ARE THERE TO CLANKERS LAIR

RAISE THE LARGE PIPE NEAR CLANKER'S CAVERN:
YOULL CEASE TO GRIPE WHEN UP GOES A PIPE

UNLOCK THE PATH NEAR CLANKER'S CAVERN THAT LEADS TO THE CLICK CLOCK WOOD PICTURE
ONCE IT SHONE BUT THE LONG TUNNEL GRILLE IS GONE

REVEAL THE PODIUM FOR THE CLICK CLOCK WOOD JIGGY
DONT DESPAIR THE TREE JIGGY PODIUM IS NOW THERE

UNLOCK THE PATH INSIDE THE GIANT WITCH STATUE, NEAR BUBBLEGLOOP SWAMP (OPEN THE GRILL)
SHES AN UGLY BAT SO LETS REMOVE HER GRILLE AND HAT

UNLOCK THE PATH TO THE FREEZEEZY PEAK PICTURE BEHIND THE ICE CUBE
ITS YOUR LUCKY DAY AS THE ICE BALL MELTS AWAY

UNLOCK PASSAGES BLOCKED BY COBWEBS
WEBS STOP YOUR PLAY SO TAKE THEM AWAY

REVEAL A JIGGY IN GRUNTILDA'S STATUE BY SMASHING THE EYE NEAR MAD MONSTER MANSION
GRUNTY WILL CRY NOW YOUVE SMASHED HER EYE

RAISE THE WATER LEVEL NEAR RUSTY BUCKET BAY
UP YOU GO WITHOUT A HITCH UP TO THE WATER LEVEL SWITCH

UNLOCK THE PATH TO THE CRYPT NEAR MAD MONSTER MANSION (REMOVE THE GATE)
YOU WONT HAVE TO WAIT NOW THERES NO CRYPT GATE

REMOVE THE COFFIN LID IN THE CRYPT
THIS SHOULD GET RID OF THE CRYPT COFFIN LID

CRUMBLE ALL BREAKABLE WALLS
THEY CAUSE TROUBLE BUT NOW THEYRE RUBBLE

ACTIVATE SPECIAL PADS

Skip the lesson from Bottles by entering these codes.

ACTIVATE THE FLY PAD
YOU WONT BE SAD NOW YOU CAN USE THE FLY PAD

ACTIVATE THE SHOCK JUMP PAD
YOULL BE GLAD TO SEE THE SHOCK JUMP PAD

EXTRA HEALTH CHEAT

Skip the note-hunt and get that extra health by entering this cheat.

AN ENERGY BAR TO GET YOU FAR

Remember, to enter a code you must first enter the word CHEAT in the Sandcastle.

BANJO-TOOIE

REGAIN ENERGY

Go to the Code Chamber in the Mayahem Temple and access the scroll on the wall. If you have been awarded this cheat by Cheato, enter HONEYBACK. If not, enter CHEATOKCABYENOH.

FALLS DON'T HURT

Go to the Code Chamber in the Mayahem Temple and access the scroll on the wall. If you have been awarded this cheat by Cheato, enter FALLPROOF. If not, enter CHEATOFOORPLLAF.

HOMING EGGS

Go to the Code Chamber in the Mayahem Temple and access the scroll on the wall. If you have been awarded this cheat, enter HOMING. If not, enter CHEATOGNIMOH.

DOUBLES MAXIMUM EGGS

Go to the Code Chamber in the Mayahem Temple and access the scroll on the wall. If you have been awarded this cheat by Cheato, enter EGGS. If not, enter CHEATOSGGE.

DOUBLES MAXIMUM FEATHERS

Go to the Code Chamber in the Mayahem Temple and access the scroll on the wall. If you have been awarded this cheat by Cheato, enter FEATHERS. If not, enter CHEATOSREHTAEF.

JOLLY ROGER LAGOON'S JUKEBOX

Go to the Code Chamber in the Mayahem Temple and access the scroll on the wall. If you have been awarded this cheat, enter JUKEBOX. If not, enter CHEATOXOBEKUJ.

SIGNS IN JIGGYWIGGY'S TEMPLE GIVE HINTS TO GET EACH JIGGY

Go to the Code Chamber in the Mayahem Temple and access the scroll on the wall. If you have been awarded this cheat, enter GETJIGGY. If not, enter CHEATOYGGIJTEG.

ALL LEVELS

Go to the Code Chamber in the Mayahem Temple and enter JIGGYWIGGYSPECIAL.

SPEED BANJO

Go to the Code Chamber in the Mayahem Temple and enter SUPERBANJO.

SPEED ENEMIES

Go to the Code Chamber in the Mayahem Temple and enter SUPERBADDY.

INFINITE EGGS AND FEATHERS

Go to the Code Chamber in the Mayahem Temple and enter NESTKING.

INFINITE HONEY

Go to the Code Chamber in the Mayahem Temple and enter HONEYKING.

BEAT'N GROOVY

ALTERNATE CONTROLS

At the title screen, press Up, Up, Down, Down, Left, Right, Left, Right, Ⓑ, Ⓐ.

™

BEN 10: ALIEN FORCE VILGAX ATTACKS

LEVEL SKIP
Pause the game and enter Portal in the Cheats menu.

UNLOCK ALL SPECIAL ATTACKS FOR ALL FORMS
Pause the game and enter Everythingproof in the Cheats menu.

UNLOCK ALL ALIEN FORMS
Pause the game and enter Primus in the Cheats menu.

TOGGLE INVULNERABILITY ON AND OFF
Pause the game and enter Xlmrsmoothy in the Cheats menu.

GIVES PLAYER FULL HEALTH
Pause the game and enter Herotime in the Cheats menu.

QUICK ENERGY REGENERATION
Pause the game and enter Generator in the Cheats menu.

BEN 10 ULTIMATE ALIEN: COSMIC DESTRUCTION

These cheats disable Achievements. To remove the cheats, you will need to start a new game.

1,000,000 DNA
Pause the game, select Cheats, and enter Cash.

REGENERATE HEALTH
Pause the game, select Cheats, and enter Health.

REGENERATE ENERGY
Pause the game, select Cheats, and enter Energy.

UPGRADE EVERYTHING
Pause the game, select Cheats, and enter Upgrade.

ALL LEVELS
Pause the game, select Cheats, and enter Levels.

ENEMIES DO DOUBLE DAMAGE/ PLAYER DOES 1/2 DAMAGE
Pause the game, select Cheats, and enter Hard.

UNLOCKS RATH
Pause the game, select Cheats, and enter Primus.

BIOLOGY BATTLE

INCREASED CONFLICT LEVEL IN GLOBAL CHALLENGE MODE
At the Global Challenge Mode lobby, press Ⓐ to access the game controls/start screen. At this screen, hold Ⓨ and press Ⓐ.

BLUR

BMW CONCEPT 1 SERIES TII CHROME
In the Multiplayer Showroom, highlight the BMW Concept 1 Series tii and press Left Trigger, Right Trigger, Left Trigger, Right Trigger.

FULLY UPGRADE FORD BRONCO
In the Multiplayer Showroom, highlight the Ford Bronco and press Left Trigger, Right Trigger, Left Trigger, Right Trigger.

AVATAR AWARDS

AWARD	EARNED BY
Wreck Tee	Earn the Been there, got the T-shirt Achievement
Friend Rechallenge Tee	Defeat a friends rechallenge.
Legend Tee	Unlock first Legend Rank in multiplayer.
Showdown Tee	Complete Showdown
Sticker Tee	Complete the Sticker Book.

BURNOUT PARADISE

BEST BUY CAR

Pause the game and select Sponsor Product Code from the Under the Hood menu. Enter Bestbuy. Need A License to use this car offline.

CIRCUIT CITY CAR

Pause the game and select Sponsor Product Code from the Under the Hood menu. Enter Circuitcity. Need Burnout Paradise License to use this car offline.

GAMESTOP CAR

Pause the game and select Sponsor Product Code from the Under the Hood menu. Enter Gamestop. Need A License to use this car offline.

LICENSES

LICENSE	NUMBER OF WINS NEEDED
D	2
C	7
B	16
A	26
Burnout Paradise	45
Elite License	All events

WALMART CAR

Pause the game and select Sponsor Product Code from the Under the Hood menu. Enter Walmart. Need Burnout Paradise License to use this car offline.

"STEEL WHEELS" GT

Pause the game and select Sponsor Product Code from the Under the Hood menu. Enter G23X 5K8Q GX2V 04B1 or E60J 8Z7T MS8L 51U6.

CARNIVAL GAMES: MONKEY SEE, MONKEY DO!

AVATAR AWARDS

AWARD	EARNED BY
Barker Bowler	Purchase Barker Bowler Prize.
Barker's Best	Purchase Barker's Best Prize.
Monkey Barker	Purchase Monkey Barker Prize.

CARS 2: THE VIDEO GAME

ALL MODES AND TRACKS

Select Enter Codes from the Options and enter 959595.

LASER GUIDED

Select Enter Codes from the Options and enter 123456. Select Cheats to toggle the cheat on and off.

UNLIMITED ENERGY

Select Enter Codes from the Options and enter 721953. Select Cheats to toggle the cheat on and off.

AVATAR AWARDS

AWARD	EARNED BY
Team Brazil Jumpsuit	Unlock this item by earning the In Your Face Achievement.
Team France Jumpsuit	Unlock this item by earning the Island Hopper Achievement.
Team Spain Jumpsuit	Unlock this item by earning the Smashing Achievement.

CARS MATER-NATIONAL

ALL ARCADE RACES, MINI-GAMES, AND WORLDS
Select Codes/Cheats from the options and enter PLAYALL.

ALL CARS
Select Codes/Cheats from the options and enter MATTEL07.

ALTERNATE LIGHTNING MCQUEEN COLORS
Select Codes/Cheats from the options and enter NCEDUDZ.

ALL COLORS FOR OTHERS
Select Codes/Cheats from the options and enter PAINTIT.

UNLIMITED TURBO
Select Codes/Cheats from the options and enter ZZOOOOM.

EXTREME ACCELERATION
Select Codes/Cheats from the options and enter OTO200X.

EXPERT MODE
Select Codes/Cheats from the options and enter VRYFAST.

ALL BONUS ART
Select Codes/Cheats from the options and enter BUYTALL.

COMIC JUMPER: THE ADVENTURES OF CAPTAIN SMILEY

AVATAR AWARDS

AWARD	EARNED BY
Captain Smiley Giant Head	Complete the whole game
Gerda T-Shirt (female only)	Complete the 1st Level
Star T-Shirt (male only)	Complete the 1st Level

COMMAND & CONQUER 3: TIBERIUM WARS

FREE NOD SHADOW SQUADS
During a NOD game, pause and press Left, Right, Up, Up, Up, Down, RB, LB, LB, B. This code does not work in Skirmish or Career.

COSTUME QUEST

AVATAR AWARDS

AWARD	EARNED BY
Pumpkin Pail	Start a new game.
Pumpkin Mask	Complete the game.

CRASH BANDICOOT: MIND OVER MUTANT

A cheat can be deactivated by re-entering the code.

FREEZE ENEMIES WITH TOUCH
Pause the game, hold Right Trigger and press Down, Down, Down, Up.

ENEMIES DROP X4 DAMAGE
Pause the game, hold Right Trigger and press Up, Up, Up, Left.

ENEMIES DROP PURPLE FRUIT
Pause the game, hold Right Trigger and press Up, Down, Down, Up.

ENEMIES DROP SUPER KICK
Pause the game, hold Right Trigger and press Up, Right, Down, Left.

ENIMIES DROP WUMPA FRUIT

Pause the game, hold Right Trigger and press Right, Right, Right, Up.

SHADOW CRASH

Pause the game, hold Right Trigger and press Left, Right, Left, Right.

DEFORMED CRASH

Pause the game, hold Right Trigger and press Left, Left, Left, Down.

CRIMSON ALLIANCE

AVATAR AWARDS

AWARD	EARNED BY
Pocket Shaman	Defeat a Primitive Shaman.
Death Knight Helm	20 Treasures.

DANCE CENTRAL 2

AVATAR AWARDS

AWARD	EARNED BY
Bring It Tee	Play every song in the game in Perform It mode.
Neon Tee	Get a solo score of at least 2,000,000 points on a song.
Ribbon Tee	Earn Gold Stars on a song.

DEAD BLOCK

AVATAR AWARDS

AWARD	EARNED BY
Construction Worker Helmet	Collect the helmet in the tutorial.
Dead Block Shirt	Beat all singleplayer levels.

DEATHSPANK

AVATAR AWARDS

AWARD	EARNED BY
Dragon Hatchling	Complete Ms. Heybenstances quest to rescue the hatchlings.
Unicorn Poop T-shirt	Kill the twin dragons guarding the artifact.

DEFENSE GRID: THE AWAKENING

The following cheats will disable Achievements.

100,000 RESOURCES

Click and hold the Right Thumbstick and press Right, Right, Right, Right

CORES CANNOT BE TAKEN

Click and hold the Right Thumbstick and press Up, Left, Down, Right

FREE CAMERA MODE

Click and hold the Right Thumbstick and press Down, Up, Down, Down

INSTANT VICTORY

Click and hold the Right Thumbstick and press Up, Up, Up, Up

KILL ALL ALIENS

Click and hold the Right Thumbstick and press Left, Right, Left, Right

KILL ALL ALIENS CARRYING CORES

Click and hold the Right Thumbstick and press Up, Down, Down, Up

LEVEL SELECT

Click and hold the Right Thumbstick and press Up, Up, Down, Down, Left, Right, Left, Right

SELF-DESTRUCT (INSTANT DEFEAT)

Click and hold the Right Thumbstick and press Down, Down, Down, Down

TOGGLE TARGET RETICULE

Click and hold the Right Thumbstick and press Down, Up, Down, Up

UNLOCK ALL TOWER TYPES

Click and hold the Right Thumbstick and press Up, Down, Left, Right

DIRT 2

Win the given events to earn the following cars:

GET THIS CAR	BY WINNING THIS EVENT
Ford RS200 Evolution	Rally Cross World Tour
Toyota Stadium Truck	Landrush World Tour
Mitsubishi Pajero Dakar 1993	Raid World Tour
Dallenbach Special	Trailblazer World Tour
1995 Subaru Impreza WRX STi	Colin McRae Challenge
Colin McRae R4 [X Games]	X Games Europe
Mitsubishi Lancer Evolution X [X Games]	X Games Asia
Subaru Impreza WRX STi [X Games]	X Games America
Ford Escort MKII and MG Metro 6R4	All X Games events

DIRT 3

AVATAR AWARDS

AVATAR	EARNED BY
Racing Shoes	Reach Fan Level 12.
Racing Gloves	Reach Fan Level 24.
Racing Suit	Complete Season 1.
Rally Helmet	Complete Season 2.

DJ HERO

Select Cheats from Options and enter the following. Some codes will disable high scores and progress. Cheats cannot be used in tutorials and online.

UNLOCK ALL CONTENT
Enter tol0.

ALL CHARACTER ITEMS
Enter uNA2.

ALL VENUES
Enter Wv1u.

ALL DECKS
Enter LAuP.

ALL HEADPHONES
Enter 62Db.

ALL MIXES
Enter 82xl.

AUTO SCRATCH
Enter it6j.

AUTO EFFECTS DIAL
Enter ab1l.

AUTO FADER
Enter sl5d.

AUTO TAPPER
Enter zith.

AUTO WIN EUPHORIA
Enter r3a9.

BLANK PLINTHS
Enter ipr0.

HAMSTER SWITCH
Enter 7geo.

HYPER DECK MODE
Enter 76st.

SHORT DECK
Enter 51uc.

BLACK AND WHITE
Enter b!99.

EDGE EFFECT
Enter 2u4u.

INVISIBLE DJ
Enter oh5t.

MIDAS
Enter 4pe5.

PITCH BLACK OUT
Enter d4kr.

PLAY IN THE BEDROOM
Enter g7nh.

RAINBOW
Enter ?jy!.

ANY DJ, ANY SETLIST
Enter 0jj8.

DAFT PUNK'S CONTENT
Enter d1g?.

DJ AM'S CONTENT
Enter k07u.

DJ JAZZY JEFF'S CONTENT
Enter n1fz.

DJ SHADOW'S CONTENT
Enter omxv.

DJ Z-TRIP'S CONTENT
Enter 5rtg.

GRANDMASTER FLASH'S CONTENT
Enter ami8.

DJ HERO 2

ALL BONUS CONTENT
Select Cheats from the Options. Choose Retail Cheats and enter VIP Pass.

DAVID GUETTA
Select Cheats from the Options. Choose Retail Cheats and enter Guetta Blaster.

DEADMAU5
Select Cheats from the Options. Choose Retail Cheats and enter Open The Trap.

INVISIBLE DJ
Select Cheats from the Options. Choose Retail Cheats and enter Now You See Me.

AUTO CROSSFADE
Select Cheats from the Options. Choose Retail Cheats and enter I Hate Crossfading. This disables Leaderboards.

AUTO SCRATCH
Select Cheats from the Options. Choose Retail Cheats and enter Soothing. This disables Leaderboards.

AUTO TAP
Select Cheats from the Options. Choose Retail Cheats and enter Look No Hands! This disables Leaderboards.

DON KING PRESENTS: PRIZEFIGHTER

Re-enter a code to disable the cheat.

INVULNERABILITY
Select Enter Unlock Code from the Extras menu and enter SHIELDOFSTEEL.

MAXIMUM STATS
Select Enter Unlock Code from the Extras menu and enter BROUSSARDMODE.

INFINITE ADRENALINE
Select Enter Unlock Code from the Extras menu and enter FISTOFTHENORTHSHIELDS.

INFINITE STAMINA
Select Enter Unlock Code from the Extras menu and enter FEELTHEBURN.

SKIP GETUP GAME
Select Enter Unlock Code from the Extras menu and enter NEVERQUIT.

PLAY AS RICARDO MAYORGA
Select Enter Unlock Code from the Extras menu and enter POTSEMAG.

GREAT MOMENTS IN BOXING VIDEO
Select Enter Unlock Code from the Extras menu and enter 1BESTBUYBEST.

DRIVER: SAN FRANCISCO

MOVIE SCENE CHALLENGES

As you collect the 130 Movie Tokens in the game, Movie Scene Challenges are unlocked as shown below.

MOVIE SCENE CHALLENGE	VEHICLE GIVEN	# MOVIE TOKENS
Gone In 60 Seconds	1973 Ford Mustang Mach I	10
Starsky & Hutch	1974 Dodge Monaco Cop	20
Bullitt	1968 Ford Mustang GT Fastback	30
The French Connection	1971 Pontiac LeMans	40
Blues Brothers	1974 Dodge Monaco	50
Cannonball Run	1978 Lamborghini Countach LP400S	60
Dukes of Hazard	1969 Dodge Charger R/T	70
Vanishing Point	1970 Dodge Challenger R/T	80
The Driver	1965 Chevrolet S-10	90
Redline	2011 McLaren MP4-12C	100
Smokey & The Bandit	1977 Pontiac TransAm Firebird	110
Test Drive	1987 RUF CT-R Yellow Bird	120
The Italian Job	1972 Lamborghini Miura	130

EARTH DEFENSE FORCE: INSECT ARMAGEDDON

HIDDEN IMAGES IN GALLERY

Select Gallery from the Extras menu. At the gallery press X, X, Y, X, Left Bumper, Right Bumper.

EVERY EXTEND EXTRA EXTREME

FINE ADJUSTMENT MENU

At the Start screen, press LB, RB, LB, RB, LB, RB, LB, RB.

FANTASTIC PETS

AVATAR AWARDS

AWARD	EARNED BY
Fantastic T-Shirt	Reach Fantastic Pet trainer rank 2.
Cute Hat (Female)	Reach Fantastic Pet trainer rank 3.
Fierce Hat (Male)	Reach Fantastic Pet trainer rank 3.
Fantastic Gloves	Reach Fantastic Pet trainer rank 4.
Fantastic Shoes	Reach Fantastic Pet trainer rank 5.
Fantastic Pet	Reach Fantastic Pet trainer rank 6.

FORZA MOTORSPORT 4

AVATAR AWARDS

AVATAR	EARNED BY
Autovista T-Shirt	Fully explore any car in Autovista.
Stopwatch Cap	Post a time in every Rivals Mode Event.

FROM DUST

AVATAR AWARDS

AVATAR	EARNED BY
The Tribal Mask	Retrieve this mask by unlocking the complete version of "From Dust".

FRUIT NINJA KINECT

AVATAR AWARDS

AVATAR	EARNED BY
Fruit Ninja T-Shirt	Equip an Item in Sensei's Swag.
Kung Fu Pants	Complete 3 Multiplayer Games.
Kung Fu Sensei Shirt	Complete 5 games of Classic, Zen or Arcade.

FUEL

CAMO ARMY HELMET
Select Bonus Codes from the Options and enter 48992519.

ROAD ADDICT JACKET
Select Bonus Codes from the Options and enter 20061977.

SPEED ANGEL SHORTS
Select Bonus Codes from the Options and enter 91031985.

BUTTERFLY LIVERY FOR THE SLUDGERAY VEHICLE
Select Bonus Codes from the Options and enter 18021974.

LIGHTNING BOLT LIVERY FOR THE MUDHOG VEHICLE
Select Bonus Codes from the Options and enter 17121973.

WARRIOR VEHICLE
Select Bonus Codes from the Options and enter 18041851.

FULL HOUSE POKER

AVATAR AWARDS

AWARD	EARNED BY
Hoodie	Level up
Bulldog Helmet	Level up to 50

GAME ROOM

SWAP KONAMI AND ASTEROIDS CABINET STYLES
During a game or at a menu, press Up, Up, Down, Down, Left, Right, Left, Right, **B**, **A**.

GAMERBOTS: THIRD-ROBOT SHOOTING

300,000 GP
Enter 24162444 as a gift code.

DEMON SWORD
Enter 39121412 as a gift code.

DUAL FLAME
Enter 34094035 as a gift code.

SPIKED CLUB
Enter 56095802 as a gift code.

STAR SLICER
Enter 55122302 as a gift code.

G.I. JOE: THE RISE OF COBRA

CLASSIC DUKE
At the main menu, press Left, Up, **X**, Up, Right, **Y**.

CLASSIC SCARLETT
At the main menu, press Right, Up, Down, Down, **Y**.

GRID

ALL DRIFT CARS
Select Bonus Codes from the Options. Then choose Enter Code and enter TUN58396.

ALL MUSCLE CARS
Select Bonus Codes from the Options. Then choose Enter Code and enter MUS59279.

BUCHBINDER EMOTIONAL ENGINEERING BMW 320SI
Select Bonus Codes from the Options. Then choose Enter Code and enter F93857372. You can use this in Race Day or in GRID World once you've started your own team.

EBAY
Select Bonus Codes from the Options. Then choose Enter Code and enter DAFJ55E01473M0. You can use this in Race Day or in GRID World once you've started your own team.

GAMESTATION BMW 320SI
Select Bonus Codes from the Options. Then choose Enter Code and enter G29782655. You can use this in Race Day or in GRID World once you've started your own team.

MICROMANIA PAGANI ZONDA R
Select Bonus Codes from the Options. Then choose Enter Code and enter M38572343. You can use this in Race Day or in GRID World once you've started your own team.

PLAY.COM ASTON MARTIN DBR9
Select Bonus Codes from the Options. Then choose Enter Code and enter P47203845. You can use this in Race Day or in GRID World once you've started your own team.

GUARDIAN HEROES

AVATAR AWARDS

AVATAR	EARNED BY
Guardian Heroes Helmet	Scored 360 points in Arcade Mode.
Guardian Heroes T-Shirt	Unlocked at least 30 characters in Story Mode.

HALF-MINUTE HERO: SUPER MEGA NEO CLIMAX

AVATAR AWARDS

AVATAR	EARNED BY
Brave Vest	Cleared 1 quest after Quest 3 in 30 seconds.
Liar T-Shirt	Cleared 10 quests after Quest 3 in 30 seconds.

HARRY POTTER AND THE DEATHLY HALLOWS: PART 1

SUPER STRENGTH POTIONS
Select Unlock Menu from the Options and enter ❌, Left, Right, Ⓐ, 🎮, 🎮.

ELITE CHALLENGES
Select Unlock Menu from the Options and enter ❤, Up, ❌, 🎮, 🎮, Ⓐ.

AUGMENTED REALITY CHEAT FROM BOX (PROTEGO TOTALUM)
Select Unlock Menu from the Options and enter ❤, Ⓑ, Up, Left, 🎮, Right.

HARRY POTTER AND THE HALF-BLOOD PRINCE

BONUS TWO-PLAYER DUELING ARENA CASTLE GATES
At the Rewards menu, press Right, Right, Down, Down, Left, Right, Left, Right, Left, Right, Start.

UNLOCK EVERYTHING
At the Rewards menu, press Down, Left, Left, Left, Left, Left, Down, Down, Right, Down, Left.

HYDRO THUNDER HURRICANE

AVATAR AWARDS

AWARD	EARNED BY
Hydro Thunder Hurricane T-Shirt	Get 500 points.
Razorback Toy Boat	Earn 18,500 points.

ILOMILO

ILOMILO SHUFFLE

At the main menu, press 🔽, 🔼, **LB**, **RB**.

AVATAR AWARDS

AWARD	EARNED BY
T-Shirt	Complete 3 levels.
Ilo And Milo	Collect enough memory fragments to unlock a full memory.

INSANELY TWISTED SHADOW PLANET

AVATAR AWARDS

AVATAR	EARNED BY
Shadow Planet Tee T-Shirt	Make it from your Homeworld to the Shadow Planet to unlock!
UFO Hero's Ship	Complete the Single-Player Campaign to unlock!

IRON MAN

CLASSIC ARMOR
Clear One Man Army vs. Mercs.

EXTREMIS ARMOR
Clear One Man Army vs. Maggia.

MARK II ARMOR
Clear One Man Army vs. Ten Rings.

HULKBUSTER ARMOR
Clear One Man Army vs. AIM-X. Can also be unlocked when clear game save data from Incredible Hulk is stored on the same console.

SILVER CENTURION ARMOR
Clear Mission 13: Showdown.

CLASSIC MARK I ARMOR
Clear One Man Army vs. AIM.

ISLANDS OF WAKFU

AVATAR AWARDS

AWARD	EARNED BY
Blue Platypus	Who's Who? Achievement
Merch T-Shirt	The Chosen One Achievement

KINECT SPORTS

AVATAR AWARDS

AWARD	EARNED BY
Classic Kinect Sports Cap	Earn the Amateur Sports Badge.
Classic Kinect Sports Tee	Earn the Professional Sports Badge.
I Heart Kinect Sports Tee	Earn the Champion Sports Badge.
Kinect Sports Champ Trophy	Earn the Legendary Sports Badge.
Kinect Sports Star Tee	Earn the Master Sports Badge.

KINECT SPORTS SEASON TWO

AVATAR AWARDS

AVATAR	EARNED BY
Kinect Sports Darts Top Hat	Stay on target throughout your career with this awesome award for reaching level 5. Woohoo!
Kinect Sports Football Hat	Show your love for all things football with this award for reaching fan level 2. I'm so jealous!
Kinect Sports Golf Green Cap	Impress everyone at the clubhouse with this award for reaching the dizzy heights of fan level 10.

KUNG FU PANDA

INFINITE CHI

Select Cheats from the Extra menu and press Down, Right, Left, Up, Down.

INVINCIBILITY

Select Cheats from the Extra menu and press Down, Down, Right, Up, Left.

FULL UPGRADES

Select Cheats from the Extra menu and press Left, Right, Down, Left, Up.

4X DAMAGE MULTIPLIER

Select Cheats from the Extra menu and press Up, Down, Up, Right, Left.

ALL MULTIPLAYER CHARACTERS

Select Cheats from the Extra menu and press Left, Down, Left, Right, Down.

DRAGON WARRIOR OUTFIT IN MULTIPLAYER

Select Cheats from the Extra menu and press Left, Down, Right, Left, Up.

ALL OUTFITS

Select Cheats from the Extra menu and press Right, Left, Down, Up, Right.

LARA CROFT AND THE GUARDIAN OF LIGHT

LARA CROFT HEAVY JUNGLE OUTFIT

Complete the game.

LARA CROFT JUNGLE OUTFIT

Score 1,410,000 points.

LARA CROFT BIKER OUTFIT

Score 1,900,000 points.

LARA CROFT LEGEND OUTFIT

Defeat Xolotl.

DOPPELGANGER OUTFIT

Score 2,400,000 points.

THE LEGEND OF SPYRO: DAWN OF THE DRAGON

UNLIMITED LIFE

Pause the game, hold LB and press Right, Right, Down, Down, Left with the Left Control Stick.

UNLIMITED MANA

Pause the game, hold RB and press Up, Right, Up, Left, Down with the Left Control Stick.

MAXIMUM XP

Pause the game, hold RB and press Up, Left, Left, Down, Up with the Left Control Stick.

ALL ELEMENTAL UPGRADES

Pause the game, hold LB and press Left, Up, Down, Up, Right with the Left Control Stick.

LEGO BATMAN

BATCAVE CODES

Using the computer in the Batcave, select Enter Code and enter the following codes.

CHARACTERS

CHARACTER	CODE
Alfred	ZAQ637
Batgirl	JKR331
Bruce Wayne	BDJ327
Catwoman (Classic)	M1AAWW
Clown Goon	HJK327
Commissioner Gordon	DDP967
Fishmonger	HGY748
Freeze Girl	XVK541
Joker Goon	UTF782
Joker Henchman	YUN924
Mad Hatter	JCA283
Man-Bat	NYU942
Military Policeman	MKL382
Nightwing	MVY759
Penguin Goon	NKA238

CHARACTER	CODE
Penguin Henchman	BJH782
Penguin Minion	KJP748
Poison Ivy Goon	GTB899
Police Marksman	HKG984
Police Officer	JRY983
Riddler Goon	CRY928
Riddler Henchman	XEU824
S.W.A.T.	HTF114
Sailor	NAV592
Scientist	JFL786
Security Guard	PLB946
The Joker (Tropical)	CCB199
Yeti	NJL412
Zoo Sweeper	DWR243

VEHICLES

VEHICLE	CODE
Bat-Tank	KNTT4B
Bruce Wayne's Private Jet	LEA664
Catwoman's Motorcycle	HPL826
Garbage Truck	DUS483
Goon Helicopter	GCH328
Harbor Helicopter	CHP735
Harley Quinn's Hammer Truck	RDT637
Mad Hatter's Glider	HS000W
Mad Hatter's Steamboat	M4DM4N
Mr. Freeze's Iceberg	ICYICE
The Joker's Van	JUK657

VEHICLE	CODE
Mr. Freeze's Kart	BCT229
Penguin Goon Submarine	BTN248
Police Bike	LJP234
Police Boat	PLC999
Police Car	KJL832
Police Helicopter	CWR732
Police Van	MAC788
Police Watercraft	VJD328
Riddler's Jet	HAHAHA
Robin's Submarine	TTF453
Two-Face's Armored Truck	EFE933

CHEATS

CHEAT	CODE
Always Score Multiply	9LRGNB
Fast Batarangs	JRBDCB
Fast Walk	ZOLM6N
Flame Batarang	D8NYWH
Freeze Batarang	XPN4NG
Extra Hearts	ML3KHP
Fast Build	EVG26J
Immune to Freeze	JXUDY6
Invincibility	WYD5CP
Minikit Detector	ZXGH9J

CHEAT	CODE
More Batarang Targets	XWP645
Piece Detector	KHJ554
Power Brick Detector	MMN786
Regenerate Hearts	HJH7HJ
Score x2	N4NR3E
Score x4	CX9MAT
Score x6	MLVNF2
Score x8	WCCDB9
Score x10	18HW07

TM

LEGO HARRY POTTER: YEARS 1-4

RED BRICK EXTRAS

Once you have access to The Leaky Cauldron, enter Wiseacre's Wizarding Supplies from Diagon Alley. Go upstairs to enter the following. Pause the game and select Extras to toggle the cheats on/off.

CHEAT	CODE	CHEAT	CODE
Carrot Wands	AUC8EH	Invincibility	QQWC6B
Character Studs	H27KGC	Red Brick Detector	7AD7HE
Character Token Detector	HA79V8	Regenerate Hearts	89ML2W
Christmas	T7PVVN	Score x2	74YKR7
Disguise	4DMK2R	Score x4	J3WHNK
Fall Rescue	ZEX7MV	Score x6	XK9ANE
Extra Hearts	J9U6Z9	Score x8	HUFV2H
Fast Dig	Z9BFAD	Score x10	H8X69Y
Fast Magic	FA3GQA	Silhouettes	HZBVX7
Gold Brick Detector	84QNQN	Singing Mandrake	BMEU6X
Hogwarts Crest Detector	TTMC6D	Stud Magnet	67FKWZ
Ice Rink	F88VUW		

WISEACRE SPELLS

Once you have access to The Leaky Cauldron, enter Wiseacre's Wizarding Supplies from Diagon Alley. Go upstairs to enter the following. You need to learn Wingardium Leviosa before you can use these cheats.

SPELL	CODE	SPELL	CODE
Accio	VE9VV7	Incarcerous	YEB9Q9
Anteoculatia	QFB6NR	Locomotor Mortis	2M2XJ6
Calvorio	6DNR6L	Multicorfors	JK6QRM
Colovaria	9GJ442	Redactum Skullus	UW8LRH
Engorgio Skullus	CD4JLX	Rictusempra	2UCA3M
Entomorphis	MYN3NB	Slugulus Eructo	U6EE8X
Flipendo	ND2L7W	Stupefy	UWDJ4Y
Glacius	ERA9DR	Tarantallegra	KWWQ44
Herbifors	H8FTHL	Trip Jinx	YZNRF6

EEYLOPS GOLD BRICKS

Once you have access to The Leaky Cauldron, enter Wiseacre's Wizarding Supplies from Diagon Alley. Go upstairs to enter the following. To access the LEGO Builder, visit Gringott's Bank at the end of Diagon Alley.

GOLD BRICK	CODE	GOLD BRICK	CODE
1	QE4VC7	7	XY6VYZ
2	FY8H97	8	TUNC4W
3	3MQT4P	9	EJ42Q6
4	PQPM7Z	10	GFJCV9
5	ZY2CPA	11	DZCY6G
6	3GMTP6		

CHARACTERS

Approach the blackboard in the Classsroom and enter the following codes.

CHARACTER	CODE	CHARACTER	CODE
Bandit	12N68W	Fedora	V75YSP
Bandit Swordsman	1MK4RT	First Mate	0GIN24
Barranca	04EM94	Grail Knight	NE6THI
Bazooka Trooper (Crusade)	MK83R7	Hovitos Tribesman	H0V1SS
Bazooka Trooper (Raiders)	S93Y5R	Indiana Jones (Desert Disguise)	4J8S4M
Belloq	CHN3YU	Indiana Jones (Officer)	VJ850S
Belloq (Jungle)	TDR197	Jungle Guide	24PF34
Belloq (Robes)	VE029L	Kao Kan	WM046L
British Commander	B73EUA	Kazim	NRH23J
British Officer	VJ5TI9	Kazim (Desert)	3M29TJ
British Soldier	DJ512W	Lao Che	2NK479
Captain Katanga	VJ3TT3	Maharajah	NFK5N2
Chatter Lal	ENW936	Major Toht	13NS01
Chatter Lal (Thuggee)	CNH4RY	Masked Bandit	N48SF0
Chen	3NK48T	Mola Ram	FJUR31
Colonel Dietrich	2K9RKS	Monkey Man	3RF6YJ
Colonel Vogel	8EAL4H	Pankot Assassin	2NKT72
Dancing Girl	C7EJ21	Pankot Guard	VN28RH
Donovan	3NFTU8	Sherpa Brawler	VJ37WJ
Elsa (Desert)	JSNRT9	Sherpa Gunner	ND762W
Elsa (Officer)	VMJ5US	Slave Child	OE3ENW
Enemy Boxer	8246RB	Thuggee	VM683E
Enemy Butler	VJ48W3	Thuggee Acolyte	T2R3F9
Enemy Guard	VJ7R51	Thuggee Slave Driver	VBS7GW
Enemy Guard (Mountains)	YR47WM	Village Dignitary	KD48TN
Enemy Officer	572E61	Village Elder	4682E1
Enemy Officer (Desert	2MK450	Willie (Dinner Suit)	VK93R7
Enemy Pilot	B84ELP	Willie (Pajamas)	MEN4IP
Enemy Radio Operator	1MF94R	Wu Han	3NSLT8
Enemy Soldier (Desert)	4NSU7Q		

EXTRAS

Approach the blackboard in the Classsroom and enter the following codes. Some cheats need to be enabled by selecting Extras from the pause menu.

CHEAT	CODE	CHEAT	CODE
Artifact Detector	VIKED7	Regenerate Hearts	MDLP69
Beep Beep	VNF59Q	Secret Characters	3X44AA
Character Treasure	VIES2R	Silhouettes	3HE85H
Disarm Enemies	VKRNS9	Super Scream	VN3R7S
Disguises	4ID1N6	Super Slap	OP1TA5
Fast Build	V83SL0	Treasure Magnet	H86LA2
Fast Dig	378RS6	Treasure x10	VI3PS8
Fast Fix	FJ59WS	Treasure x2	VM4TS9
Fertilizer	B1GW1F	Treasure x4	VLWEN3
Ice Rink	33GM7J	Treasure x6	V84RYS
Parcel Detector	VUT673	Treasure x8	A72E1M
Poo Treasure	WWQ1SA		

LEGO INDIANA JONES 2: THE ADVENTURE CONTINUES

Pause the game, select Enter Secret Code from the Extras menu, and enter the following.

CHARACTERS

CHARACTER	CODE	CHARACTER	CODE
Bellog (Priest)	FTL48S	Indiana Jones (Officer)	3FQFKS
Dovchenko	WL4T6N	Interdimensional Being	PXT4UP
Enemy Boxer	7EQF47	Lao Che	7AWX3J
Henry Jones	4CSAKH	Mannequin (Boy)	2UJQWC
Indiana Jones	PGWSEA	Mannequin (Girl)	3PGSEL
Indiana Jones: 2	FGLKYS	Mannequin (Man)	QPWDMM
Indiana Jones (Collect)	DZFY9S	Mannequin (Woman)	U7SMVK
Indiana Jones (Desert)	M4C34K	Mola Ram	82RMC2
Indiana Jones (Desert Disguise)	2W8QR3	Mutt	2GKS62
Indiana Jones (Dinner Suit)	QUNZUT	Salah	E88YRP
Indiana Jones (Kali)	J2XS97	Willie	94RUAJ

EXTRAS

EFFECT	CODE	EFFECT	CODE
Beep Beep	UU3VSC	Score x3	PEHHPZ
Disguise	Y9TE98	Score x4	UXGTB3
Fast Build	SNXC2F	Score X6	XWLJEY
Fast Dig	XYAN83	Score x8	S5UZCP
Fast Fix	3Z7PJX	Score x10	V7JYBU
Fearless	TUXNZF	Silhouettes	FQGPYH
Ice Rink	TY9P4U	Snake Whip	2U7YCV
Invincibility	6JBB65	Stud Magnet	EGSM5B
Poo Money	SZFAAE		

LEGO PIRATES OF THE CARIBBEAN: THE VIDEO GAME

CODES

Pause the game and select Extras. Choose Enter Code and enter the following codes:

EFFECT	PASSWORD	EFFECT	PASSWORD
Ammand the Corsair	EW8T6T	Jack Sparrow (Musical)	VDJSPW
Angelica (Disguised)	DLRR45	Jacoby	BWO656
Angry Cannibal	VGF32C	Jimmy Legs	13GLW5
Blackbeard	D3DWOD	King George	RKED43
Clanker	ZM37GT	Koehler	RT093G
Clubba	644THF	Mistress Ching	GDETDE
Davy Jones	4DJLKR	Phillip	WEVO40
Govorner Weatherby Swann	LD9454	Quartermaster	RX58HU
Gunner	Y611WB	The Spaniard	P861JO
Hungry Cannibal	64BNHG	Twigg	KDLFKD

The following still need to be purchase after entering the codes.

CHARACTERS

ADMIRAL ACKBAR

At the bar in Mos Eisley Cantina, select Enter Code and enter ACK646.

BATTLE DROID (COMMANDER)

At the bar in Mos Eisley Cantina, select Enter Code and enter KPF958.

BOBA FETT (BOY)

At the bar in Mos Eisley Cantina, select Enter Code and enter GGF539.

BOSS NASS

At the bar in Mos Eisley Cantina, select Enter Code and enter HHY697.

CAPTAIN TARPALS

At the bar in Mos Eisley Cantina, select Enter Code and enter QRN714.

COUNT DOOKU

At the bar in Mos Eisley Cantina, select Enter Code and enter DDD748.

DARTH MAUL

At the bar in Mos Eisley Cantina, select Enter Code and enter EUK421.

EWOK

At the bar in Mos Eisley Cantina, select Enter Code and enter EWK785.

GENERAL GRIEVOUS

At the bar in Mos Eisley Cantina, select Enter Code and enter PMN576.

GREEDO

At the bar in Mos Eisley Cantina, select Enter Code and enter ZZR636.

IG-88

At the bar in Mos Eisley Cantina, select Enter Code and enter GIJ989.

IMPERIAL GUARD

At the bar in Mos Eisley Cantina, select Enter Code and enter GUA850.

JANGO FETT

At the bar in Mos Eisley Cantina, select Enter Code and enter KLJ897.

KI-ADI MUNDI

At the bar in Mos Eisley Cantina, select Enter Code and enter MUN486.

LUMINARA

At the bar in Mos Eisley Cantina, select Enter Code and enter LUM521.

PADMÉ

At the bar in Mos Eisley Cantina, select Enter Code and enter VBJ322.

R2-Q5

At the bar in Mos Eisley Cantina, select Enter Code and enter EVILR2.

STORMTROOPER

At the bar in Mos Eisley Cantina, select Enter Code and enter NBN431.

TAUN WE

At the bar in Mos Eisley Cantina, select Enter Code and enter PRX482.

VULTURE DROID

At the bar in Mos Eisley Cantina, select Enter Code and enter BDC866.

WATTO

At the bar in Mos Eisley Cantina, select Enter Code and enter PLL967.

ZAM WESELL

At the bar in Mos Eisley Cantina, select Enter Code and enter 584HJF.

SKILLS

DISGUISE

At the bar in Mos Eisley Cantina, select Enter Code and enter BRJ437.

FORCE GRAPPLE LEAP

At the bar in Mos Eisley Cantina, select Enter Code and enter CLZ738.

VEHICLES

DROID TRIFIGHTER

At the bar in Mos Eisley Cantina, select Enter Code and enter AAB123.

IMPERIAL SHUTTLE

At the bar in Mos Eisley Cantina, select Enter Code and enter HUT845.

TIE INTERCEPTOR

At the bar in Mos Eisley Cantina, select Enter Code and enter INT729.

TIE FIGHTER

At the bar in Mos Eisley Cantina, select Enter Code and enter DBH897.

ZAM'S AIRSPEEDER

At the bar in Mos Eisley Cantina, select Enter Code and enter UUU875.

LEGO STAR WARS II: THE ORIGINAL TRILOGY

BEACH TROOPER

At Mos Eisley Canteena, select Enter Code and enter UCK868. You still need to select Characters and purchase this character for 20,000 studs.

BEN KENOBI (GHOST)

At Mos Eisley Canteena, select Enter Code and enter BEN917. You still need to select Characters and purchase this character for 1,100,000 studs.

BESPIN GUARD

At Mos Eisley Canteena, select Enter Code and enter VHY832. You still need to select Characters and purchase this character for 15,000 studs.

BIB FORTUNA

At Mos Eisley Canteena, select Enter Code and enter WTY721. You still need to select Characters and purchase this character for 16,000 studs.

BOBA FETT

At Mos Eisley Canteena, select Enter Code and enter HLP221. You still need to select Characters and purchase this character for 175,000 studs.

DEATH STAR TROOPER

At Mos Eisley Canteena, select Enter Code and enter BNC332. You still need to select Characters and purchase this character for 19,000 studs.

EWOK

At Mos Eisley Canteena, select Enter Code and enter TTT289. You still need to select Characters and purchase this character for 34,000 studs.

GAMORREAN GUARD

At Mos Eisley Canteena, select Enter Code and enter YZF999. You still need to select Characters and purchase this character for 40,000 studs.

GONK DROID

At Mos Eisley Canteena, select Enter Code and enter NFX582. You still need to select Characters and purchase this character for 1,550 studs.

GRAND MOFF TARKIN

At Mos Eisley Canteena, select Enter Code and enter SMG219. You still need to select Characters and purchase this character for 38,000 studs.

GREEDO

At Mos Eisley Canteena, select Enter Code and enter NAH118. You still need to select Characters and purchase this character for 60,000 studs.

HAN SOLO (HOOD)

At Mos Eisley Canteena, select Enter Code and enter YWM840. You still need to select Characters and purchase this character for 20,000 studs.

IG-88

At Mos Eisley Canteena, select Enter Code and enter NXL973. You still need to select Characters and purchase this character for 30,000 studs.

IMPERIAL GUARD

At Mos Eisley Canteena, select Enter Code and enter MMM111. You still need to select Characters and purchase this character for 45,000 studs.

IMPERIAL OFFICER

At Mos Eisley Canteena, select Enter Code and enter BBV889. You still need to select Characters and purchase this character for 28,000 studs.

IMPERIAL SHUTTLE PILOT

At Mos Eisley Canteena, select Enter Code and enter VAP664. You still need to select Characters and purchase this character for 29,000 studs.

IMPERIAL SPY

At Mos Eisley Canteena, select Enter Code and enter CVT125. You still need to select Characters and purchase this character for 13,500 studs.

JAWA

At Mos Eisley Canteena, select Enter Code and enter JAW499. You still need to select Characters and purchase this character for 24,000 studs.

LOBOT

At Mos Eisley Canteena, select Enter Code and enter UUB319. You still need to select Characters and purchase this character for 11,000 studs.

PALACE GUARD

At Mos Eisley Canteena, select Enter Code and enter SGE549. You still need to select Characters and purchase this character for 14,000 studs.

REBEL PILOT

At Mos Eisley Canteena, select Enter Code and enter CYG336. You still need to select Characters and purchase this character for 15,000 studs.

REBEL TROOPER (HOTH)

At Mos Eisley Canteena, select Enter Code and enter EKU849. You still need to select Characters and purchase this character for 16,000 studs.

SANDTROOPER

At Mos Eisley Canteena, select Enter Code and enter YDV451. You still need to select Characters and purchase this character for 14,000 studs.

SKIFF GUARD

At Mos Eisley Canteena, select Enter Code and enter GBU888. You still need to select Characters and purchase this character for 12,000 studs.

SNOWTROOPER

At Mos Eisley Canteena, select Enter Code and enter NYU989. You still need to select Characters and purchase this character for 16,000 studs.

STROMTROOPER

At Mos Eisley Canteena, select Enter Code and enter PTR345. You still need to select Characters and purchase this character for 10,000 studs.

THE EMPEROR

At Mos Eisley Canteena, select Enter Code and enter HHY382. You still need to select Characters and purchase this character for 275,000 studs.

TIE FIGHTER

At Mos Eisley Canteena, select Enter Code and enter HDY739. You still need to select Characters and purchase this character for 60,000 studs.

TIE FIGHTER PILOT

At Mos Eisley Canteena, select Enter Code and enter NNZ316. You still need to select Characters and purchase this character for 21,000 studs.

TIE INTERCEPTOR

At Mos Eisley Canteena, select Enter Code and enter QYA828. You still need to select Characters and purchase this character for 40,000 studs.

TUSKEN RAIDER

At Mos Eisley Canteena, select Enter Code and enter PEJ821. You still need to select Characters and purchase this character for 23,000 studs.

UGNAUGHT

At Mos Eisley Canteena, select Enter Code and enter UGN694. You still need to select Characters and purchase this character for 36,000 studs.

TM

LEGO STAR WARS III: THE CLONE WARS

Pause the game, select Enter Code from Extras and enter the following:

CHARACTERS

CHARACTER	CODE	CHARACTER	CODE
Aayla Secura	2VG95B	Heavy Weapons Clone Trooper	WXUTWY
Adi Gallia	G2BFEN	HELIOS 3D	4AXTY4
Admiral Ackbar (Classic)	272Y9Q	Hevy	EUB8UG
Admiral Yularen	NG6PYX	Hondo Ohnaka	5A7XYX
Ahsoka	2VJ9TH	IG-86	EABPCP
Anakin Skywalker	F9VUYJ	Imperial Guard (Classic)	5W6FGD
Anakin Skywalker (Geonosian Arena)	9AA4DW	Jango Fett	5KZQ4D
Asajj Ventress	YG9DD7	Jar Jar Binks	MESPTS
Aurra Sing	M2V1JV	Jek	AYREC9
Bail Organa	GEHX6C	Ki-Adi-Mundi	HGBCTQ
Barriss Offee	BTVTZ5	Kit Fitso	PYWJ6N
Battle Droid	5Y7MA4	Lando Calrissian (Classic)	ERAEWE
Battle Droid Commander	LSU4LJ	LEP Servent Droid	SM3Y9B
Bib Fortuna	9U4TF3	Lieutenant Thire	3NEUXC
Boba Fett (Classic)	TY2BYJ	Lok Durd	TKCYUZ
Boil	Q5Q39P	Luke Skywalker (Classic)	PG73HF
Bossk	2KLW5R	Luminara Unduli	MKUYQ8
C-3PO	574226	Lurmen Villager	R35Y7N
Cad Bane	NHME85	Luxury Droid	V4WMJN
Captain Antilles (Classic)	D8SNGJ	Mace Windu	8NVRWJ
Captain Rex	MW3QYH	MagnaGuard	2KEF2D
Captain Typho	GD6FX3	MSE-6	S6GRNZ
Chancellor Palpatine	5C62YQ	Nahdar Vebb	ZKXG43
Chewbacca (Classic)	66UU3T	Neimoidian	BJB94J
Clone Pilot	HQ7BVD	Nute Gunray	QFYXMC
Clone Shadow Trooper (Classic)	7GFNCQ	Obi-Wan Kenobi	J9HNF9
Clone Trooper	NP5GTT	Obi-Wan Kenobi (Classic)	FFBU5M
Commander Bly	7CB6NS	Obi-Wan Kenobi (Geonosian Arena)	5U9FJK
Commander Cody	SMN259	OG-9 Homing Spider Droid	7NEC36
Commander Fil	U25HFC	Onaconda Farr	DB7ZQN
Commander Ponds	JRPR2A	Padmé Amidala (Geonosian Arena)	SZ824Q
Commander Stone	5XZQSV	Padmé Amidala	8X87U6
Commando Droid	QEGU64	Pirate Ruffian	BH2EHU
Count Dooku	EWR7WM	Plo Koon	BUD4VU
Darth Maul (Classic)	QH68AK	Poggle The Lesser	4592WM
Darth Sidious (Classic)	QXY5XN	Princess Leia (Classic)	2D3D3L
Darth Vader (Classic)	FM4JB7	Probe Droid	U2T4SP
Darth Vader Battle Damaged (Classic)	NMJFBL	Queen Neeyutnee	ZQRN85
Destroyer Droid	9MUTS2	Qui-Gon Jinn (Classic)	LKHD3B
Dr. Nuvo Vindi	MB9EMW	R2-D2	RZ5HUV
Echo	JB9E5S	R3-S6	Z87PAU
Eeth Koth	WUFDYA	R4-P17	5MXSYA
Gammorean Guard	WSFZZQ	R6-H5	7PMC3C
General Grievous	7FNU4T	Rebel Commando (Classic)	PZMQNK
Geonosian Guard	GAFZUD	Robonino	2KLW5R
Gold Super Battle Droid	2C8NHP	Rys	4PTP53
Gonk Droid	C686PK	Savage Oppress	MELL07
Grand Moff Tarkin	NH2405	Senate Commando	EPBPLK
Greedo (Classic)	FUW4C2	Senate Commando (Captain)	S4Y7VW
Hailfire Droid	T7XF9Z	Senator Kharrus	EA4E9S
Han Solo (Classic)	KFDBXF	Senator Philo	9Q7YCT
Heavy Super Battle Droid	G65KJJ	Shahan Alama	G4N7C2

CHARACTER	CODE
Sionver Boll	5C62YQ
Stormtrooper (Classic)	HPE7PZ
Super Battle Droid	MJKDV5
Tee Watt Kaa	FYVSHD
Turk Falso	HEBHW5
Tusken Raider (Classic)	GC2XSA
TX-20	PE7FGD
Undead Geonosian	QGENFD

CHARACTER	CODE
Vader's Apprentice (Classic)	EGQQ4V
Waq Too	VRUVSZ
Wat Tambor	ZP8XVH
Waxer	BNJE79
Wedge Antilles (Classic)	DRGLWS
Whorm Loathsom	4VVYQV
Workout Clone Trooper	MP9DRE
Yoda	CSQTMB

VEHICLES

VEHICLE	CODE
Dwarf Spider Droid	NACMGG
Geonosian Solar Sailor	PJ2U3R
Geonosian Starfighter	EDENEC

VEHICLE	CODE
Slave I	KDDQVD
The Twilight	T4K5L4
Vulture Droid	7W7K7S

RED BRICKS

CHEAT	CODE
Character Studs	QD2C31
Dark Side	X1V4N2
Dual Wield	C4ES4R
Fast Build	GCHP7S
Glow in the Dark	4GT3VQ
Invincibility	J46P7A
Minikit Detector	CSD5NA
Perfect Deflect	3F5L56
Regenerate Hearts	2D7JNS

CHEAT	CODE
Score x2	YZPHUV
Score x4	43T5E5
Score x6	SEBHGR
Score x8	BYFSAQ
Score x10	N1CKR1
Stud Magnet	6MZ5CH
Super Saber Cut	BS828K
Super Speeders	B1D3W3

LOONEY TUNES: ACME ARSENAL

UNLMITED AMMO

At the cheat menu, press Down, Left, Up, Right, Down, Left, Up, Right, Down.

LUCHA LIBRE AAA HEROES DEL RING

LITTLE ONES

At the character select, press Up, Up, Down, Down, Left, Right, Left, Right. Play with them to unlock the Little Ones Can Too Achievement.

MADDEN NFL 12

MADDEN NFL 12 DEVELOPERS TEAM IN EXHIBITION

Select Exhibition from Play Now. At the team select, press the Random Team button, Left Trigger, until the Developers team shows up. Once you have entered a game as the team, they will always be on the list.

MARVEL ULTIMATE ALLIANCE

UNLOCK ALL SKINS
At the Team menu, press Up, Down, Left, Right, Left, Right, Start.

UNLOCKS ALL HERO POWERS
At the Team menu, press Left, Right, Up, Down, Up, Down, Start.

ALL HEROES TO LEVEL 99
At the Team menu, press Up, Left, Up, Left, Down, Right, Down, Right, Start.

UNLOCK ALL HEROES
At the Team menu, press Up, Up, Down, Down, Left, Left, Left, Start.

UNLOCK DAREDEVIL
At the Team menu, press Left, Left, Right, Right, Up, Down, Up, Down, Start.

UNLOCK SILVER SURFER
At the Team menu, press Down, Left, Left, Up, Right, Up, Down, Left, Start.

GOD MODE
During gameplay, press Up, Down, Up, Down, Up, Left, Down, Right, Start.

TOUCH OF DEATH
During gameplay, press Left, Right, Down, Down, Right, Left, Start.

SUPER SPEED
During gameplay, press Up, Left, Up, Right, Down, Right, Start.

FILL MOMENTUM
During gameplay, press Left, Right, Right, Left, Up, Down, Down, Up, Start.

UNLOCK ALL COMICS
At the Review menu, press Left, Right, Right, Left, Up, Up, Right, Start.

UNLOCK ALL CONCEPT ART
At the Review menu, press Down, Down, Down, Right, Right, Left, Down, Start.

UNLOCK ALL CINEMATICS
At the Review menu, press Up, Left, Left, Up, Right, Right, Up, Start.

UNLOCK ALL LOAD SCREENS
At the Review menu, press Up, Down, Right, Left, Up, Up Down, Start.

UNLOCK ALL COURSES
At the Comic Missions menu, press Up, Right, Left, Down, Up, Right, Left, Down, Start.

MARVEL ULTIMATE ALLIANCE 2

These codes will disable the ability to save.

GOD MODE
During a game, press Up, Down, Up, Down, Up, Left, Down, Right, Start.

UNLIMITED FUSION
During a game, press Right, Right, Up, Down, Up, Up, Left, Start.

UNLOCK ALL POWERS
During a game, press Left, Right, Up, Down, Up, Down, Start.

UNLOCK ALL HEROES
During a game, press Up, Up, Down, Down, Left, Left, Left, Start.

UNLOCK ALL SKINS
During a game, press Up, Down, Left, Right, Left, Right, Start.

UNLOCK JEAN GREY
During a game, press Left, Left, Right, Right, Up, Down, Up, Down, Start.

UNLOCK HULK
During a game, press Down, Left, Left, Up, Right, Up, Down, Left, Start.

UNLOCK THOR
During a game, press Up, Right, Right, Down, Right, Down, Left, Right, Start.

UNLOCK ALL AUDIO LOGS
At the main menu, press Left, Right, Right, Left, Up, Up, Right, Start.

UNLOCK ALL DOSSIERS
At the main menu, press Down, Down, Down, Right, Right, Left, Down, Start.

UNLOCK ALL MOVIES
At the main menu, press Up, Left, Left, Up, Right, Right, Up, Start.

MX VS. ATV REFLEX

MX VEHICLES FOR PURCHASE
Select Enter Cheat Code from the Options and enter brapbrap.

JUSTIN BRAYTON, KTM MX BIKES AND ATVS IN ARCADE MODE
Select Enter Cheat Code from the Options and enter readytorace.

ALL EVENT LOCATIONS IN ARCADE MODE
Select Enter Cheat Code from the Options and enter whereto.

ALL AI OPPONENTS
Select Enter Cheat Code from the Options and enter allai.

ATV VEHICLES FOR PURCHASE
Select Enter Cheat Code from the Options and enter couches.

ALL AVAILABLE RIDER GEAR
Select Enter Cheat Code from the Options and enter gearedup.

ALL AVAILABLE HELMETS
Select Enter Cheat Code from the Options and enter skullcap.

ALL AVAILABLE BOOTS
Select Enter Cheat Code from the Options and enter kicks.

ALL AVAILABLE GOGGLES
Select Enter Cheat Code from the Options and enter windows.

MX VS. ATV UNTAMED

ALL RIDING GEAR
Select Cheat Codes from the Options and enter crazylikea.

ALL HANDLEBARS
Select Cheat Codes from the Options and enter nohands.

27 GRAPHICS
Select Cheat Codes from the Options and enter STICKE🅰.

NARUTO: THE BROKEN BOND

NEW SASUKE
At The Character Select press Up, Down, ❎, ❎, ❎, ❎, 🅨, 🅑.

NINE TAILS NARUTO
At the Character Select press ❎, ❎, ❎, 🅨, ❎, 🅨, ❎, 🅨, ❎, ❎.

UCHIHA MADARA
At the Character Select press ❎, ❎, ❎, 🅨, ❎, 🅑, 🅑, 🅐, 🅐, 🅨.

NASCAR 09

ALL FANTASY DRIVERS
Select EA Extras from My Nascar, choose Cheat Codes and enter CHECKERED FLAG.

WALMART TRACK AND THE WALMART CAR
Select EA Extras from My Nascar, choose Cheat Codes and enter Walmart Everyday.

NASCAR THE GAME 2011

MARK MARTIN PAINT SCHEMES
At the garage main menu, press Down, Down, Up, Up, Right, Left, Right, Left. Enter godaddy.com.

KYLE BUSH NOS ENERGY DRINK CAR
At the garage main menu, press Down, Down, Up, Up, Right, Left, Right, Left. Enter drinknos.

NBA 2K10

ABA BALL
Select Codes from Options and enter payrespect.

2K CHINA TEAM
Select Codes from Options and enter 2kchina.

NBA 2K TEAM
Select Codes from Options and enter nba2k.

2K SPORTS TEAM
Select Codes from Options and enter 2ksports.

VISUAL CONCEPTS TEAM
Select Codes from Options and enter vcteam.

CAVFANATICS JERSEY FOR THE CAVALIERS
Select Codes from the Options menu and enter aifnaatccv.

HARDWOOD CLASSIC JERSEYS
Select Codes from the Options menu and enter wasshcicsl. This code gives Hardwood Classic Jerseys for the Cavaliers, Jazz, Magic, Raptors, timberwolves, Trail Blazers, and Warriors.

LATIN NIGHTS JERSEYS
Select Codes from the Options menu and enter aihinntslgt. This code gives Latin Nights jerseys for Bulls, Heat, Knicks, Lakers, Mavericks, Rockets, Spurs, and Suns.

NBA ALL-STAR JERSEYS
Select Codes from the Options menu and enter otnresla.

NBA GREEN JERSEYS
Select Codes from the Options menu and enter nreogge. This code gives green uniforms for the Bobcats, Bulls, and Nuggets.

MARDI GRAS JERSEY FOR THE HORNETS
Select Codes from the Options menu and enter asrdirmga.

RACING JERSEY FOR THE BOBCATS
Select Codes from the Options menu and enter agsntrccai.

RIP CITY JERSEY FOR THE BLAZERS
Select Codes from the Options menu and enter ycprtii.

SECOND ROAD JERSEYS
Select Codes from the Options menu and enter eydonscar. This code gives Second Road Jerseys for the Grizzlies, Hawks, Mavericks, and Rockets.

ST. PATRICK'S DAY JERSEYS
Select Codes from the Options menu and enter riiasgerh. This code gives St. Patrick's Day jerseys for the Bulls, Celtics, Knicks, and Raptors.

NBA 2K11

MJ: CREATING A LEGEND
In Features, select Codes from the Extras menu. Choose Enter Code and enter icanbe23.

2K CHINA TEAM
In Features, select Codes from the Extras menu. Choose Enter Code and enter 2kchina.

2K SPORTS TEAM
In Features, select Codes from the Extras menu. Choose Enter Code and enter 2Ksports.

NBA 2K TEAM
In Features, select Codes from the Extras menu. Choose Enter Code and enter nba2k.

VC TEAM

In Features, select Codes from the Extras menu. Choose Enter Code and enter vcteam.

ABA BALL

In Features, select Codes from the Extras menu. Choose Enter Code and enter payrespect.

2011 ALL-STAR UNIFORMS

In Features, select Codes from the Extras menu. Choose Enter Code and enter wydololoh.

SECONDARY ROAD UNIFORM

In Features, select Codes from the Extras menu. Choose Enter Code and enter ronoilnm. This unlocks the secondary road uniform for the Hornets, Magic, and Timberwolves.

ORANGE SPLIT DUNK

In Features, select Codes from the Extras menu. Choose Enter Code and enter SPRITEDUNK1. Go to Sprite Slam Dunk Showdown and use the help menu to find out more.

SPIN TOMMY DUNK

In Features, select Codes from the Extras menu. Choose Enter Code and enter SPRITEDUNK2. Go to Sprite Slam Dunk Showdown and use the help menu to find out more.

THE VILLAIN DUNK

In Features, select Codes from the Extras menu. Choose Enter Code and enter SPRITEDUNK3. Go to Sprite Slam Dunk Showdown and use the help menu to find out more.

NBA 2K12

ABA BALL

Select Extras from the Features menu. Choose Codes and enter payrespect. This can be toggled on and off from this Codes menu.

2K CHINA TEAM

Select Extras from the Features menu. Choose Codes and enter 2kchina.

2K SPORTS TEAM

Select Extras from the Features menu. Choose Codes and enter 2ksports.

UNLOCK NBA 2K TEAM

Select Extras from the Features menu. Choose Codes and enter nba2k.

VC TEAM

Select Extras from the Features menu. Choose Codes and enter vcteam.

JORDAN RETRO COLLECTION

Select Extras from the Features menu. Choose Codes and enter 23.

NBA JAM

BEASTIE BOYS

At the title screen, press Up, Up, Down, Down, Left, Right, Left, Right, **B**, **A**. This team includes Ad Rock, MCA, and Mike D.

J. COLE AND 9TH WONDER

At the title screen, press Up, Left, Down, Right, Up, Left, Down, Right, Circle, **A**.

DEMOCRATS TEAM

At the title screen, press Left (x13), **A**. This team includes Barack Obama, Joe Biden, Bill Clinton, and Hillary Clinton.

REPUBLICANS TEAM

At the title screen, press Right (x13), **A**. The team includes George W. Bush, Sarah Palin, Dick Cheney, and John McCain.

ESPN'S SPORTSNATION

Select Play Now. When entering the initials, enter ESP for P1 and NSN for P2. Advance to the Choose Teams screen to find the team. This team includes the hosts of the show; Colin Cowherd and Michelle Beadle.

NBA MASCOTS

Select Play Now. When entering the initials, enter MAS for P1 and COT for P2.

ORIGINAL GENERATION JAM

Select Play Now. When entering the initials, enter MJT for P1. Advance to the Choose Teams screen to find the team. This team includes Mark Turmell and Tim Kitzrow.

NBA LIVE 09

SUPER DUNKS MODE

Use the Sprite vending machine in the practice area and enter spriteslam.

NBA LIVE 10

CHARLOTTE BOBCATS' 2009/2010 RACE DAY ALTERNATE JERSEYS

Select Options from My NBA Live and go to Select Codes. Enter ceobdabacarstcy.

NEW ORLEANS HORNETS' 2009/2010 MARDI GRAS ALTERNATE JERSEYS

Select Options from My NBA Live and go to Select Codes. Enter nishrag1rosmad0.

ALTERNATE JERSEYS

Select Options from My NBA Live and go to Select Codes. Enter ndnba1rooaesdc0. This unlocks alternate jerseys for Atlanta Hawks, Dallas Mavericks, Houston Rockets, and Memphis Grizzlies.

MORE HARDWOOD CLASSICS NIGHTS JERSEYS

Select Options from My NBA Live and go to Select Codes. Enter hdogdrawhoticns. This unlocks Hardwood Classics Nights jerseys for Cleveland Cavaliers, Golden State Warriors, Minnesota Timberwolves, Orlando Magic, Philadelphia 76ers.

ADIDAS EQUATIONS

Select Options from My NBA Live and go to Select Codes. Enter adaodqavieints1.

ADIDAS TS CREATORS WITH ANKLE BRACES

Select Options from My NBA Live and go to Select Codes. Enter atciadsstsdhecf.

ADIDAS TS SUPERNATURAL COMMANDERS

Select Options from My NBA Live and go to Select Codes. Enter andsicdsmatdnsr.

ADIDAS TS SUPERNATURAL CREATORS

Select Options from My NBA Live and go to Select Codes. Enter ard8siscdnatstr.

AIR MAX LEBRON VII

Select Options from My NBA Live and go to Select Codes. Enter ere1nbvlaoeknii, 2ovnaebnkrielei, 3rioabeneikenvl, ri4boenanekilve, ivl5brieekaeonn, or n6ieirvalkeeobn.

KOBE V

Select Options from My NBA Live and go to Select Codes. Enter ovze1bimenkoko0, m0kveokoiebozn2, eev0nbimokk3ozo, or bmo4inozeeo0kvk.

JORDAN CP3 IIIS

Select Options from My NBA Live and go to Select Codes. Enter iaporcdian3ejis.

JORDAN MELO M6S

Select Options from My NBA Live and go to Select Codes. Enter emlarmeoo6ajdsn.

JORDAN SIXTY PLUSES

Select Options from My NBA Live and go to Select Codes. Enter aondsuilyjrspxt.

NIKE HUARACHE LEGIONS

Select Options from My NBA Live and go to Select Codes. Enter aoieuchrahelgn.

NIKE KD 2S

Select Options from My NBA Live and go to Select Codes. Enter kk2tesaosepinrd.

NIKE ZOOM FLIP'NS

Select Options from My NBA Live and go to Select Codes. Enter epfnozaeminolki.

NEED FOR SPEED PROSTREET

$2,000
Select Career and then choose Code Entry. Enter 1MA9X99.

$4,000
Select Career and then choose Code Entry. Enter W2IOLL01.

$8,000
Select Career and then choose Code Entry. Enter L1IS97A1.

$10,000
Select Career and then choose Code Entry. Enter 1MI9K7E1.

$10,000
Select Career and then choose Code Entry. Enter CASHMONEY.

$10,000
Select Career and then choose Code Entry. Enter REGGAME.

AUDI TT
Select Career and then choose Code Entry. Enter ITSABOUTYOU.

CHEVELLE SS
Select Career and then choose Code Entry. Enter HORSEPOWER.

COKE ZERO GOLF GTI
Select Career and then choose Code Entry. Enter COKEZERO.

DODGE VIPER
Select Career and then choose Code Entry. Enter WORLDSLONGESTLASTING.

MITSUBISHI LANCER EVOLUTION
Select Career and then choose Code Entry. Enter MITSUBISHIGOFAR.

UNLOCK ALL BONUSES
Select Career and then choose Code Entry. Enter UNLOCKALLTHINGS.

5 REPAIR MARKERS
Select Career and then choose Code Entry. Enter SAFETYNET.

ENERGIZER VINYL
Select Career and then choose Code Entry. Enter ENERGIZERLITHIUM.

CASTROL SYNTEC VINYL
Select Career and then choose Code Entry. Enter CASTROLSYNTEC. This also gives you $10,000.

TM

NEED FOR SPEED UNDERCOVER

$10,000
Select Secret Codes from the Options menu and enter $EDSOC.

DIE-CAST BMW M3 E92
Select Secret Codes from the Options menu and enter)B7@B=.

DIE-CAST LEXUS IS F
Select Secret Codes from the Options menu and enter 0;5M2;.

NEEDFORSPEED.COM LOTUS ELISE
Select Secret Codes from the Options menu and enter -KJ3=E.

DIE-CAST NISSAN 240SX (S13)
Select Secret Codes from the Options menu and enter ?P:COL.

DIE-CAST PORSCHE 911 TURBO
Select Secret Codes from the Options menu and enter >8P:I;.

SHELBY TERLINGUA
Select Secret Codes from the Options menu and enter NeedForSpeedShelbyTerlingua.

DIE-CAST VOLKWAGEN R32
Select Secret Codes from the Options menu and enter!2ODBJ:.

NHL 10

THIRD JERSEYS
At the EA Extras screen, enter rwyhafwh6ekyjcmr

NHL 2K8

2007-2008 NHL REEBOK EDGE JERSEYS
From the Features menu, select Unlock 2007-2008/Enter Password. Enter S6j83RMk01.

NHL 2K9

3RD JERSEYS
From the Features menu, enter R6y34bsH52 as a code.

NHL 2K10

THIRD JERSEYS
Select Cheats from the Extras menu and enter G8r23Bty56.

VISUAL CONCEPTS TEAM
Select Cheats from the Extras menu and enter vcteam.

NPPL CHAMPIONSHIP PAINTBALL 2009

TIPPMANN X-7 AK-47 SCENARIO PAINTBALL MARKER
Select Field Gear and press Up, Up, Right, Right, Down, Down, Left, Left.

ORCS MUST DIE!

AVATAR AWARDS

AVATAR	EARNED BY
OMD Logo Tee	Complete Act 1 of Orcs Must Die!
OMD Skull Hat	Kill 1,000 enemies in Orcs Must Dies!

PINBALL FX 2

AVATAR AWARDS

AWARD	EARNED BY
Pinball FX 2 T-Shirt	Achieve 5,000 Wizard Score.
Pinball Sorceress Dress (Female)	Achieve 100,000 Wizard Score.
Pinball Wizard Robe (Male)	Achieve 100,000 Wizard Score.

PLANTS VS. ZOMBIES

During a game, press ⬛, ⬛, ⬛, ⬛. Now you can enter the following codes. You must be given a code before it can be used.

MUSTACHES FOR ZOMBIE
Enter mustache.

SHADES FOR ZOMBIES
Enter future.

ZOMBIES DANCE
Enter dance.

CANDY WHEN ZOMBIE DIES
Enter piñata.

DEAD ZOMBIES LEAVE DAISIES
Enter daisies.

ALTERNATE LAWN MOWER
Enter trickedout.

PORTAL 2

AVATAR AWARDS

AWARD	EARNED BY
Companion Cube	Complete Portal 2 Single Player.
Love Shirt	Hug 3 friends in Portal 2 Coop.
Portal 2 Hat	Survive the manual override.
Portal 2 Shirt	Complete Portal 2 Coop
Turret Shirt	Complete Test Chamber 10 in less than 70 seconds.

PRINCE OF PERSIA

SANDS OF TIME PRINCE/FARAH SKINS
Select Skin Manager from the Extras menu. Press ❤ and enter 52585854. This gives you the Sands of Time skin for the Prince and Farah from Sands of Time for the Princess. Access them from the Skin Manager

PRINCE ALTAIR IBN LA-AHAD SKIN
At the main menu, press ❤ for Exclusive Content. Create an Ubisoft account. Then select "Altair Skin for Prince" to unlock.

RESONANCE OF FATE

Once you have reached Chapter 7, search Leanne's closet. As she speaks her first line enter the following codes to unlock more outfits.

8-BIT GIRL SHIRT

Up, Up, Down, Down, Left, Right, Left, Right, Y, ❌

CLUB FAMITSU SHIRT

Y, Y, Up, Up, ❌, ❌, Left, Left, 🎮, 🎮

GEMAGA SHIRT

Right Trigger, Left Trigger, 🎮, 🎮, ❤,
❤, ❤, ❌, ❌, Up

HIRAKOU SHIRT

❌, ❤, 🎮, 🎮, 🎮, 🎮, Click Left
Thumbstick, Click Left Thumbstick, Up, Down

PLATFORM LOGO SHIRT

Left, Up, Right, Down, 🎮, 🎮, 🎮, 🎮,
❤, Click Left Thumbstick

POLITAN SUIT

Click Right Thumbstick (x3), Right, Left, ❤,
❌, Left Trigger, Right Trigger, 🎮. This
requires you to have the Reindeer Suit first.

ROCK BAND 3

GUILD X-79 GUITAR

At the main menu, press Blue, Orange, Orange, Blue, Orange, Orange, Blue, Blue.

OVATION D-2010 GUITAR

At the main menu, press Orange, Blue, Orange, Orange, Blue, Blue, Orange, Blue.

STOP! GUITAR

At the main menu, press Orange, Orange, Blue, Blue, Orange, Blue, Blue, Orange.

ROCKET KNIGHT

ALL CHARACTER SKINS

At the title screen, press Up, Up, Down, Down, Left, Right, Left, Right, Ⓐ, Ⓑ, Start.

SAMURAI SHODOWN 2

PLAY AS KUROKO IN 2-PLAYER

At the character select, press Up, Down, Left, Up, Down, Right + ❌.

SCOTT PILGRIM VS. THE WORLD: THE GAME

PLAY AS SAME CHARACTER

At the title screen, press Down, 🎮, Up, 🎮, ❤, Ⓑ.

HEART SWORD

At the title screen, press ❌, ❌, ❌, Ⓐ, Ⓑ, Ⓐ, ❤, ❤.

BLOOD MODE

At the title screen, press Ⓐ, Ⓑ, Ⓐ, ❌, Ⓐ, Ⓑ, Ⓑ.

BOSS RUSH MODE

Pause the game on the overworld and press Right, Right, Ⓑ, 🎮, Right, Right, Ⓑ, 🎮.

ZOMBIE MODE

At the title screen, press Down, Up, Right, Down, Up, Right, Down, Up, Right, Right, Right.

SOUND CHECK BONUS LEVEL

Pause the game on the overworld and press **LB**, **LB**, **LB**, **RB**, **RB**, **RB**, **LB**, **RB**.

CHANGE MONEY TO ANIMALS

At the title screen, press Up, Up, Down, Down, Up, Up, Up, Up.

SEGA BASS FISHING

AVATAR AWARDS

AVATAR	EARNED BY
Sega Bass Fishing Tee	Play the game for 5 hours.
Sega Bass Fishing Rod	Play the game for 10 hours.

SEGA SUPERSTARS TENNIS

UNLOCK CHARACTERS

Complete the following missions to unlock the corresponding character.

CHARACTER	MISSION TO COMPLETE
Alex Kidd	Mission 1 of Alex Kidd's World
Amy Rose	Mission 2 of Sonic the Hedgehog's World
Gilius	Mission 1 of Golden Axe's World
Gum	Mission 12 of Jet Grind Radio's World
Meemee	Mission 8 of Super Monkey Ball's World
Pudding	Mission 1 of Space Channel 5's World
Reala	Mission 2 of NiGHTs' World
Shadow The Hedgehog	Mission 14 of Sonic the Hedgehog's World

THE SIMPSONS GAME

After unlocking the following, the outfits can be changed at the downstairs closet in the Simpson's house. The Trophies can be viewed at different locations in the house: Bart's room, Lisa's room, Marge's room, and the garage.

BART'S OUTFITS AND TROPHIES (POSTER COLLECTION)

At the main menu, press Right, Left, ❌, ❌, ❌, Right Thumb Stick.

HOMER'S OUTFITS AND TROPHIES (BEER BOTTLE COLLECTION)

At the main menu, press Left, Right, ❌, ❌, ❌, Left Thumb Stick.

LISA'S OUTFITS AND TROPHIES (DOLLS)

At the main menu, press ❌, ❌, ❌, ❌, ❌, Left Thumb Stick.

MARGE'S OUTFITS AND TROPHIES (HAIR PRODUCTS)

At the main menu, press ❌, ❌, ❌, ❌, ❌, Right Thumb Stick.

THE SIMS 3

CHEATS

Load your family, press Start, and hold ⓛ + Left Trigger + ⓡ + Right Trigger. The game prompts you to save another file before activating the cheats. Spoot the Llama is now available in Misc Décor. Place it in your lot and click it to access the cheats. This disables Achievements and challenges.

THE SIMS 3: PETS

CREATION MODE

Pause the game and press Left Trigger + Left Bumper + Right Trigger + Right Bumper. This disables achievements.

SKATE 2

BIG BLACK

Select Enter Cheat from the Extras menu and enter letsdowork.

3D MODE

Select Enter Cheat from the Extras menu and enter strangeloops. Use glasses to view in 3D.

SKATE 3

HOVERBOARD MODE

In Free Play, select Extras from the Options. Choose Enter Cheat Code and enter mcfly.

MINI SKATER MODE

In Free Play, select Extras from the Options. Choose Enter Cheat Code and enter miniskaters.

ZOMBIE MODE

In Free Play, select Extras from the Options. Choose Enter Cheat Code and enter zombie.

ISAAC CLARK FROM DEADSPACE

In Free Play, select Extras from the Options. Choose Enter Cheat Code and enter deadspacetoo.

DEM BONES

Beat most of the Hall of Meat Challenges.

MEAT MAN

Beat all Hall of Meat Challenges.

RESETS OBJECTS TO ORIGINAL POSITIONS

In Free Play, select Extras from the Options. Choose Enter Cheat Code and enter streetsweeper.

SONIC FREE RIDERS

AVATAR AWARDS

AWARD	EARNED BY
Sonic Free Riders Shirt	Watch the credits in their entirety.
E-10000 G Shirt	Place 1st on every course with E-10000 G.
Jet Shirt	Place 1st on every course with Jet.
Sonic Shirt	Place 1st on every course with Sonic.

CHAOS EMERALD BOARD

Get S-rank on all Story Missions.

PROFESSIONAL BOARD

Complete all Trial Missions.

SONIC THE HEDGEHOG 4: EPISODE I

AVATAR AWARDS

AWARD	EARNED BY
Sonic Costume (Body)	After collecting the 7 Chaos Emeralds, defeat the final boss 1 more time
Sonic Costume (Head)	Collect all rings during ending after the final stage.

SOULCASTER

PASSWORD

Select Continue and enter JUSTIN BAILEY ------ ------ as a password. This starts you midway through the game, on hard difficulty, with plenty of money. This password is a reference to a password from Metroid.

SPACE CHANNEL 5 PART 2

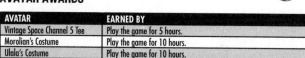

AVATAR AWARDS

AVATAR	EARNED BY
Vintage Space Channel 5 Tee	Play the game for 5 hours.
Morolian's Costume	Play the game for 10 hours.
Ulala's Costume	Play the game for 10 hours.

LET CPU TAKE OVER

Pause the game, hold Left Bumper + Right Bumper and press B, B, Up, Left, A, Left, A, Left, A. The CPU takes over, but achievements are disabled.

SPIDER-MAN: EDGE OF TIME

SHATTERED DIMENSIONS BONUS SUITS

If you have a saved game data for Spider-Man: Shattered Dimensions on your system, eight new Alternate Suits become available in the Bonus Gallery.

AMAZING SPIDER-MAN #500 SUIT (AMAZING)

Select Enter Code from VIP Unlock Code and enter laststand. Go to the Bonus Gallery to access the alternate suits.

POISON SUIT (2099)

Select Enter Code from VIP Unlock Code and enter innerspider. Go to the Bonus Gallery to access the alternate suits.

135

BIG TIME SUIT (2099)

At the main menu, press Right, Down, Down, Up, Left, Down, Down, Right.

FUTURE FOUNDATION SUIT (AMAZING)

At the main menu, press Up, Down, Left, Up, Down, Left, Right, Left.

SPIDER-MAN: SHATTERED DIMENSIONS

The following can be entered after completing the tutorial.

IRON SPIDER SUIT

At the main menu, press Up, Right, Right, Right, Left, Left, Left, Down, Up.

NEGATIVE ZONE SUIT

At the main menu, press Left, Right, Right, Down, Right, Down, Up, Left.

SCARLET SPIDER SUIT

At the main menu, press Right, Up, Left, Right, Up, Left, Right, Up, Left, Right.

SPLIT/SECOND

HANZO FX350 CX (COMPUTER SPIELE) IN QUICK PLAY

At the Options menu, press ✗, Up, ✗, Up, ✗, Up.

RYBACK COYOTE AMX IN QUICK PLAY

At the Options menu, press Left, ✗, Left, ✗, Left, ✗, Left, ✗, Left, ✗, Left, ✗, Right.

RYBACK MOHAWK XDX (DISNEY XD) IN QUICK PLAY

At the Options menu, press ✗, Down, ✗, Down, ✗, Down.

STAR WARS THE CLONE WARS: REPUBLIC HEROES

BIG HEAD MODE

Pause the game, select Shop, and enter Up, Down, Left, Right, Left, Right, Down, Up in Cheats.

MINI-GUN

Pause the game, select Shop, and enter Down, Left, Right, Up, Right, Up, Left, Down in Cheats.

ULTIMATE LIGHTSABER

Pause the game, select Shop, and enter Right, Down, Down, Up, Left, Up, Up, Down in Cheats.

LIGHTSABER THROW UPGRADE

Pause the game, select Shop, and enter Left, Left, Right, Right, Up, Down, Down, Up in Combat Upgrades.

SPIDER DROID UPGRADE

Pause the game, select Shop, and enter Up, Left, Down, Left, Right, Left, Left, Left in Droid-Jak Upgrades.

STAR WARS: THE FORCE UNLEASHED

CHEAT CODES

Pause the game and select Input Code. Here you can enter the following codes. Activating any of the following cheat codes will disable some unlockables, and you will be unable to save your progress.

CHEAT	CODE	CHEAT	CODE
All Force Powers at Max Power	KATARN	All Saber Crystals	HURRIKANE
All Force Push Ranks	EXARKUN	All Talents	JOCASTA
All Saber Throw Ranks	ADEGAN	Deadly Saber	LIGHTSABER
All Repulse Ranks	DATHOMIR		

COMBOS

Pause the game and select Input Code. Here you can enter the following codes. Activating any of the following cheat codes will disable some unlockables, and you will be unable to save your progress.

COMBO	CODE	COMBO	CODE
All Combos	MOLDYCROW	Saber Slam	PLOKOON
Aerial Ambush	VENTRESS	Saber Sling	KITFISTO
Aerial Assault	EETHKOTH	Sith Saber Flurry	LUMIYA
Aerial Blast	YADDLE	Sith Slash	DARAGON
Impale	BRUTALSTAB	Sith Throw	SAZEN
Lightning Bomb	MASSASSI	New Combo	FREEDON
Lightning Grenade	RAGNOS	New Combo	MARAJADE

ALL DATABANK ENTRIES

Pause the game and select Input Code. Enter OSSUS.

MIRRORED LEVEL

Pause the game and select Input Code. Enter MINDTRICK. Re-enter the code to return level to normal.

SITH MASTER DIFFICULTY

Pause the game and select Input Code. Enter SITHSPAWN.

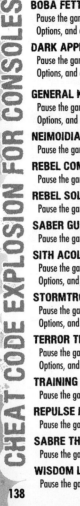

COSTUMES

Pause the game and select Input Code. Here you can enter the following codes.

COSTUME	CODE
All Costumes	SOHNDANN
Bail Organa	VICEROY
Ceremonial Jedi Robes	DANTOOINE
Drunken Kota	HARDBOILED
Emperor	MASTERMIND
Incinerator Trooper	PHOENIX
Jedi Adventure Robe	HOLOCRON
Kashyyyk Trooper	TK421GREEN
Kota	MANDALORE

COSTUME	CODE
Master Kento	WOOKIEE
Proxy	PROTOTYPE
Scout Trooper	FERRAL
Shadow Trooper	BLACKHOLE
Sith Stalker Armor	KORRIBAN
Snowtrooper	SNOWMAN
Stormtrooper	TK421WHITE
Stormtrooper Commander	TK421BLUE

STAR WARS: THE FORCE UNLEASHED II

BOBA FETT COSTUME

Pause the game, select Cheat Codes from the Options, and enter MANDALORE.

DARK APPRENTICE COSTUME

Pause the game, select Cheat Codes from the Options, and enter VENTRESS.

GENERAL KOTA COSTUME

Pause the game, select Cheat Codes from the Options, and enter RAHM.

NEIMOIDIAN COSTUME

Pause the game, select Cheat Codes from the Options, and enter GUNRAY.

REBEL COMMANDO COSTUME

Pause the game, select Cheat Codes from the Options, and enter SPECFORCE.

REBEL SOLDIER COSTUME

Pause the game, select Cheat Codes from the Options, and enter REBELSCUM.

SABER GUARD COSTUME

Pause the game, select Cheat Codes from the Options, and enter MORGUKAI.

SITH ACOLYTE COSTUME

Pause the game, select Cheat Codes from the Options, and enter HAAZEN.

STORMTROOPER COSTUME

Pause the game, select Cheat Codes from the Options, and enter TK421.

TERROR TROOPER COSTUME

Pause the game, select Cheat Codes from the Options, and enter SHADOW.

TRAINING DROID COSTUME

Pause the game, select Cheat Codes from the Options, and enter HOLODROID.

REPULSE FORCE POWER

Pause the game, select Cheat Codes from the Options, and enter MAREK.

SABRE THROW

Pause the game, select Cheat Codes from the Options, and enter TRAYA.

WISDOM LIGHTSABER CRYSTALS

Pause the game, select Cheat Codes from the Options, and enter SOLARI.

TRAINING GEAR
Have a save game from Star Wars: The Force Unleashed.

CEREMONIAL ROBES
Have a save game from Star Wars: The Force Unleashed with the Light Side ending.

SITH STALKER ARMOR
Have a save game from Star Wars: The Force Unleashed with the Dark Side ending.

SUPER STREET FIGHTER IV

BARREL BUSTER AND CAR CRUSHER BONUS STAGES
Beat Arcade Mode in any difficulty

COLORS AND TAUNTS
Colors 1 and 2 plus the first taunt for each fighter are available from the start. For colors 11 & 12, start a game with a Street Fighter IV save game on your system. To earn the rest of the colors and taunts, you need to fight a certain number of matches with that character.

COLOR	# OF MATCHES
3	2
4	4
5	6
6	8
7	10
8	12
9	14
10	16

TAUNT	# OF MATCHES
2	1
3	3
4	5
5	7
6	9
7	11
8	13
9	15
10	16

TIGER WOODS PGA TOUR 09

SPECTATORS BIG HEAD MODE
Select EA SPORTS Extras from My Tiger '09, choose Password and enter cephalus.

TOM CLANCY'S HAWX

A-12 AVENGER II
At the hangar, hold Left Trigger and press ❌, 🅛🅑, ❌, 🅡🅑, 🅨, ❌.

F-18 HARV
At the hangar, hold Left Trigger and press 🅛🅑, 🅨, 🅛🅑, 🅨, 🅛🅑, ❌.

FB-22 STRIKE RAPTOR
At the hangar, hold Left Trigger and press 🅡🅑, ❌, 🅡🅑, ❌, 🅡🅑, 🅨.

TONY HAWK RIDE

RYAN SHECKLER
Select Cheats from the Options menu and enter SHECKLERSIG.

QUICKSILVER 80'S LEVEL
Select Cheats from the Options menu and enter FEELINGEIGHTIES.

TOY SOLDIERS: COLD WAR

COMMANDO GAMER PICTURE
Buy the game.

RUSSIAN GAMER PICTURE
Complete the game.

AVATAR AWARDS

AVATAR	EARNED BY
Flight Jacket	Complete the first section of Basic Training.
Mullet	Survive until Wave 9 in Basic Training.
Toy Soldiers T-Shirt	Play a survival match to Round 5.

TRANSFORMERS: DARK OF THE MOON

RATCHET IN MULTIPLAYER
At the Unlockables screen, press Up, Right, Down, Left, Up, Start.

TRANSFORMERS REVENGE OF THE FALLEN

LOW GRAVITY MODE
Select Cheat Code and enter Ⓐ, Ⓧ, Ⓨ, ⓛ, Ⓨ, ⓛ.

NO WEAPON OVERHEAT
Select Cheat Code and enter ⓛ, Ⓧ, Ⓐ, ⓛ, Ⓨ, ⓛⒷ.

ALWAYS IN OVERDRIVE MODE
Select Cheat Code and enter ⓛⒷ, Ⓑ, ⓛⒷ, Ⓐ, Ⓧ, ⓡ.

UNLIMITED TURBO
Select Cheat Code and enter Ⓑ, ⓛ, Ⓧ, ⓡ, Ⓐ, Ⓨ.

NO SPECIAL COOLDOWN TIME
Select Cheat Code and enter ⓡ, Ⓧ, ⓡ, ⓡ, Ⓧ, Ⓐ.

INVINCIBILITY
Select Cheat Code and enter ⓛ, Ⓐ, Ⓧ, ⓛ, Ⓧ, Ⓧ.

4X ENERGON FROM DEFEATED ENEMIES
Select Cheat Code and enter Ⓨ, Ⓧ, Ⓑ, ⓡ, Ⓐ, Ⓨ.

INCREASED WEAPON DAMAGE IN ROBOT FORM
Select Cheat Code and enter Ⓨ, Ⓨ, ⓡ, Ⓐ, ⓛⒷ, Ⓨ.

INCREASED WEAPON DAMAGE IN VEHICLE FORM
Select Cheat Code and enter Ⓨ, Ⓑ, ⓡⒷ, Ⓧ, ⓡ, ⓛ.

MELEE INSTANT KILLS
Select Cheat Code and enter ⓡ, Ⓐ, ⓛⒷ, Ⓑ, ⓡ, ⓛⒷ.

LOWER ENEMY ACCURACY
Select Cheat Code and enter Ⓧ, ⓛ, ⓡ, ⓛ, ⓡ, ⓡⒷ.

INCREASED ENEMY HEALTH
Select Cheat Code and enter Ⓑ, Ⓧ, ⓛⒷ, Ⓑ, ⓡ, Ⓨ.

INCREASED ENEMY DAMAGE
Select Cheat Code and enter ⓛⒷ, Ⓨ, Ⓐ, Ⓨ, ⓡ, ⓡ.

INCREASED ENEMY ACCURACY
Select Cheat Code and enter Ⓨ, Ⓨ, Ⓑ, Ⓐ, Ⓧ, ⓛⒷ.

SPECIAL KILLS ONLY MODE
Select Cheat Code and enter Ⓑ, Ⓑ, ⓡⒷ, Ⓑ, Ⓐ, ⓛ.

UNLOCK ALL SHANGHAI MISSIONS AND ZONES
Select Cheat Code and enter Ⓨ, ⓛ, ⓡ, ⓛⒷ, Ⓨ, Ⓐ.

UNLOCK ALL WEST COAST MISSIONS AND ZONES
Select Cheat Code and enter ⓛⒷ, ⓡⒷ, ⓡ, Ⓨ, ⓡ, Ⓑ.

UNLOCK ALL DEEP SIX MISSIONS AND ZONES
Select Cheat Code and enter Ⓧ, ⓡⒷ, Ⓨ, Ⓑ, Ⓐ, ⓛⒷ.

UNLOCK ALL EAST COAST MISSIONS AND ZONES

Select Cheat Code and enter 🅐, 🅑, 🆁🅱, 🅐, 🅑, 🅧.

UNLOCK ALL CAIRO MISSIONS AND ZONES

Select Cheat Code and enter 🅐, 🆈, 🅐, 🆈, 🅑, 🅻🅱.

UNLOCK AND ACTIVATE ALL UPGRADES

Select Cheat Code and enter 🅻🅱, 🆈, 🅻🅱, 🅑, 🅧, 🅧.

TRENCHED

AVATAR AWARDS

AVATAR	EARNED BY
Trenched T-Shirt	Complete Mobile Trench certification.
Trenchie	Wrest control of Europe back from the Northern Pylon.

TROPICO 3

CHEAT MENU

During a game, click the Left Thumbstick and Right Thumbstick and hold them down. Add Back + Start to open the cheat menu. Activating any cheats disables achievements.

VIVA PINATA: PARTY ANIMALS

CLASSIC GAMER AWARD ACHIEVEMENT

At the START screen, press Up, Up, Down, Down, Left, Right, Left, Right, 🅑, 🅐. This earns you 10 points toward your Gamerscore.

VIVA PINATA: TROUBLE IN PARADISE

CREDITS

Select Play Garden and name your garden Piñata People. This unlocks the ability to view the credits on the main menu.

WIPEOUT: IN THE ZONE

AVATAR AWARDS

AWARD	EARNED BY
Wipeout Life Jacket	At the main menu, press Left, B, Down, Y, A, B, Right, Up.
Wipeout Safety Helmet	At the main menu, press Y, A, B, Up, Down, Left, Y, Right.

WIPEOUT 2

AVATAR AWARDS

AVATAR	EARNED BY
Winter Vest	Complete episode 6 to unlock this sweet avatar item.
Ice Helmet	Complete episode 8 to unlock this stylish avatar item.
Snow Helmet	Complete episode 8 to unlock this stylish avatar item.

A WORLD OF KEFLINGS

AVATAR AWARDS

AWARD	EARNED BY
Baby Dragon	Make friends with the baby dragon released from an egg in the Ice Kingdom.
Winged Hat Of Kefkimo	Talk to the Chief at the great Hall in the Ice Kingdom.

WORLD OF OUTLAWS: SPRINT CARS

$5,000,000
Enter your name as CHICMCHIM.

ALL DRIVERS
Enter your name as MITYMASTA.

ALL TRACKS
Enter your name as JOEYJOEJOE.

WORMS ULTIMATE MAYHEM

AVATAR AWARDS

AVATAR	EARNED BY
Ultimate Mayhem Tee	Earn any Achievement in Worms: Ultimate Mayhem.
Worm Tee	Locate the 5 hidden Easter Eggs in Worms: Ultimate Mayhem.

WWE ALL STARS

UNLOCK ARENAS, WRESTLERS, AND ATTIRE
At the main menu, press Left, ⓨ, Down, Left, ⓨ, ⓧ, Left, ⓧ, ⓨ, Down, Right, ⓧ, Left, Up, ⓧ, Right.

AUSTIN AND PUNK ATTIRES
At the main menu, press Left, Left, Right, Right, Up, Down, Up, Down.

ROBERTS AND ORTON ATTIRES
At the main menu, press Up, Down, Left, Right, Up, Up, Down, Down.

SAVAGE AND MORRISON ATTIRES
At the main menu, press Down, Left, Up, Right, Right, Up, Left, Down.

WWE SMACKDOWN! VS. RAW 2008

HBK AND HHH'S DX OUTFIT
Select Cheat Codes from the Options and enter DXCostume69K2.

KELLY KELLY'S ALTERNATE OUTFIT
Select Cheat Codes from the Options and enter KellyKG12R.

BRET HART
Complete the March 31, 1996 Hall of Fame challenge by defeating Bret Hart with Shawn Michaels in a One-On-One 30-Minute Iron Man Match on Legend difficulty. Purchase from WWE Shop for $210,000.

MICK FOLEY
Complete the June 28, 1998 Hall of Fame challenge by defeating Mick Foley with The Undertaker in a H*** In a Cell Match on Legend difficulty. Purchase from WWE Shop for $210,000.

MR. MCMAHON

Win or successfully defend a championship (WWE or World Heavyweight) at WrestleMania in WWE 24/7 GM Mode. Purchase from WWE Shop for $110,000.

THE ROCK

Complete the April 1, 2001 Hall of Fame challenge by defeating The Rock with Steve Austin in a Single Match on Legend Difficulty. Purchase from WWE Shop for $210,000.

STEVE AUSTIN

Complete the March 23, 1997 Hall of Fame challenge by defeating Steve Austin with Bret Hart in a Submission Match on Legend Difficulty. Purchase from WWE Shop for $210,000.

TERRY FUNK

Complete the April 13, 1997 Hall of Fame challenge by defeating Tommy Dreamer, Sabu and Sandman with any Superstar in an ECW Extreme Rules 4-Way Match on Legend difficulty. Purchase from WWE Shop for $210,000.

MR. MCMAHON BALD

Must unlock Mr. McMahon as a playable character first. Purchase from WWE Shop for $60,000.

WWE SMACKDOWN VS. RAW 2009

BOOGEYMAN

Select Cheat Codes from My WWE and enter BoogeymanEatsWorms!!.

GENE SNITSKY

Select Cheat Codes from My WWE and enter UnlockSnitskySvR2009.

HAWKINS & RYDER

Select Cheat Codes from My WWE and enter Ryder&HawkinsTagTeam.

JILLIAN HALL

Select Cheat Codes from My WWE and enter PlayAsJillianHallSvR.

LAYLA

Select Cheat Codes from My WWE and enter UnlockECWDivaLayla09.

RIC FLAIR

Select Cheat Codes from My WWE and enter FlairWooooooooooooooo.

TAZZ

Select Cheat Codes from My WWE and enter UnlockECWTazzSvR2009.

VINCENT MCMAHON

Select Cheat Codes from My WWE and enter VinceMcMahonNoChance.

HORNSWOGGLE AS MANAGER

Select Cheat Codes from My WWE and enter HornswoggleAsManager.

CHRIS JERICHO COSTUME B

Select Cheat Codes from My WWE and enter AltJerichoModelSvR09.

CM PUNK COSTUME B

Select Cheat Codes from My WWE and enter CMPunkAltCostumeSvR!.

REY MYSTERIO COSTUME B

Select Cheat Codes from My WWE and enter BooyakaBooyaka619SvR.

SATURDAY NIGHT'S MAIN EVENT ARENA

Select Cheat Codes from My WWE and enter SatNightMainEventSvR.

WWE SMACKDOWN VS. RAW 2010

THE ROCK

Select Cheat Codes from the Options menu and enter The Great One.

DIRT SHEET BRAWL AND OFFICE STAGE BRAWL

Select Cheat Codes from the Options menu and enter BonusBrawl.

JOHN CENA'S NEW COSTUME

Select Cheat Codes from the Options menu and enter CENATION.

RANDY ORTON'S NEW COSTUME

Select Cheat Codes from the Options menu and enter ViperRKO.

SANTINO MARELLA'S NEW COSTUME

Select Cheat Codes from the Options menu and enter Milan Miracle.

SHAWN MICHAELS' NEW COSTUME

Select Cheat Codes from the Options menu and enter Bow Down.

TRIPLE H'S NEW COSTUME

Select Cheat Codes from the Options menu and enter Suck IT!.

WWE SMACKDOWN VS. RAW 2011

JOHN CENA (ENTRANCE/CIVILIAN)

In My WWE, select Cheat Codes from the Options and enter SLURPEE.

ALL OF RANDY ORTON'S COSTUMES

In My WWE, select Cheat Codes from the Options and enter apexpredator.

TRIBUTE TO THE TROOPS ARENA

In My WWE, select Cheat Codes from the Options and enter 8thannualtribute.

CRUISERWEIGHT TITLE, HARDCORE TITLE, AND MILLION DOLLAR TITLE

In My WWE, select Cheat Codes from the Options and enter Historicalbelts.

X-MEN DESTINY

JUGGERNAUT SUIT

At the title screen, hold Left Bumper + Right Bumper and press Down, Right, Up, Left, Y, B.

EMMA FROST SUIT

At the title screen, hold Left Bumper + Right Bumper and press Up, Down, Right, Left, B, Y.

PLAYSTATION® 2

CONTENTS

ASTRO BOY: THE VIDEO GAME

INVULNERABLE
Pause the game and press Up, Down, Down, Up, L1, R1.

MAX STATS
Pause the game and press Left, Left, R1, Down, Down, L1.

INFINITE SUPERS
Pause the game and press Left, L1, Right, L1, Up, Down.

INFINITE DASHES
Pause the game and press R1, R1, L1, R1, Left, Up.

DISABLE SUPERS
Pause the game and press L1, L1, R1, R1, L1, Left.

COSTUME SWAP (ARENA AND CLASSIC COSTUMES)
Pause the game and press R1, Up, L1, Up, Down, R1.

UNLOCK LEVELS
Pause the game and press Up, L1, Right, L1, Down, L1. This allows you to travel to any level from the Story menu.

AVATAR: THE LAST AIRBENDER-THE BURNING EARTH

1 HIT DISHONOR
At the Main menu, press L1 and select Code Entry. Enter 28260.

ALL BONUS GAME
At the Main menu, press L1 and select Code Entry. Enter 99801.

ALL GALLERY ITEMS
At the Main menu, press L1 and select Code Entry. Enter 85061.

DOUBLE DAMAGE
At the Main menu, press L1 and select Code Entry. Enter 90210.

INFINITE HEALTH
At the Main menu, press L1 and select Code Entry. Enter 65049.

MAX LEVEL
At the Main menu, press L1 and select Code Entry. Enter 89121.

UNLIMITED SPECIAL ATTACKS
At the Main menu, press L1 and select Code Entry. Enter 66206.

AVATAR - THE LAST AIRBENDER: INTO THE INFERNO

ALL CHAPTERS
Select Game Secrets at Ember Islands and enter 52993833.

MAX COINS
Select Game Secrets at Ember Islands and enter 66639224.

ALL ITEMS AVAILABLE AT SHOP
Select Game Secrets at Ember Islands and enter 34737253.

ALL CONCEPT ART
Select Game Secrets at Ember Islands and enter 27858343.

BAKUGAN BATTLE BRAWLERS

1,000 BP
Enter 33204429 as your name.

5,000 BP
Enter 42348294 as your name.

10,000 BP
Enter 46836478 as your name.

100,000 BP
Enter 18499753 as your name.

500,000 BP
Enter 26037947 as your name.

BEN 10: ALIEN FORCE THE GAME

LEVEL LORD
Enter Gwen, Kevin, Big Chill, Gwen as a code.

INVINCIBILITY
Enter Kevin, Big Chill, Swampfire, Kevin as a code.

ALL COMBOS
Enter Swampfire, Gwen, Kevin, Ben as a code.

INFINITE ALIENS
Enter Ben, Swampfire, Gwen, Big Chill as a code.

BEN 10: ALIEN FORCE VILGAX ATTACKS

LEVEL SKIP
Pause the game and enter Portal in the Cheats menu.

UNLOCK ALL SPECKAL ATTACKS FOR ALL FORMS
Pause the game and enter Everythingproof in the Cheats menu.

UNLOCK ALL ALIEN FORMS
Pause the game and enter Primus in the Cheats menu.

TOGGLE INVULNERABILITY ON AND OFF
Pause the game and enter Xlmrsmoothy in the Cheats menu.

GIVES PLAYER FULL HEALTH
Pause the game and enter Herotime in the Cheats menu.

QUICK ENERGY REGENERATION
Pause the game and enter Generator in the Cheats menu.

BEN 10: PROTECTOR OF EARTH

INVINCIBILITY
Select a game from the Continue option. Go to the Map Selection screen, press Start and choose Extras. Select Enter Secret Code and enter XLR8, Heatblast, Wildvine, Fourarms.

ALL COMBOS
Select a game from the Continue option. Go to the Map Selection screen, press Start and choose Extras. Select Enter Secret Code and enter Cannonblot, Heatblast, Fourarms, Heatblast.

ALL LOCATIONS
Select a game from the Continue option. Go to the Map Selection screen, press Start and choose Extras. Select Enter Secret Code and enter Heatblast, XLR8, XLR8, Cannonblot.

DNA FORCE SKINS
Select a game from the Continue option. Go to the Map Selection screen, press Start and choose Extras. Select Enter Secret Code and enter Wildvine, Fourarms, Heatblast, Cannonbolt.

DARK HEROES SKINS
Select a game from the Continue option. Go to the Map Selection screen, press Start and choose Extras. Select Enter Secret Code and enter Cannonbolt, Cannonbolt, Fourarms, Heatblast.

ALL ALIEN FORMS
Select a game from the Continue option. Go to the Map Selection screen, press Start and enter Extras. Select Enter Secret Code and enter Wildvine, Fourarms, Heatblast, Wildvine.

MASTER CONTROL
Select a game from the Continue option. Go to the Map Selection screen, press Start and choose Extras. Select Enter Secret Code and enter Cannonbolt, Heatblast, Wildvine, Fourarms.

BEN 10 ULTIMATE ALIEN: COSMIC DESTRUCTION

To remove the cheats, you will need to start a new game.

1,000,000 DNA
Pause the game, select Cheats, and enter Cash.

REGENERATE HEALTH
Pause the game, select Cheats, and enter Health.

REGENERATE ENERGY
Pause the game, select Cheats, and enter Energy.

UPGRADE EVERYTHING
Pause the game, select Cheats, and enter Upgrade.

ALL LEVELS
Pause the game, select Cheats, and enter Levels.

ENEMIES DO DOUBLE DAMAGE/ PLAYER DOES ½ DAMAGE
Pause the game, select Cheats, and enter Hard.

BOLT

Some of the following cheats can be toggled on/off by selecting Cheats from the pause menu.

ALL GAME LEVELS
Select Cheats from the Extras menu and enter Right, Up, Left, Right, Up, Right.

ALL MINI GAMES
Select Cheats from the Extras menu and enter Right, Up, Right, Right.

ENCHANCED VISION
Select Cheats from the Extras menu and enter Left, Right, Up, Down.

UNLIMITED GAS MINES
Select Cheats from the Extras menu and enter Right, Left, Left, Up, Down, Right.

UNLIMITED GROUND POUND
Select Cheats from the Extras menu and enter Right, Up, Right, Up, Left, Down.

UNLIMITED INVULNERABILITY
Select Cheats from the Extras menu and enter Down, Down, Up, Left.

UNLIMITED LASER EYES
Select Cheats from the Extras menu and enter Left, Left, Up, Right.

UNLIMITED STEALTH CAMO
Select Cheats from the Extras menu and enter Left, Down, Down, Down.

UNLIMITED SUPERBARK
Select Cheats from the Extras menu and enter Right, Left -Left, Up, Down, Up.

BRATZ: THE MOVIE

FEELIN' PRETTY CLOTHING LINE
In the Bratz office at the laptop computer, enter PRETTY.

HIGH SCHOOL CLOTHING LINE
In the Bratz office at the laptop computer, enter SCHOOL.

PASSION 4 FASHION CLOTHING LINE
In the Bratz office at the laptop computer, enter ANGELZ.

SWEETZ CLOTHING LINE
In the Bratz office at the laptop computer, enter SWEETZ.

CAPCOM CLASSICS COLLECTION VOL. 2

UNLOCK EVERYTHING
At the Title screen, press Left, Right, Up, Down, **L1**, **R1**, **L1**, **R1**. This code unlocks Cheats, Tips, Art, and Sound Tests.

CARS MATER-NATIONAL

ALL ARCADE RACES, MINI-GAMES, AND WORLDS
Select Codes/Cheats from the options and enter PLAYALL.

ALL CARS
Select Codes/Cheats from the options and enter MATTEL07.

ALTERNATE LIGHTNING MCQUEEN COLORS
Select Codes/Cheats from the options and enter NCEDUDZ.

ALL COLORS FOR OTHERS
Select Codes/Cheats from the options and enter PAINTIT.

UNLIMITED TURBO
Select Codes/Cheats from the options and enter ZZOOOOM.

EXTREME ACCELERATION
Select Codes/Cheats from the options and enter 0TO200X.

EXPERT MODE
Select Codes/Cheats from the options and enter VRYFAST.

ALL BONUS ART
Select Codes/Cheats from the options and enter BUYTALL.

CARS RACE-O-RAMA

ALL ARCADE MODE EVENTS
Select Cheats from the Options menu and enter SLVRKEY.

ALL STORY MODE EVENTS
Select Cheats from the Options menu and enter GOLDKEY.

ALL OF LIGHTNING MCQUEEN'S FRIENDS
Select Cheats from the Options menu and enter EVRYBDY.

ALL LIGHTNING MCQUEEN CUSTOM KIT PARTS
Select Cheats from the Options menu and enter GR8MODS.

ALL PAINT JOBS FOR ALL NON-LIGHTNING MCQUEEN CHARACTERS
Select Cheats from the Options menu and enter CARSHOW.

CORALINE

BUTTON EYE CORALINE
Select Cheats from Options and enter Cheese.

THE DA VINCI CODE

GOD MODE
Select Codes from the Options and enter VITRUVIAN MAN.

EXTRA HEALTH
Select Codes from the Options and enter SACRED FEMININE.

MISSION SELECT
Select Codes from the Options and enter CLOS LUCE 1519.

ONE-HIT FIST KILL
Select Codes from the Options and enter PHILLIPS EXETER.

ONE-HIT WEAPON KILL
Select Codes from the Options and enter ROYAL HOLLOWAY.

ALL VISUAL DATABASE
Select Codes from the Options and enter APOCRYPHA.

ALL VISUAL DATABASE AND CONCEPT ART
Select Codes from the Options and enter ET IN ARCADIA EGO.

DISNEY PRINCESS: ENCHANTED JOURNEY

BELLE'S KINGDOM
Select Secrets and enter GASTON.

GOLDEN SET
Select Secrets and enter BLUEBIRD.

FLOWER WAND
Select Secrets and enter SLEEPY.

HEART WAND
Select Secrets and enter BASHFUL.

SHELL WAND
Select Secrets and enter RAJAH.

SHIELD WAND
Select Secrets and enter CHIP.

STAR WAND
Select Secrets and enter SNEEZY.

DJ HERO

Select Cheats from Options and enter the following. Some codes will disable high scores and progress. Cheats cannot be used in tutorials and online.

UNLOCK ALL CONTENT
Enter tol0.

ALL CHARACTER ITEMS
Enter uNA2.

ALL VENUES
Enter Wv1u.

ALL DECKS
Enter LAuP.

ALL HEADPHONES
Enter 62Db.

ALL MIXES
Enter 82xl.

AUTO SCRATCH
Enter IT6j.

AUTO EFFECTS DIAL
Enter ab1L.

AUTO FADER
Enter SL5d.

AUTO TAPPER
Enter ZitH.

AUTO WIN EUPHORIA
Enter r3a9.

BLANK PLINTHS
Enter ipr0.

HAMSTER SWITCH
Enter 7geo.

HYPER DECK MODE
Enter 76st.

SHORT DECK
Enter 51uC.

INVISIBLE DJ
Enter oh5T.

PITCH BLACK OUT
Enter d4kR.

PLAY IN THE BEDROOM
Enter g7nH.

ANY DJ, ANY SETLIST
Enter 0jj8.

DAFT PUNK'S CONTENT
Enter d1g?.

DJ AM'S CONTENT
Enter k07u.

DJ JAZZY JEFF'S CONTENT
Enter n1fz.

DJ SHADOW'S CONTENT
Enter oMxV.

DJ Z-TRIP'S CONTENT
Enter 5rtg.

GRANDMASTER FLASH'S CONTENT
Enter ami8.

FLATOUT 2

ALL CARS AND 1,000,000 CREDITS
Select Enter Code from the Extras and enter GIEVEPIX.

1,000,000 CREDITS
Select Enter Code from the Extras and enter GIVECASH.

PIMPSTER CAR
Select Enter Code from the Extras and enter RUTTO.

FLATMOBILE CAR
Select Enter Code from the Extras and enter WOTKINS.

MOB CAR
Select Enter Code from the Extras and enter BIGTRUCK.

SCHOOL BUS
Select Enter Code from the Extras and enter GIEVCARPLZ.

ROCKET CAR
Select Enter Code from the Extras and enter KALJAKOPPA.

TRUCK
Select Enter Code from the Extras and enter ELPUEBLO.

FUNKMASTER FLEX'S DIGITAL HITZ FACTORY

EXTRA SKIN 1

At the main menu, press Select, Left, Right, Left, Right, Left, Right, Left, Right, Left, Right, Left, Right.

EXTRA SKIN 2

At the main menu, press Select, Left, Left, Right, Right, Left, Left, Right, Right, Left, Left, Right, Right.

EXTRA SKIN 3

At the main menu, press Select, Left, Left, Left, Right, Right, Right, Left, Left, Left, Right, Right, Right.

EXTRA SKIN 4

At the main menu, press Select, Left, Left, Left, Left, Right, Left, Right, Right, Right, Left, Left, Left, Left.

EXTRA SONG – MUDDY BY MOTLEY

At the main menu, press Select, Up, Down, Left, Right, Up, Down, Left, Right, Up, Down, Left, Right.

G.I. JOE: THE RISE OF COBRA

CLASSIC DUKE

At the main menu, press Left, Up, ✕, Up, Right, ▲.

CLASSIC SCARLETT

At the main menu, press Right, Up, Down, Down, ▲.

THE GOLDEN COMPASS

The following codes are entered in the order of top/left, bottom/left, top/right. The Featurettes can then be accessed through the Extras menu.

VOICE SESSION 1 FETUREETE

In Extras, select Enter Code from the Game Secrets menu and enter Compass, Sun, Madonna.

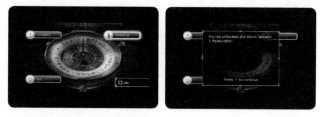

VOICE SESSION 2 FEATURETTE

In Extras, select Enter Code from the Game Secrets menu and enter Compass, Moon, Wild Man.

BEHIND THE SCENES FEATURETTE

In Extras, select Enter Code from the Game Secrets menu and enter Alpha/Omega, Alpha/Omega, Compass.

WILDLIFE WAYSTATION FEATURETTE

In Extras, select Enter Code from the Game Secrets menu and enter Griffin, Elephant, Owl.

POLAR BEARS IN MOTION FEATURETTE

In Extras, select Enter Code from the Game Secrets menu and enter Sun, Moon, Wild Man.

HARRY POTTER AND THE HALF-BLOOD PRINCE

BONUS TWO-PLAYER DUELING ARENA CASTLE GATES

At the Rewards menu, press Right, Right, Down, Down, Left, Right, Left, Right, Left, Right, Start.

ICE AGE 2: THE MELTDOWN

INFINITE PEBBLES

Pause the game and press Down, Down, Left, Up, Up, Right, Up, Down.

INFINITE ENERGY

Pause the game and press Down, Left, Right, Down, Down, Right, Left, Down.

INFINITE HEALTH

Pause the game and press Up, Right, Down, Up, Left, Down, Right, Left.

IRON MAN

ARMOR SELECTION

Iron Man's different armor suits are unlocked by completing certain missions. Refer to the following tables for when each is unlocked. After selecting a mission to play, you can pick the armor you wish to use.

COMPLETE MISSION	SUIT UNLOCKED
1: Escape	Mark I
2: First Flight	Mark II
3: Fight Back	Mark III
6: Flying Fortress	Comic Tin Can
9: Home Front	Classic
13: Showdown	Silver Centurion

CONCEPT ART

Concept Art is unlocked after finding certain numbers of Weapon Crates.

CONCEPT ART UNLOCKED	NUMBER OF WEAPON CRATES FOUND
Environments Set 1	6
Environments Set 2	12
Iron Man	18
Environments Set 3	24
Enemies	30
Environments Set 4	36
Villains	42
Vehicles	48
Covers	50

KUNG FU PANDA

INVULNERABILITY

Select Cheats from the Extras menu and enter Down, Down, Right, Up, Left.

INFINITE CHI

Select Cheats from the Extras menu and enter Down, Right, Left, Up, Down.

BIG HEAD MODE

Select Cheats from the Extras menu and enter Down, Up, Left, Right, Right.

ALL MULTIPLAYER CHARACTERS

Select Cheats from the Extras menu and enter Left, Down, Left, Right, Down.

DRAGON WARRIOR OUTFIT IN MULTIPLAYER

Select Cheats from the Extras menu and enter Left, Down, Right, Left, Up.

THE LEGEND OF SPYRO: THE ETERNAL NIGHT

INFINITE MAGIC

Pause the game and press Up, Up, Down, Down, Left, Right, Left, Right, L1, R1, L1, R1.

THE LEGEND OF SPYRO: DAWN OF THE DRAGON

INFINITE HEALTH
Pause the game, hold **L1** and press Right, Right, Down, Down, Left with the Left Analog Stick.

INFINITE MANA
Pause the game, hold **L1** and press Up, Right, Up, Left, Down with the Left Analog Stick.

MAX XP
Pause the game, hold **L1** and press Up, Left, Left, Down, Up with the Left Analog Stick.

ALL ELEMENTAL UPGRADES
Pause the game, hold **L1** and press Left, Up, Down, Up, Right with the Left Analog Stick.

LEGO BATMAN

BATCAVE CODES
Using the computer in the Batcave, select Enter Code and enter the following codes.

CHARACTERS

CHARACTER	CODE	CHARACTER	CODE
Alfred	ZAQ637	Penguin Henchman	BJH782
Batgirl	JKR331	Penguin Minion	KJP748
Bruce Wayne	BDJ327	Poison Ivy Goon	GTB899
Catwoman (Classic)	M1AAWW	Police Marksman	HKG984
Clown Goon	HJK327	Police Officer	JRY983
Commissioner Gordon	DDP967	Riddler Goon	CRY928
Fishmonger	HGY748	Riddler Henchman	XEU824
Freeze Girl	XVK541	S.W.A.T.	HTF114
Joker Goon	UTF782	Sailor	NAV592
Joker Henchman	YUN924	Scientist	JFL786
Mad Hatter	JCA283	Security Guard	PLB946
Man-Bat	NYU942	The Joker (Tropical)	CCB199
Military Policeman	MKL382	Yeti	NJL412
Nightwing	MVY759	Zoo Sweeper	DWR243
Penguin Goon	NKA238		

VEHICLES

VEHICLE	CODE	VEHICLE	CODE
Bat-Tank	KNTT4B	Mr. Freeze's Kart	BCT229
Bruce Wayne's Private Jet	LEA664	Penguin Goon Submarine	BTN248
Catwoman's Motorcycle	HPL826	Police Bike	LJP234
Garbage Truck	DUS483	Police Boat	PLC999
Goon Helicopter	GCH328	Police Car	KJL832
Harbor Helicopter	CHP735	Police Helicopter	CWR732
Harley Quinn's Hammer Truck	RDT637	Police Van	MAC788
Mad Hatter's Glider	HS000W	Police Watercraft	VJD328
Mad Hatter's Steamboat	M4DM4N	Riddler's Jet	HAHAHA
Mr. Freeze's Iceberg	ICYICE	Robin's Submarine	TTF453
The Joker's Van	JUK657	Two-Face's Armored Truck	EFE933

CHEATS

CHEAT	CODE	CHEAT	CODE
Always Score Multiply	9LRGNB	Extra Hearts	ML3KHP
Fast Batarangs	JRBDCB	Fast Build	EVG26J
Fast Walk	ZOLM6N	Immune to Freeze	JXUDY6
Flame Batarang	D8NYWH	Invincibility	WYD5CP
Freeze Batarang	XPN4NG	Minikit Detector	ZXGH9J

CHEAT	CODE
More Batarang Targets	XWP645
Piece Detector	KHJ554
Power Brick Detector	MMM786
Regenerate Hearts	HJH7HJ
Score x2	N4NR3E

CHEAT	CODE
Score x4	CX9MAT
Score x6	MLVNF2
Score x8	WCCDB9
Score x10	18HW07

LEGO STAR WARS II: THE ORIGINAL TRILOGY

BEACH TROOPER

At Mos Eisley Canteena, select Enter Code and enter UCK868. You still need to select Characters and purchase this character for 20,000 studs.

BEN KENOBI (GHOST)

At Mos Eisley Canteena, select Enter Code and enter BEN917. You still need to select Characters and purchase this character for 1,100,000 studs.

BESPIN GUARD

At Mos Eisley Canteena, select Enter Code and enter VHY832. You still need to select Characters and purchase this character for 15,000 studs.

BIB FORTUNA

At Mos Eisley Canteena, select Enter Code and enter WTY721. You still need to select Characters and purchase this character for 16,000 studs.

BOBA FETT

At Mos Eisley Canteena, select Enter Code and enter HLP221. You still need to select Characters and purchase this character for 175,000 studs.

DEATH STAR TROOPER

At Mos Eisley Canteena, select Enter Code and enter BNC332. You still need to select Characters and purchase this character for 19,000 studs.

EWOK

At Mos Eisley Canteena, select Enter Code and enter TTT289. You still need to select Characters and purchase this character for 34,000 studs.

GAMORREAN GUARD

At Mos Eisley Canteena, select Enter Code and enter YZF999. You still need to select Characters and purchase this character for 40,000 studs.

GONK DROID

At Mos Eisley Canteena, select Enter Code and enter NFX582. You still need to select Characters and purchase this character for 1,550 studs.

GRAND MOFF TARKIN

At Mos Eisley Canteena, select Enter Code and enter SMG219. You still need to select Characters and purchase this character for 38,000 studs.

GREEDO

At Mos Eisley Canteena, select Enter Code and enter NAH118. You still need to select Characters and purchase this character for 60,000 studs.

HAN SOLO (HOOD)

At Mos Eisley Canteena, select Enter Code and enter YWM840. You still need to select Characters and purchase this character for 20,000 studs.

IG-88

At Mos Eisley Canteena, select Enter Code and enter NXL973. You still need to select Characters and purchase this character for 30,000 studs.

IMPERIAL GUARD

At Mos Eisley Canteena, select Enter Code and enter MMM111. You still need to select Characters and purchase this character for 45,000 studs.

IMPERIAL OFFICER

At Mos Eisley Canteena, select Enter Code and enter BBV889. You still need to select Characters and purchase this character for 28,000 studs.

IMPERIAL SHUTTLE PILOT

At Mos Eisley Canteena, select Enter Code and enter VAP664. You still need to select Characters and purchase this character for 29,000 studs.

IMPERIAL SPY

At Mos Eisley Canteena, select Enter Code and enter CVT125. You still need to select Characters and purchase this character for 13,500 studs.

JAWA

At Mos Eisley Canteena, select Enter Code and enter JAW499. You still need to select Characters and purchase this character for 24,000 studs.

LOBOT

At Mos Eisley Canteena, select Enter Code and enter UUB319. You still need to select Characters and purchase this character for 11,000 studs.

PALACE GUARD

At Mos Eisley Canteena, select Enter Code and enter SGE549. You still need to select Characters and purchase this character for 14,000 studs.

REBEL PILOT

At Mos Eisley Canteena, select Enter Code and enter CYG336. You still need to select Characters and purchase this character for 15,000 studs.

REBEL TROOPER (HOTH)

At Mos Eisley Canteena, select Enter Code and enter EKU849. You still need to select Characters and purchase this character for 16,000 studs.

SANDTROOPER

At Mos Eisley Canteena, select Enter Code and enter YDV451. You still need to select Characters and purchase this character for 14,000 studs.

SKIFF GUARD

At Mos Eisley Canteena, select Enter Code and enter GBU888. You still need to select Characters and purchase this character for 12,000 studs.

SNOWTROOPER

At Mos Eisley Canteena, select Enter Code and enter NYU989. You still need to select Characters and purchase this character for 16,000 studs.

STROMTROOPER

At Mos Eisley Canteena, select Enter Code and enter PTR345. You still need to select Characters and purchase this character for 10,000 studs.

THE EMPEROR

At Mos Eisley Canteena, select Enter Code and enter HHY382. You still need to select Characters and purchase this character for 275,000 studs.

TIE FIGHTER

At Mos Eisley Canteena, select Enter Code and enter HDY739. You still need to select Characters and purchase this character for 60,000 studs.

TIE FIGHTER PILOT

At Mos Eisley Canteena, select Enter Code and enter NNZ316. You still need to select Characters and purchase this character for 21,000 studs.

TIE INTERCEPTOR

At Mos Eisley Canteena, select Enter Code and enter QYA828. You still need to select Characters and purchase this character for 40,000 studs.

TUSKEN RAIDER

At Mos Eisley Canteena, select Enter Code and enter PEJ821. You still need to select Characters and purchase this character for 23,000 studs.

UGNAUGHT

At Mos Eisley Canteena, select Enter Code and enter UGN694. You still need to select Characters and purchase this character for 36,000 studs.

LOONEY TUNES: ACME ARSENAL

UNLIMITED AMMUNITION

At the cheats menu, enter Down, Left, Up, Right, Down, Left, Up, Right, Down.

MAJOR LEAGUE BASEBALL 2K8

BIG HEAD MODE

Select Enter Cheat Code from the My 2K8 menu and enter Black Sox. This unlocks the Smart Choice cheat. Go to My Cheats to toggle the cheat on and off.

MAJOR LEAGUE BASEBALL 2K9

BIG HEADS

At the cheats menu, enter Black Sox.

MARVEL SUPER HERO SQUAD

IRON MAN, BONUS COSTUME "WAR MACHINE"

Select Enter Code from the Options and enter 111111.

HULK, BONUS COSTUMES "GREY HULK" & "RED HULK"

Select Enter Code from the Options and enter 222222.

WOLVERINE, BONUS COSTUMES "WOLVERINE (BROWN COSTUME)" & "FERAL WOLVERINE"

Select Enter Code from the Options and enter 333333.

THOR, BONUS COSTUMES "THOR (CHAIN ARMOR)" & "LOKI-THOR"

Select Enter Code from the Options and enter 444444.

SILVER SURFER, BONUS COSTUMES "ANTI-SURFER" & "GOLD SURFER"

Select Enter Code from the Options and enter 555555.

FALCON, BONUS COSTUME "ULTIMATES FALCON"

Select Enter Code from the Options and enter 666666.

CHEAT "SUPER KNOCKBACK"

Select Enter Code from the Options and enter 777777.

CHEAT "NO BLOCK MODE"

Select Enter Code from the Options and enter 888888.

DOCTOR DOOM, BONUS COSTUMES "ULTIMATES DOCTOR DOOM" & "PROFESSOR DOOM"

Select Enter Code from the Options and enter 999999.

CAPTAIN AMERICA, BONUS COSTUME "ULTIMATE CAPTAIN AMERICA COSTUME"

Select Enter Code from the Options and enter 177674

A.I.M. AGENT, BONUS COSTUME "BLUE SUIT A.I.M."

Select Enter Code from the Options and enter 246246

CHEAT "GROUNDED"

Select Enter Code from the Options and enter 476863

CHEAT "ONE-HIT TAKEDOWN"

Select Enter Code from the Options and enter 663448

CHEAT "INFINITE SHARD DURATION"

Select Enter Code from the Options and enter 742737

CHEAT "THROWN OBJECT TAKEDOWN"

Select Enter Code from the Options and enter 847936

MARVEL ULTIMATE ALLIANCE

UNLOCK ALL SKINS

At the Team Menu, press Up, Down, Left, Right, Left, Right, Start.

UNLOCKS ALL HERO POWERS

At the Team Menu, press Left, Right, Up, Down, Up, Down, Start.

UNLOCK ALL HEROES

At the Team Menu, press Up, Up, Down, Down, Left, Left, Left, Start.

UNLOCK DAREDEVIL

At the Team Menu, press Left, Left, Right, Right, Up, Down, Up, Down, Start.

UNLOCK SILVER SURFER

At the Team Menu, press Down, Left, Left, Up, Right, Up, Down, Left, Start.

GOD MODE

During gameplay, press Up, Down, Up, Down, Up, Left, Down, Right, Start.

TOUCH OF DEATH

During gameplay, press Left, Right, Down, Down, Right, Left, Start.

SUPER SPEED

During gameplay, press Up, Left, Up, Right, Down, Right, Start.

FILL MOMENTUM

During gameplay, press Left, Right, Right, Left, Up, Down, Down, Up, Start.

UNLOCK ALL COMICS

At the Review menu, press Left, Right, Right, Left, Up, Up, Right, Start.

UNLOCK ALL CONCEPT ART

At the Review menu, press Down, Down, Down, Right, Right, Left, Down, Start.

UNLOCK ALL MOVIES

At the Review menu, press Up, Left, Left, Up, Right, Right, Up, Start.

UNLOCK ALL LOAD SCREENS

At the Review menu, press Up, Down, Right, Left, Up, Up Down, Start.

UNLOCK ALL COURSES

At the Comic Missions menu, press Up, Right, Left, Down, Up, Right, Left, Down, Start.

MARVEL ULTIMATE ALLIANCE 2

GOD MODE

At any point during a game, press Up, Up, Down, Down, Left, Right, Down.

GIVE MONEY

At the Team Select or Hero Details screen press Up, Up, Down, Down, Up, Up, Up, Down.

UNLOCK ALL POWERS

At the Team Select or Hero Details screen press Up, Up, Down, Down, Left, Right, Right, Left.

ADVANCE ALL CHARACTERS TO L99

At the Hero Details screen press Down, Up, Left, Up, Right, Up, Left, Down.

UNLOCK ALL BONUS MISSIONS

While using the Bonus Mission Simulator, press Up, Right, Down, Left, Left, Right, Up, Up.

ADD 1 CHARACTER LEVEL

During a game, press Down, Up, Right, Up, Right, Up, Right, Down.

ADD 10 CHARACTER LEVELS

During a game, press Down, Up, Left, Up, Left, Up, Left, Down.

MLB 08: THE SHOW

ALL CLASSIC STADIUMS

At the main menu, press Down, Right, ●, ■, Left, ▲, Up, L1. The controller will vibrate if entered correctly.

ALL GOLDEN & SILVER ERA PLAYERS IN EXHIBITION

At the main menu, press L1, L2, ●, ■, ▲, ●, Down. The controller will vibrate if entered correctly.

MLB POWER PROS

VIEW MLB PLAYERS AT CREATED PLAYERS MENU

Select View or Delete Custom Players/Password Display from the My Data menu. Press Up, Up, Down, Down, Left, Right, Left Right, L1, R1.

ALVIN LOCKHART'S BATTING STANCE AND PITCHING FORM

At the main menu, press Right, Left, Up, Down, Down, Right, Right, Up, Up, Left, Down, Left. These will be available at the shop.

MX VS. ATV UNTAMED

EVERYTHING

Select Cheat Codes from the options menu and enter YOUGOTIT.

1,000,000 STORE POINTS

Select Cheat Codes from the options menu and enter MANYZEROS.

50CC BIKE CLASS

Select Cheat Codes from the options menu and enter LITTLEGUY.

ALL BIKES

Select Cheat Codes from the options menu and enter ONRAILS.

ALL CHALLENGES

Select Cheat Codes from the options menu and enter MORESTUFF.

ALL FREESTYLE TRACKS

Select Cheat Codes from the options menu and enter ALLSTYLE.

ALL GEAR

Select Cheat Codes from the options menu and enter WELLDRESSED.

ALL MACHINES

Select Cheat Codes from the options menu and enter MCREWHEELS.

ALL RIDERS

Select Cheat Codes from the options menu and enter WHOSTHAT.

ALL TRACKS

Select Cheat Codes from the options menu and enter FREETICKET.

MONSTER TRUCK

Select Cheat Codes from the options menu and enter PWNAGE.

NARUTO: ULTIMATE NINJA 2

In Naruto's house, select Input Password. This is where you can enter an element, then three signs. Enter the following here:

1,000 RYO

Water, Hare, Monkey, Monkey
Water, Ram, Horse, Dog
Water, Horse, Horse, Horse
Water, Rat, Rooster, Boar
Water, Rat, Monkey, Rooster
Fire, Rat, Dragon, Dog

5,000 RYO

Water, Tiger, Dragon, Tiger
Water, Snake, Rooster, Horse

10,000 RYO

Fire, Tiger, Tiger, Rooster
Fire, Tiger, Dragon, Hare

158

NASCAR 08

ALL CHASE MODE CARS
Select Cheat Codes from the Options menu and enter checkered flag.

EA SPORTS CAR
Select Cheat Codes from the Options menu and enter ea sports car.

FANTASY DRIVERS
Select Cheat Codes from the Options menu and enter race the pack.

WALMART CAR AND TRACK
Select Cheat Codes from the Options menu and enter walmart everyday.

NASCAR 09

WALMART TRACK AND THE WALMART CAR
In Chase for the Sprint Cup, enter the driver's name as WalMart EveryDay.

NBA 09 THE INSIDE

ALL-STAR 09 EAST
Select Trophy Room from the Options. Press L1, then ◉, and enter SHPNV2K699.

ALL-STAR 09 WEST
Select Trophy Room from the Options. Press L1, then ◉, and enter K8AV6YMLNF.

ALL TROPHIES
Select Trophy Room from the Options. Press L1, then ◉, and enter K@ZZ@@M!.

LA LAKERS LATIN NIGHTS
Select Trophy Room from the Options. Press L1, then ◉, and enter NMTWCTC84S.

MIAMI HEAT LATIN NIGHTS
Select Trophy Room from the Options. Press L1, then ◉, and enter WCTGSA8SPD.

PHOENIX SUNS LATIN NIGHTS
Select Trophy Room from the Options. Press L1, then ◉, and enter LKUTSENFJH.

SAN ANTONIO LATIN NIGHTS
Select Trophy Room from the Options. Press L1, then ◉, and enter JFHSY73MYD.

NBA 2K10

ABA BALL
Select Codes from Options and enter payrespect.

NBA 2K TEAM
Select Codes from Options and enter nba2k.

2K SPORTS TEAM
Select Codes from Options and enter 2ksports.

VISUAL CONCEPTS TEAM
Select Codes from Options and enter vcteam.

NBA 2K11

2K CHINA TEAM
In Features, select Codes from the Extras menu. Choose Enter Code and enter 2kchina.

2K SPORTS TEAM
In Features, select Codes from the Extras menu. Choose Enter Code and enter 2Ksports.

NBA 2K TEAM
In Features, select Codes from the Extras menu. Choose Enter Code and enter nba2k.

VC TEAM
In Features, select Codes from the Extras menu. Choose Enter Code and enter vcteam.

ABA BALL
In Features, select Codes from the Extras menu. Choose Enter Code and enter payrespect.

NBA LIVE 08

ADIDAS GIL II ZERO SHOE CODES

Select NBA Codes from My NBA Live and enter the following:

SHOES	CODE
Agent Zero	ADGILLIT6BE
Black President	ADGILLIT7BF
Cuba	ADGILLIT4BC
Cust0mize Shoe	ADGILLIT5BD
GilWood	ADGILLIT1B9
TS Lightswitch Away	ADGILLIT0B8
TS Lightswitch Home	ADGILLIT2BA

NCAA FOOTBALL 08

PENNANT CODES

Go to My Shrine and select Pennants. Press Select and enter the following:

PENNANT	CODE	PENNANT	CODE
#200 1st & 15 Cheat	Thanks	#278 All-Clemson Team	Death Valley
#201 Blink Cheat	For	#279 All-Colorado Team	Glory
#202 Boing Cheat	Registering	#281 All-FSU Team	Uprising
#204 Butter Fingers Cheat	With EA	#282 All-Georgia Team	Hunker Down
#205 Crossed The Line Cheat	Tiburon	#283 All-Iowa Team	On Iowa
#206 Cuffed Cheat	EA Sports	#285 All-LSU Team	Geaux Tigers
#207 Extra Credit Cheat	Touchdown	#287 All-Michigan Team	Go Blue
#208 Helium Cheat	In The Zone	#288 All-Mississippi State Team	Hail State
#209 Hurricane Cheat	Turnover	#289 All-Nebraska Team	Go Big Red
#210 Instant FrePlay Cheat	Impact	#291 All-Notre Dame Team	Golden Domer
#211 Jumbalaya Cheat	Heisman	#292 All-Ohio State Team	Killer Nuts
#212 Molasses Cheat	Game Time	#293 All-Oklahoma Team	Boomer
#213 Nike Free Cheat	Break Free	#294 All-Oklahoma State Team	Go Pokes
#214 Nike Magnigrip Cheat	Hand Picked	#296 All-Penn State Team	We Are
#215 Nike Pro Cheat	No Sweat	#298 All-Purdue Team	Boiler Up
#219 QB Dud Cheat	Elite 11	#300 All-Tennessee Team	Big Orange
#221 Steel Toe Cheat	Gridiron	#301 All-Texas Team	Hook Em
#222 Stiffed Cheat	NCAA	#302 All-Texas A&M Team	Gig Em
#223 Super Dive Cheat	Upset	#303 All-UCLA Team	Mighty
#226 Tough As Nail Cheat	Offense	#304 All-USC Team	Fight On
#228 What A Hit Cheat	Blitz	#305 All-Virginia Team	Wahoos
#229 Kicker Hex Cheat	Sideline	#307 All-Washington Team	Bow Down
#273 2004 All-American Team	Fumble	#308 All-Wisconsin Team	U Rah Rah
#274 All-Alabama Team	Roll Tide	#344 MSU Mascot Team	Mizzou Rah
#276 All-Arkansas Team	Woopigsooie	#385 Wyo Mascot	All Hail
#277 All-Auburn Team	War Eagle	#386 Zips Mascot	Hail WV

NEED FOR SPEED PROSTREET

$2,000
Select Career and then choose Code Entry. Enter 1MA9X99.

$4,000
Select Career and then choose Code Entry. Enter W2IOLL01.

$8,000
Select Career and then choose Code Entry. Enter L1IS97A1.

$10,000
Select Career and then choose Code Entry. Enter 1MI9K7E1.

$10,000
Select Career and then choose Code Entry. Enter CASHMONEY.

$10,000
Select Career and then choose Code Entry. Enter REGGAME.

AUDI TT
Select Career and then choose Code Entry.
Enter ITSABOUTYOU.

CHEVELLE SS
Select Career and then choose Code Entry.
Enter HORSEPOWER.

COKE ZERO GOLF GTI
Select Career and then choose Code Entry.
Enter COKEZERO.

DODGE VIPER
Select Career and then choose Code Entry.
Enter WORLDSLONGESTLASTING.

MITSUBISHI LANCER EVOLUTION
Select Career and then choose Code Entry.
Enter MITSUBISHIGOFAR.

UNLOCK ALL BONUSES
Select Career and then choose Code Entry.
Enter UNLOCKALLTHINGS.

5 REPAIR MARKERS
Select Career and then choose Code Entry.
Enter SAFETYNET.

ENERGIZER VINYL
Select Career and then choose Code Entry.
Enter ENERGIZERLITHIUM.

CASTROL SYNTEC VINYL
Select Career and then choose Code Entry.
Enter CASTROLSYNTEC. This also gives you
$10,000.

NHL 08

ALL RBK EDGE JERSEYS
At the RBK Edge Code option, enter h3oyxpwksf8ibcgt.

NHL 09

UNLOCK 3RD JERSEYS
At the cheat menu, enter xe6377uyrwm48frf.

NICKTOONS: ATTACK OF THE TOYBOTS

DAMAGE BOOST
Select Cheats from the Extras menu. Choose
Enter Cheat Code and enter 456645.

INVULNERABILITY
Select Cheats from the Extras menu. Choose
Enter Cheat Code and enter 313456.

UNLOCK EXO-HUGGLES 9000
Select Cheats from the Extras menu. Choose
Enter Cheat Code and enter 691427.

UNLOCK MR. HUGGLES
Select Cheats from the Extras menu. Choose
Enter Cheat Code and enter 654168.

UNLIMITED LOBBER GOO
Select Cheats from the Extras menu. Choose
Enter Cheat Code and enter 118147.

UNLIMITED SCATTER GOO
Select Cheats from the Extras menu. Choose
Enter Cheat Code and enter 971238.

UNLIMITED SPLITTER GOO
Select Cheats from the Extras menu. Choose
Enter Cheat Code and enter 854511.

RATATOUILLE

Select Gusteau's Shop from the Extras menu. Choose Secrets, select the appropriate code
number, and then enter the code. Once the code is entered, select the cheat you want to
activate it.

CODE NUMBER	CODE	EFFECT
1	Pieceocake	Very Easy difficulty mode
2	Myhero	No impact and no damage from enemies
3	Asobo	Plays the Asobo logo
4	Shielded	No damage from enemies
5	Spyagent	Move undetected by any enemy
6	Ilikeonions	Release air every time Remy jumps
7	Hardfeelings	Head butt when attacking instead of tailswipe
8	Slumberparty	Multiplayer mode
9	Gusteauart	All Concept Art
10	Gusteauship	All four championship modes
11	Mattelme	All single player and multiplayer mini-games
12	Gusteauvid	All Videos
13	Gusteaures	All Bonus Artworks
14	Gusteaudream	All Dream Worlds in Gusteau's Shop
15	Gusteauslide	All Slides in Gusteau's Shop
16	Gusteaulevel	All single player mini-games
17	Gusteaucombo	All items in Gusteau's Shop
18	Gusteaupot	5,000 Gusteau points
19	Gusteaujack	10,000 Gusteau points
20	Gusteauomni	50,000 Gusteau points

SCOOBY-DOO! FIRST FRIGHTS

DAPHNE'S SECRET COSTUME
Select Codes from the Extras menu and enter 2839.

FRED'S SECRET COSTUME
Select Codes from the Extras menu and enter 4826.

SCOOBY DOO'S SECRET COSTUME
Select Codes from the Extras menu and enter 1585.

SHAGGY'S SECRET COSTUME
Select Codes from the Extras menu and enter 3726.

VELMA'S SECRET COSTUME
Select Codes from the Extras menu and enter 6588.

THE SECRET SATURDAYS: BEASTS OF THE 5TH SUN

ALL LEVELS
Select Enter Secret Code from the Secrets menu and enter Zon, Zon, Zon, Zon.

UNLOCK AMAROK TO BE SCANNED IN LEVEL 2
Select Enter Secret Code from the Secrets menu and enter Fiskerton, Zak, Zon, Komodo.

UNLOCK BISHOPVILLE LIZARDMAN TO BE SCANNED IN LEVEL 3
Select Enter Secret Code from the Secrets menu and enter Komodo, Zon, Zak, Komodo.

UNLOCK NAGA TO BE SCANNED IN LEVEL 7
Select Enter Secret Code from the Secrets menu and enter Zak, Zak, Zon, Fiskerton.

UNLOCK RAKSHASA TO BE SCANNED IN LEVEL 8
Select Enter Secret Code from the Secrets menu and enter Zak, Komodo, Fiskerton, Fiskerton.

UNLOCK BILOKO TO BE SCANNED IN LEVEL 9
Select Enter Secret Code from the Secrets menu and enter Zon, Zak, Zon, Fiskerton.

SEGA SUPERSTARS TENNIS

UNLOCK CHARACTERS

Complete the following missions to unlock the corresponding character.

CHARACTER	MISSION TO COMPLETE
Alex Kidd	Mission 1 of Alex Kidd's World
Amy Rose	Mission 2 of Sonic the Hedgehog's World
Gilius	Mission 1 of Golden Axe's World
Gum	Mission 12 of Jet Grind Radio's World
Meemee	Mission 8 of Super Monkey Ball's World
Pudding	Mission 1 of Space Channel 5's World
Reala	Mission 2 of NiGHTs' World
Shadow The Hedgehog	Mission 14 of Sonic the Hedgehog's World

SHREK THE THIRD

10,000 GOLD COINS

At the gift shop, press Up, Up, Down, Up, Right, Left.

THE SIMPSONS GAME

UNLIMITED POWER FOR ALL CHARACTERS

At the Extras menu, press ●, Left, Right, ●, ●, L1.

ALL CLICHÉS.

At the Extras menu, press Left, ●, Right, ●, Right, L1.

ALL MOVIES

At the Extras menu, press ●, Left, ●, Right, ●, R1.

THE SIMS 2: CASTAWAY

CHEAT GNOME

During a game, press **R1**, **L1**, Down, ●, **R2**. You can now use this Gnome to get the following:

MAX ALL MOTIVES

During a game, press **R2**, Up, ⊗, ●, L1.

MAX CURRENT INVENTORY

During a game, press Left, Right, ●, **R2**, ●.

MAX RELATIONSHIPS

During a game, press **L1**, Up, **R2**, Left, ▲.

ALL RESOURCES

During a game, press ●, ▲, Down, ⊗, Left.

ALL CRAFTING PLANS

During a game, press ⊗, ▲, **L2**, ●, **R1**.

ADD 1 TO SKILL

During a game, press ▲, **L1**, **L1**, Left, ▲.

EXCLUSIVE VEST AND TANKTOP

Pause the game and go to Fashion and Grooming. Press ●, **R2**, **R2**, ▲, Down.

THE SIMS 2: PETS

CHEAT GNOME

During a game, press **L1**, **L1**, **R1**, ⊗, ⊗, Up.

GIVE SIM PET POINTS

After activating the Cheat Gnome, press ▲, ●, ⊗, ●, **L1**, **R1** during a game. Select the Gnome to access the cheat.

ADVANCE 6 HOURS

After activating the Cheat Gnome, press Up, Left, Down, Right, **R1** during a game. Select the Gnome to access the cheat.

GIVE SIM SIMOLEONS

After activating the Cheat Gnome, enter the Advance 6 Hours cheat. Access the Gnome

and exit. Enter the cheat again. Now, Give Sim Simoleons should be available from the Gnome.

CAT AND DOG CODES

When creating a family, press ⬤ to Enter Unlock Code. Enter the following for new fur patterns.

FUR PATTERN/CAT OR DOG	UNLOCK CODE
Bandit Mask Cats	EEGJ2YRQZZAIZ9QHA64
Bandit Mask Dogs	EEGJ2YRQZQARQ9QHA64
Black Dot Cats	EEGJ2YRQZQQ1IQ9QHA64
Black Dot Dogs	EEGJ2YRQZZ1IQ9QHA64
Black Smiley Cats	EEGJ2YRQQQZ1RQ9QHA64
Black Smiley Dogs	EEGJ2YRZQQARQ9QHA64
Blue Bones Cats	EEGJ2YRQZZZARQ9QHA64
Blue Bones Dogs	EEGJ2YRZZZ1IZ9QHA64
Blue Camouflage Cats	EEGJ2YRZZQ1IQ9QHA64
Blue Camouflage Dogs	EEGJ2YRZZZ1RQ9QHA64
Blue Cats	EEGJ2YRQZZAIQ9QHA64
Blue Dogs	EEGJ2YRQQQ1IZ9QHA64
Blue Star Cats	EEGJ2YRQQZ1IZ9QHA64
Blue Star Dogs	EEGJ2YRQZQ1IQ9QHA64
Deep Red Cats	EEGJ2YRQQQAIQ9QHA64
Deep Red Dogs	EEGJ2YRQZQ1RQ9QHA64
Goofy Cats	EEGJ2YRQZQ1IZ9QHA64
Goofy Dogs	EEGJ2YRZZZARQ9QHA64
Green Cats	EEGJ2YRZQQAIZ9QHA64
Green Dogs	EEGJ2YRQZQAIQ9QHA64
Green Flower Cats	EEGJ2YRQZQAIQ9QHA64
Green Flower Dogs	EEGJ2YRQQZZ1RQ9QHA64
Light Green Cats	EEGJ2YRZZQ1RQ9QHA64
Light Green Dogs	EEGJ2YRQQQ1RQ9QHA64
Navy Hearts Cats	EEGJ2YRZQZ1IQ9QHA64
Navy Hearts Dogs	EEGJ2YRQQZ1IQ9QHA64
Neon Green Cats	EEGJ2YRZZQAIQ9QHA64
Neon Green Dogs	EEGJ2YRZQQAIQ9QHA64
Neon Yellow Cats	EEGJ2YRZZQARQ9QHA64
Neon Yellow Dogs	EEGJ2YRQQQAIZ9QHA64
Orange Diagonal Cats	EEGJ2YRQQZAIQ9QHA64
Orange Diagonal Dogs	EEGJ2YRZQZ1IZ9QHA64
Panda Cats	EEGJ2YRQZQAIZ9QHA64
Pink Cats	EEGJ2YRQQZZ1IZ9QHA64
Pink Dogs	EEGJ2YRZQZ1RQ9QHA64
Pink Vertical Strip Cats	EEGJ2YRQQQARQ9QHA64
Pink Vertical Strip Dogs	EEGJ2YRZZZAIQ9QHA64
Purple Cats	EEGJ2YRQQZARQ9QHA64
Purple Dogs	EEGJ2YRQQZAIZ9QHA64
Star Cats	EEGJ2YRZQZARQ9QHA64
Star Dogs	EEGJ2YRZQZAIZ9QHA64
White Paws Cats	EEGJ2YRQQQ1RQ9QHA64
White Paws Dogs	EEGJ2YRZQQ1IZ9QHA64
White Zebra Stripe Cats	EEGJ2YRZZQ1IZ9QHA64
White Zebra Stripe Dogs	EEGJ2YRZZZ1IQ9QHA64
Zebra Stripes Dogs	EEGJ2YRZQQAIZ9QHA64

SLY 3: HONOR AMONG THIEVES

TOONAMI PLANE
While flying the regular plane, pause the game and press R1, R1, Right, Down, Down, Right.

RESTART EPISODES
Pause the game during the Episode and enter the following codes to restart that Episode. You must first complete that part of the Episode to use the code.

EPISODE	CODE
Episode 1, Day 1	Left, R2, Right, L1, R2, L1
Episode 1, Day 2	Down, L2, Up, Left, R2, L2
Episode 2, Day 1	Right, L2, Left, Up, Right, Down
Episode 2, Day 2	Down, Up, R1, Up, R2, L2
Episode 3, Day 1	R2, R1, L1, Left, L1, Down
Episode 3, Day 2	L2, R1, R2, L2, L1, Up
Episode 4, Day 1	Left, Right, L1, R2, Right, R2
Episode 4, Day 2	L1, Left, L2, Left, Up, L1
Episode 5, Day 1	Left, R2, Right, Up, L1, R2
Episode 5, Day 2	R2, R1, L1, R1, R2, R1
Operation Laptop Retrieval	L2, Left, R1, L2, L1, Down
Operation Moon Crash	L2, Up, Left, L1, L2, L1
Operation Reverse Double Cross	Right, Left, Up, Left, R2, Left
Operation Tar Be-Gone	Down, L2, R1, L2, R1, Right
Operation Turbo Dominant Eagle	Down, Right, Left, L2, R1, Right
Operation Wedding Crasher	L2, R2, Right, Down, L1, R2

SPIDER-MAN: FRIEND OR FOE

NEW GREEN GOBLIN AS A SIDEKICK
While standing in the Helicarrier between levels, press Left, Down, Right, Right, Down, Left.

SANDMAN AS A SIDEKICK
While standing in the Helicarrier between levels, press Right, Right, Right, Up, Down, Left.

VENOM AS A SIDEKICK
While standing in the Helicarrier between levels, press Left, Left, Right, Up, Down, Down.

5000 TECH TOKENS
While standing in the Helicarrier between levels, press Up, Up, Down, Down, Left, Right.

THE SPIDERWICK CHRONICLES

INVULNERABILITY
During the game, hold L1 + R1 and press ▲, ▲, ▲, ▲, ✕, ✕, ▲, ▲.

HEAL
During the game, hold L1 + R1 and press ▲, ■, ✕, ●, ▲, ■, ✕, ●.

COMBAT LOADOUT
During the game, hold L1 + R1 and press ▲, ▲, ✕, ✕, ■, ■, ●, ●.

INFINITE AMMO
During the game, hold L1 + R1 and press ■, ■, ■, ●, ✕, ✕, ✕, ▲.

FIELD GUIDE UNLOCKED
During the game, hold L1 + R1 and press ●, ●, ●, ■, ▲, ▲, ▲, ✕.

SPRITE A
During the game, hold L2 + R2 and press ▲, ✕, ●, ■, ✕, ▲, ■, ●.

SPRITE B
During the game, hold L2 + R2 and press ✕, ✕, ▲, ■, ■, ●, ▲, ✕.

SPRITE C
During the game, hold L2 + R2 and press ●, ▲, ■, ✕, ●, ▲, ■, ✕.

SPONGEBOB SQUAREPANTS FEATURING NICKTOONS: GLOBS OF DOOM

When entering the following codes, the order of the characters going down is: SpongeBob SquarePants, Nicolai Technus, Danny Phantom, Dib, Zim, Tlaloc, Tak, Beautiful Gorgeous, Jimmy Neutron, Plankton. These names are shortened to the first name in the following.

ATTRACT COINS

Using the Upgrade Machine on the bottom level of the lair, select "Input cheat codes here". Enter Tlaloc, Plankton, Danny, Plankton, Tak. Coins are attracted to you making them much easier to collect.

DON'T LOSE COINS

Using the Upgrade Machine on the bottom level of the lair, select "Input cheat codes here". Enter Plankton, Jimmy, Beautiful, Jimmy, Plankton. You don't lose coins when you get knocked out.

GOO HAS NO EFFECT

Using the Upgrade Machine on the bottom level of the lair, select "Input cheat codes here". Enter Danny, Danny, Danny, Nicolai, Nicolai. Goo does not slow you down.

MORE GADGET COMBO TIME

Using the Upgrade Machine on the bottom level of the lair, select "Input cheat codes here". Enter SpongeBob, Beautiful, Danny, Plankton, Nicolai. You have more time to perform gadget combos.

STAR WARS THE CLONE WARS: REPUBLIC HEROES

BIG HEAD MODE

Pause the game, select Shop, and enter Up, Down, Left, Right, Left, Right, Down, Up in Cheats.

MINI-GUN

Pause the game, select Shop, and enter Down, Left, Right, Up, Right, Up, Left, Down in Cheats.

ULTIMATE LIGHTSABER

Pause the game, select Shop, and enter Right, Down, Down, Up, Left, Up, Up, Down in Cheats.

LIGHTSABER THROW UPGRADE

Pause the game, select Shop, and enter Left, Left, Right, Right, Up, Down, Down, Up in Combat Upgrades.

SPIDER DROID UPGRADE

Pause the game, select Shop, and enter Up, Left, Down, Left, Right, Left, Left, Left in Droid-Jak Upgrades.

STAR WARS: THE FORCE UNLEASHED

CHEATS

Once you have accessed the Rogue Shadow, select Enter Code from the Extras menu. Now you can enter the following codes:

CHEAT	CODE
Invincibility	CORTOSIS
Unlimited Force	VERGENCE
1,000,000 Force Points	SPEEDER
All Force Powers	TYRANUS

CHEAT	CODE
Max Force Power Level	KATARN
Max Combo Level	COUNTDOOKU
Stronger Lightsaber	LIGHTSABER

COSTUMES

Once you have accessed the Rogue Shadow, select Enter Code from the Extras menu. Now you can enter the following codes:

COSTUME	CODE
All Costumes	GRANDMOFF
501st Legion	LEGION
Aayla Secura	AAYLA
Admiral Ackbar	ITSATWAP

COSTUME	CODE
Anakin Skywalker	CHOSENONE
Asajj Ventress	ACOLYTE
Ceremonial Jedi Robes	DANTOOINE
Chop'aa Notimo	NOTIMO

COSTUME	CODE	COSTUME	CODE
Classic stormtrooper	TK421	Luke Skywalker	T16WOMPRAT
Count Dooku	SERENNO	Luke Skywalker (Yavin)	YELLOWJCKT
Darth Desolous	PAUAN	Mace Windu	JEDIMASTER
Darth Maul	ZABRAK	Mara Jade	MARAJADE
Darth Phobos	HIDDENFEAR	Maris Brook	MARISBROOD
Darth Vader	SITHLORD	Navy commando	STORMTROOP
Drexl Roosh	DREXLROOSH	Obi Wan Kenobi	BENKENOBI
Emperor Palpatine	PALPATINE	Proxy	HOLOGRAM
General Rahm Kota	MANDALORE	Qui Gon Jinn	MAVERICK
Han Solo	NERFHERDER	Shaak Ti	TOGRUTA
Heavy trooper	SHOCKTROOP	Shadow trooper	INTHEDARK
Juno Eclipse	ECLIPSE	Sith Robes	HOLOCRON
Kento's Robe	WOOKIEE	Sith Stalker Armor	KORRIBAN
Kleef	KLEEF	Twi'lek	SECURA
Lando Calrissian	SCOUNDREL		

STREET FIGHTER ALPHA ANTHOLOGY

STREET FIGHTER ALPHA

PLAY AS DAN

At the Character Select screen in Arcade Mode, hold the Start button and place the cursor on the Random Select space then input one of the following commands within 1 second:

LP LK MK HK HP MP
HP HK MK LK LP MP
LK LP MP HP HK MK
HK HP MP LP LK HK

PLAY AS M.BISON

At the Character Select screen, hold the Start button, place the cursor on the random select box, and input:

1P side: Down, Down, Back, Back, Down, Back, Back + LP + HP

2P side: Down, Down, Forward, Forward, Down, Forward, Forward + LP + HP

PLAY AS AKUMA

At the Character Select screen, hold the Start button, place the cursor on the random select box, and input:

1P side: Down, Down, Down, Back, Back, Back + LP + HP

2P side: Down, Down, Down, Forward, Forward, Forward + LP + HP

AKUMA MODE

Select your character in Arcade mode, then press and hold Start + MP + MK as the Character Selection screen ends.

RYU AND KEN VS. M.BISON

On both the 1p and 2p side in Arcade mode, press and hold Start, then:

1P side: place the cursor on Ryu and input Up, Up, release Start, Up, Up + LP

2P side: place the cursor on Ken and input Up, Up, release Start, Up, Up + HP

LAST BOSS MODE

Select Arcade mode while holding ●, ⊗, and R1.

DRAMATIC BATTLE MODE

Select Dramatic Battle mode while holding ●, ⊗, and R2.

RANDOM BATTLE MODE

Select Versus mode while holding ●, ⊗, and R2.

STREET FIGHTER ALPHA 2

PLAY AS ORIGINAL CHUN-LI

Highlight Chun-Li on the Character Select screen, hold the Start button for 3 seconds, then select Chun-Li normally.

PLAY AS SHIN AKUMA

Highlight Akuma on the Character Select screen, hold the Start button for 3 seconds, then select Akuma normally.

PLAY AS EVIL RYU

Highlight Ryu on the Character Select screen, hold the Start button, input Forward, Up, Down, Back, then select Ryu normally.

PLAY AS EX DHALSIM

Highlight Dhalsim on the Character Select screen, hold the Start button, input Back, Down, Forward, Up, then select Dhalsim normally.

PLAY AS EX ZANGIEF

Highlight Zangief on the Character Select screen, hold the Start button, input Down, Back, Back, Back, Back, Up, Up, Forward, Forward, Forward, Forward, Down, then select Zangief normally.

LAST BOSS MODE

Select Arcade mode while holding the ●, ●, and R1 buttons.

DRAMATIC BATTLE MODE

Select Dramatic Battle mode while holding the ● + ✖ + R2.

SELECT SPECIAL ROUTE IN SURVIVAL MODE

Select Survival Battle while holding the R1 or R2.

RANDOM BATTLE MODE

Select Versus mode while holding the ● + ✖ + R2.

STREET FIGHTER ALPHA 2 GOLD

PLAY AS EX RYU

Highlight Ryu and press the Start button once before selecting normally.

PLAY AS EVIL RYU

Highlight Ryu and press the Start button twice before selecting normally.

PLAY AS ORIGINAL CHUN-LI

Highlight Chun-Li and press the Start button once before selecting normally.

PLAY AS EX CHUN-LI

Highlight Chun-Li and press the Start button twice before selecting normally.

PLAY AS EX KEN

Highlight Ken and press the Start button once before selecting normally.

PLAY AS EX DHALSIM

Highlight Dhalsim and press the Start button once before selecting normally.

PLAY AS EX ZANGIEF

Highlight Zangief and press the Start button once before selecting normally.

PLAY AS EX SAGAT

Highlight Sagat and press the Start button once before selecting normally.

PLAY AS EX M.BISON

Highlight M.Bison and press the Start button once before selecting normally.

PLAY USING SAKURA'S ALTERNATE COLORS

Highlight Sakura and press the Start button five times before selecting normally.

PLAY AS SHIN AKUMA

Highlight Akuma and press the Start button five times before selecting normally.

PLAY AS CAMMY

Highlight M.Bison and press the Start button twice before selecting normally.

LAST BOSS MODE

Select Arcade mode while holding ● + ● + R1.

SELECT SPECIAL ROUTE IN SURVIVAL MODE

Select Survival Battle while holding the R1 or R2.

DRAMATIC BATTLE MODE

Select Dramatic Battle mode while holding ● + ✖ + R2.

RANDOM BATTLE MODE

Select Versus mode while holding ● + ✖ + R2.

STREET FIGHTER ALPHA 3

PLAY AS BALROG

Highlight Karin for one second, then move the cursor to the random select box and hold Start before selecting normally.

PLAY AS JULI

Highlight Karin for one second, then move the cursor to the random select box and press Up, or Down, while selecting normally.

PLAY AS JUNI

Highlight Karin for one second, then move the cursor to the random select box and press Back, or Forward, while selecting normally.

CLASSICAL MODE

Press and hold HP + HK while starting game.

SPIRITED MODE

Press and hold MP + MK while starting game.

SAIKYO MODE

Press and hold LP + LK while starting game.

SHADALOO MODE

Press and hold LK + MK + HK while starting game.

SELECT SPECIAL ROUTE IN SURVIVAL MODE

Select Survival mode while holding R1 or R2.

DRAMATIC BATTLE MODE

Select Dramatic Battle mode while holding ● + ✖ + R2.

RANDOM BATTLE MODE

Select Versus mode while holding ● + ✖ + R2.

STUNTMAN IGNITION

3 PROPS IN STUNT CREATOR MODE

Select Cheats from Extras and enter COOLPROP.

ALL ITEMS UNLOCKED FOR CONSTRUCTION MODE

Select Cheats from Extras and enter NOBLEMAN.

MVX SPARTAN

Select Cheats from Extras and enter fastride.

ALL CHEATS

Select Cheats from Extras and enter Wearefrozen. This unlocks the following cheats: Slo-mo Cool, Thrill Cam, Vision Switcher, Nitro Addiction, Freaky Fast, and Ice Wheels.

ALL CHEATS

Select Cheats from Extras and enter Kungfoopete.

ICE WHEELS CHEAT

Select Cheats from Extras and enter IceAge.

NITRO ADDICTION CHEAT

Select Cheats from Extras and enter TheDuke.

VISION SWITCHER CHEAT

Select Cheats from Extras and enter GFXMODES.

TAK AND THE GUARDIANS OF GROSS

INVULNERABILITY

Select Cheat Codes from the Extras menu and enter KRUNKIN.

INFINITE NOVA

Select Cheat Codes from the Extras menu and enter CAKEDAY.

WEAK ENEMIES

Select Cheat Codes from the Extras menu and enter CODMODE.

ALL LEVELS

Select Cheat Codes from the Extras menu and enter GUDGEON.

ALL MINI GAMES

Select Cheat Codes from the Extras menu and enter CURLING.

ALL AWARDS

Select Cheat Codes from the Extras menu and enter SNEAKER.

ALL CONCEPT ART

Select Cheat Codes from the Extras menu and enter FRIVERS.

RAINBOW TRAIL

Select Cheat Codes from the Extras menu and enter UNICORN.

TEENAGE MUTANT NINJA TURTLES: SMASH-UP

CYBER SHREDDER
At the Bonus Content menu, press Up, Down, Right, Up, Down, Right, Left, Up, Right, Down.

4 NINJA TURTLES' ALTERNATE COSTUMES
At the Bonus Content menu, press Up, Left, Down, Right, Up, Down, Left, Up, Left, Left.

TIGER WOODS PGA TOUR 08

ALL GOLFERS
Select Passwords from the Options and enter GAMEFACE.

BRIDGESTONE ITEMS
Select Passwords from the Options and enter SHOJIRO.

COBRA ITEMS
Select Passwords from the Options and enter SNAKEKING.

GRAFALLOY ITEMS
Select Passwords from the Options and enter JUSTSHAFTS.

MACGREGOR ITEMS
Select Passwords from the Options and enter MACTEC.

MIZUNO ITEMS
Select Passwords from the Options and enter RIHACHINRIZO.

NIKE ITEMS
Select Passwords from the Options and enter JUSTDOIT.

OAKLEY ITEMS
Select Passwords from the Options and enter JANNARD.

PING ITEMS
Select Passwords from the Options and enter SOLHEIM.

PRECEPT ITEMS
Select Passwords from the Options and enter GUYSAREGOOD.

TAYLORMADE ITEMS
Select Passwords from the Options and enter MRADAMS.

TIGER WOODS PGA TOUR 09

$1,000,000
Select Passwords from the Extras menu and enter JACKPOT.

MAX SKILL POINTS
Select Passwords from the Extras menu and enter IAMRUBBISH.

ALL CLOTHING & EQUIPMENT
Select Passwords from the Extras menu and enter SHOP2DROP.

ALL PGA TOUR EVENTS
Select Passwords from the Extras menu and enter BEATIT.

ALL COVER STORIES
Select Passwords from the Extras menu and enter HEADLINER.

TONY HAWK'S PROVING GROUND

CHEAT CODES
Select Cheat Codes from the Options and enter the following cheats. Some codes need to be enabled by selecting Cheats from the Options during a game.

UNLOCK	CHEAT
Unlocks Bosco	MOREMILK
Unlocks Cam	NOTACAMERA
Unlocks Cooper	THECOOP
Unlocks Eddie X	SKETCHY
Unlocks El Patinador	PILEDRIVER
Unlocks Eric	FLYAWAY

UNLOCK	CHEAT
Unlocks Judy Nails	LOVEROCKNROLL
Unlocks Mad Dog	RABBIES
Unlocks MCA	INTERGALACTIC
Unlocks Mel	NOTADUDE
Unlocks Rube	LOOKSSMELLY
Unlocks Spence	DAPPER
Unlocks Shayne	MOVERS
Unlocks TV Producer	SHAKER
Unlock FDR	THEPREZPARK
Unlock Lansdowne	THELOCALPARK
Unlock Air & Space Museum	THEINDOORPARK
Unlocks all Fun Items	OVERTHETOP
Unlock all Game Movies	WATCHTHIS
Unlock all Rigger Pieces	IMGONNABUILD
All specials unlocked and in player's special list	LOTSOFTRICKS
Full Stats	BEEFEDUP
Give player +50 skill points	NEEDSHELP
Unlocks Perfect Manual	STILLAINTFALLIN
Unlocks Perfect Rail	AINTFALLIN
Unlocks Unlimited Focus	MYOPIC
Invisible Man	THEMISSING
Mini Skater	TINYTATER

UP

You will need to activate the following cheats at the pause menu after entering them.

RUSSELL ATTRACTS ALL BUTTERFLIES
Select Cheats from the Bonuses menu and enter BUTTERFLY.

MUNTZ'S AVIATOR GOGGLES FOR CARL
Select Cheats from the Bonuses menu and enter AVIATORGOGGLES.

CARL JUMPS FROM TEETER TOTTER TO LIFT RUSSEL
Select Cheats from the Bonuses menu and enter CARLHEAVYWEIGHT.

BALLOONS WHEN CARL JUMPS
Select Cheats from the Bonuses menu and enter BALLOONPARTY.

WWE SMACKDOWN VS. RAW 2009

BOOGEYMAN
Select Cheat Codes from My WWE and enter BoogeymanEatsWorms!!.

GENE SNITSKY
Select Cheat Codes from My WWE and enter UnlockSnitskySvR2009.

HAWKINS & RYDER
Select Cheat Codes from My WWE and enter Ryder&HawkinsTagTeam.

JILLIAN HALL
Select Cheat Codes from My WWE and enter PlayAsJillianHallSvR.

LAYLA
Select Cheat Codes from My WWE and enter UnlockECWDivaLayla09.

RIC FLAIR
Select Cheat Codes from My WWE and enter FlairWooooooooooooooo.

TAZZ
Select Cheat Codes from My WWE and enter UnlockECWTazzSvR2009.

VINCENT MCMAHON
Select Cheat Codes from My WWE and enter VinceMcMahonNoChance.

HORNSWOGGLE AS MANAGER
Select Cheat Codes from My WWE and enter HornswoggleAsManager.

CHRIS JERICHO COSTUME B
Select Cheat Codes from My WWE and enter AltJerichoModelSvR09.

CM PUNK COSTUME B
Select Cheat Codes from My WWE and enter CMPunkAltCostumeSvR!.

REY MYSTERIO COSTUME B
Select Cheat Codes from My WWE and enter BooyakaBooyaka619SvR.

SATURDAY NIGHT'S MAIN EVENT ARENA
Select Cheat Codes from My WWE and enter SatNightMainEventSvR.

WWE SMACKDOWN VS. RAW 2010

THE ROCK
Select Cheat Codes from the Options and enter The Great One.

VINCE'S OFFICE AND DIRT SHEET FOR BACKSTAGE BRAWL
Select Cheat Codes from the Options menu and enter BonusBrawl.

SHAWN MICHAELS' NEW COSTUME
Select Cheat Codes from the Options menu and enter Bow Down.

RANDY ORTON'S NEW COSTUME
Select Cheat Codes from the Options menu and enter ViperRKO.

TRIPLE H'S NEW COSTUME
Select Cheat Codes from the Options menu and enter Suck IT!.

WWE SMACKDOWN VS. RAW 2011

JOHN CENA (ENTRANCE/CIVILIAN)
In My WWE, select Cheat Codes from the Options and enter SLURPEE.

ALL OF RANDY ORTON'S COSTUMES
In My WWE, select Cheat Codes from the Options and enter apexpredator.

TRIBUTE TO THE TROOPS ARENA
In My WWE, select Cheat Codes from the Options and enter 8thannualtribute.

CRUISERWEIGHT TITLE, HARDCORE TITLE, AND MILLION DOLLAR TITLE
In My WWE, select Cheat Codes from the Options and enter Historicalbelts.

X-MEN: THE OFFICIAL GAME

DANGER ROOM ICEMAN
At the Cerebro Files menu, press Right, Right, Left, Left, Down, Up, Down, Up, Start.

DANGER ROOM NIGHTCRAWLER
At the Cerebro Files menu, press Up, Up, Down, Down, Left, Right, Left, Right, Start.

DANGER ROOM WOLVERINE
At the Cerebro Files menu, press Down, Down, Up, Up, Right, Left, Right, Left, Start.